The Transformation

of American

Industrial Relations

THE

TRANSFORMATION

OF AMERICAN

INDUSTRIAL

RELATIONS

————

THOMAS A. KOCHAN
HARRY C. KATZ
ROBERT B. McKERSIE

————

Basic Books, Inc., Publishers   *New York*

Library of Congress Cataloging-in-Publication Data

Kochan, Thomas A.
    The transformation of American industrial relations.

    Bibliographical references: p. 254
    Includes index.
    1. Industrial relations—United States—History—
20th century.   2. Labor policy—United States—
1951–   . II. McKersie, Robert B.   III. Title.
HD8072.K67   1986   331′.0973   85–47502
ISBN   0–465–08696–9 (cloth)
ISBN   0–465–08697–7 (paper)

Contents

Preface to the Paperback Edition   vii

Acknowledgments   xv

Chapter 1   *A Strategic Choice Perspective on Industrial Relations*   3

Chapter 2   *Historical Evolution of the U.S. Collective Bargaining System*   21

Chapter 3   *The Emergence of the Nonunion Industrial Relations System*   47

Chapter 4   *Industrial Relations Systems at the Workplace*   81

Chapter 5   *The Process and Results of Negotiations*   109

Chapter 6   *Changing Workplace Industrial Relations in Unionized Settings*   146

Chapter 7   *Union Engagement of Strategic Business Decisions*   178

Chapter 8   *American Workers and Industrial Relations Institutions*   206

Chapter 9   *Strategic Choices Shaping the Future*   226

Notes   254

Index   275

Preface to the Paperback Edition

WE HAVE BEEN PLEASED by the amount of debate, discussion, and critical appraisal that this book has received from our fellow researchers and practitioners in industrial relations. While not everyone has agreed completely with our analysis and interpretation of developments in contemporary industrial relations, the book appears to have stimulated others to reappraise and crystallize their own views and to join the debate over the future of American industrial relations. In this brief preface we will provide a flavor of the current debates and update our own perspectives, based on recent developments and further research we have conducted since the publication of the original volume.*

Most of the writing for this book was completed by the spring of 1986. Much has happened in American industrial relations since then. We remain convinced of the usefulness of the framework presented in this book and would argue that recent events provide further substantiation for our analysis of fundamental changes in our system of industrial relations. There is continuing evidence that the focus of activity in American industrial relations has shifted to the strategic and workplace levels. For example, at a number of airlines, including Eastern (now Texas Air), Pan Am, and United, unions are trying to influence corporate financial affairs by searching for "white knights" to finance restructuring. Financial machinations on Wall Street represent a glamorous and well-publicized forum for union strategic involvement, but our discussions with various unions and firms suggest that many other unions are now regularly confronted by and involved in similar strategic issues. Extensive corporate restructuring and attendant changes in production have forced unions to be concerned with strategic issues.

Some commentators have suggested that recent events evidence a return to more conventional collective bargaining rather than a transition to a new industrial relations system. Similarities in the 1987 agreements at

* We would like to express our appreciation to the participants of a conference organized by James Dworkin and Richard Peterson at Purdue University in May of 1988; in large part, the material contained in this preface has been derived from that stimulating discussion and critique of this book.

Ford, General Motors, and Chrysler, for example, typify a return to pattern bargaining and, more generally, to traditional collective bargaining. We disagree. While the company agreements among the Big Three and the UAW in 1987 did include similar wage settlements, we believe collective bargaining in the auto industry has continued to manifest the breakdown of the New Deal collective bargaining system as described in chapters 5, 6, and 7. Note, for example, that although the wage settlements were similar across the Big Three, auto worker earnings have varied substantially as a product of the diverse payouts in the profit-sharing plans of the three companies.

More generally, auto bargaining has revealed a continuing emphasis on strategic and workplace issues. On the shop floor there has been extensive experimentation with a new industrial relations system that includes the features we describe in this volume. This restructuring is accompanied by enormous debate between and within the ranks of labor and management, due in part to the depth of the changes under way and the parties' quest for a coherent view of how these developments fit together in a new system. Our work as instructors in a training program at General Motors for local UAW officials, in which these events and debates are openly discussed, convinces us that there is little sign of a return to traditional patterns of industrial relations in the auto industry. Our knowledge of events in other industries suggests the same conclusion.

The terms and scope of the debate under way within unions are interesting in their own right and provide further evidence that the union strategic cell in our three-tier framework is not an empty one. Unions are struggling to define whether and how they should position themselves in the new system of industrial relations and on what terms they should accept participation in such a system. The debates in the auto industry mentioned above are but one illustration of these discussions.

There are also interesting and important debates under way within the ranks of national trade-union leadership. National unions, just as their local unions, are reassessing their representation and organizing strategies in response to the managerial initiatives that prevail. In particular, national unions appear to be searching for a way to encourage an institutionalized forum for their involvement in and regulation of work teams and participatory processes. Some recent discussions within the AFL-CIO imply that the labor movement is asking itself whether there is an American form of works councils and codetermination that might be feasible and attractive. We have participated in some of these discussions and it is clear that the issues are complex and there are no easy formulations to recommend. It is especially difficult to think of codetermination possibilities that should be recommended, given the legitimate doubts union leaders have regarding the steadfastness of management's willingness to share information and authority. A view often expressed by union leaders is that management is only willing to share information about losses and problems (presumably as a prelude to concession bargaining) and that over the long term, management will not behave in a way that supports involvement of unions at the strategic level.

National union leaders also appear to be reassessing the political agendas of unions, given the changes under way in collective bargaining and the world economy. Traditional policy approaches, while still supported by many union leaders, do not appear to confront economic changes and the persistent fact that traditional union appeals are not attractive to the increasingly diverse American workforce. The realization of these facts has led some union leaders to advocate fundamental changes in labor and employment policies that support union efforts to organize workers in ways that respond to their diverse needs and provide them with real influence in the governance of the workplace. For example, unions are searching for ways to link their appeal to the many unsettled employee "rights" issues that stem from the demographic changes of the workforce and an ever-expanding agenda of concerns. While unions have seen little recent organizing success, even in the face of the dislocation confronted by the workforce, it does appear that employees are not satisfied with the status quo, by either the protections currently provided by public policy or the assurances offered by employers. It is significant that 80 percent of the population expressed support for federal legislation requiring advance notification of plant closings and major layoffs; and the acquiescence of President Reagan to the enactment of a sixty-day requirement reflected recognition of this political reality.

The workforce appears to have unsatisfied demands concerning such issues as pay equity, career development, day care, and maternity leave. We believe there is a potential role for unions as the coalescing agent and voice for these various rights issues. The challenge for unions is to reassert their place in these new domains and to link the rights issues to the still important pay and employment-security concerns felt by the workforce.

The vacillation and debate taking place within the ranks of trade unions are paralleled by the variety of strategic responses within management's ranks to economic pressures. The employers' current dilemma is much as we described it in the book. American management continues to be torn between, on the one hand, business strategies that compete on the basis of low costs and the minimization of labor input, and on the other hand, product and technological strategies focused around innovative capabilities, high skill content, and a commitment to human resource development. In the last several years, a number of firms have pursued the first option through aggressive downsizing and increased outsourcing, with little concern for the effects that these actions have on employee motivation. In some instances this strategy of pushing quickly to lower labor costs has been accompanied by hard, confrontational bargaining that has involved operating plants in the face of strikes and replacing the workers, with the eventual result that the union has been decertified.

At the same time, other firms in auto and telecommunications, for example, have reorganized to confront competitive pressures but have done so while addressing employee career development and redeployment. A variety of joint programs have been instituted by the parties to the auto-UAW and AT&T-CWA relationships. With names such as Employee Development and Training and the Alliance for Employee Growth and Development, these programs have made it possible for workers affected by change to be retrained for continuing employment and for workers to prepare themselves for a future of new technology and work structures requiring substantially more responsibility and initiative. For example, over half of Ford's workforce has participated in various educational programs sponsored by the Ford-UAW Fund. These joint training efforts are also bringing about more access by the unions involved to the strategic decisions that are the "drivers" of the skills and capabilities that will be required of the workforce in the years ahead.

At the same time that we observe these contrasting strategies that are being pursued in terms of corporate strategy and collective-bargaining policies, we also observe an intensification of the trends affecting the workplace level of industrial relations. We have continued to track developments for a number of union-management relationships. It is clear that an increasing number of firms and unions are experimenting with key elements of what we refer to as a new industrial relations system: team forms of work organization, contingent compensation, employment security, and enhanced worker and union participation in business and strategic decision making. Our research suggests that in some cases this new system has generated favorable economic performance relative to nonunion alternatives. However, we were not (and, as will be pointed out below, still are not) convinced that this new industrial relations system will spread naturally across the economy. Our final chapter discusses the many public, union, and management policies needed to encourage such a development.

In addition, it is clear that the alternate nonunion system also continues to expand. This packaging of sophisticated HRM personnel policies represents a very different industrial relations system as compared to traditional "paternalistic" or "bureaucratic" nonunion systems. In fact, it is the nature and appeal of these HRM policies that is behind many of the organizing difficulties confronted by unions. Further evidence on this score has been provided by the fact that unions have had only modest success in recent organizing campaigns even when those campaigns have followed layoffs or plant closings. We interpret these difficulties as testament to our claim that unions will have to make substantial changes in their organizing and representational strategies in order to organize the workers of a sophisticated HRM employer.

We see the emergence of this alternative nonunion system as one of the key developments contributing to the transformative nature of recent American industrial relations. In this connection, a full account of the evolution of the various nonunion personnel policies followed by an accurate assessment of their implications is one of the major research agendas for the field of industrial relations.

A question that we are frequently asked is whether the framework and key propositions of this book are applicable beyond the borders of the United States. While we viewed the task of understanding the changes taking place within the U.S. context as a major project in its own right, we see international industrial relations (along with the nonunion sector) as the major under-researched topic of the day. International comparisons provide an opportunity to test the roles played by different institutions and strategies by looking across countries (or industries) facing similar economic pressures. Recent commonalities in economic pressures among countries have made such tests particularly interesting.

Will the three-tiered framework and the related hypotheses offered in our book be useful in explaining international developments? Our preliminary analysis of events in Europe suggests that the framework does hold, yet clearly a much more detailed comparative analysis is required. We also expect that such analysis will require amendments to our framework. For example, when applied to the analysis of European developments, the three-tiered framework would have to be modified to account for the greater reliance on national and multi-industry bargaining and more extensive governmental regulation of *substantive* employment conditions.

In many ways we are struck by the extent to which European industrial relations is being transformed along lines similar to changes under way in the United States even though most European unions entered the 1980s with a larger fraction of the workforce organized and with greater substantive involvement by the government in the determination of employment conditions. Our reading of the evidence suggests, for example, that a shift in industrial relations activity to the strategic and workplace levels is occurring in a number of European countries in a manner not that different from events in the United States. In particular, on the shop floor it appears that unions are struggling to find their place in the midst of experiments to institute team systems of work and new channels of communication and participation in a manner remarkably similar to American unions. As we and others pursue comparative research, the challenge is to search for the sources of that similarity as well as for the influences that national institutions exert as important sources of diversity.

Some of the reviews that have appeared have criticized us for saying little about the role of the "state" (public policy) in realizing the transformation to a new industrial relations system. One reason for giving little emphasis to the role of the government was that at the time the book was written we interpreted events of the early 1980s as very much those of a "pre–public policy" period of experimentation, or trial and error, on the part of labor and management, acting largely without an active government role.

Much of our work since the publication of the book has focused more directly on the role of government policy in diffusing and institutionalizing innovations in industrial relations. This work has convinced us that broad diffusion and institutionalization of a new industrial relations system will indeed require an active government policy—one that endorses the new model and treats it as a necessary microfoundation for broader macroeconomic and social policies.

A debate over the relevance of industrial relations practice to the future of national labor and human-resource policy is now beginning to be joined. The anticipation of a new administration in Washington in 1989 has spurred discussion of the relationship of labor and human-resource policies to macroeconomic and social policies designed to revitalize the economy. Our position in these debates is that the features of the transformed industrial relations system that we describe in this book can provide a more suitable microfoundation for the economy and workforce of the future than would either a return to the traditional New Deal system or a continuation of the present situation of cautious experimentation and limited diffusion of the new model. Moreover, we believe that the labor, human-resource, and economic policies of government will determine the extent to which diffusion and institutionalization of a new model will in fact occur.

However, the decision by some future administration to adopt an activist labor policy that endorses and supports diffusion of a new model of industrial relations would itself constitute a strategic choice as dramatic and important as any of the choices or events discussed in this book. Thus, there is no guarantee, nor even a discernible trend, that would predict such a development. Perhaps this further validates the importance of providing for such strategic choices in models of industrial relations.

While the union, employer, and government strategies that will shape the future are not yet clearly articulated, it is clear that actions both above and below the traditional level of collective bargaining are continuing to reshape American industrial relations. We hope this book makes a contribution to the way we think about these developments.

THOMAS KOCHAN
HARRY KATZ
ROBERT MCKERSIE

October 1988

Acknowledgments

THIS BOOK has been at least five years in the making. It summarizes the findings, conclusions, and implications for theory, policy, and practice we have drawn from a collaborative research project conducted at MIT under the title: "U.S. Industrial Relations in Transition." This project started in 1981 with a vague belief on our part that important but as yet uncertain changes were beginning to take place in the U.S. industrial relations system. With the generous support and assistance of the individuals and organizations listed below we have been able to study unfolding developments and search for a better understanding and interpretation as industrial relations moved through a fascinating period of crisis, experimentation, and debate. While a number of articles and interim books have reported on specific issues and findings, our purpose here is to draw together these findings and to explore their implications for the future of industrial relations in the United States.

A journey of this length could not have been pursued without considerable resources and many collaborators. We would like to begin our acknowledgments by thanking the Sloan School of Management and our colleagues, especially those in the Industrial Relations Section, for providing the intellectual atmosphere that gives academic life its special quality. The Alfred P. Sloan Foundation and the U.S. Department of Labor deserve special thanks for providing the financial resources that made it possible to undertake a project of this scope and duration.

Auspices and dollars are important factors in the research equation, but willing and stimulating co-investigators are the key ingredient. Given the collaborative nature of the project and the significance of their contributions, all the members of our MIT research team should be listed on the title page in bold letters, but space does not permit this display.

We would like to acknowledge the invaluable assistance of the following individuals who completed their Ph.D. programs during the course of the project: Casey Ichniowski (Columbia University), Jan Klein (Harvard Business School), and Anil Verma (University of British Columbia). In addition, Peter Cappelli (University of Pennsylvania) spent a year working on the project with us as a postdoctoral fellow. Others joined the project in its later stages and are currently in residence at MIT completing their Ph.D.s. They include John Chalykoff, Joel Cutcher-Gershenfeld, Richard Locke, John-Paul McDuffie, Boaz Tamir, and Kirsten Wever. As will be evident to the reader, we have drawn heavily on their work and they have been vital participants in our own quality circle.

We also have benefited from the research, insights, and comments of Michael Piore and Henry Farber of the MIT Economics Department, Charles Sabel of the MIT Political Science Department, and Richard Walton and E. Robert Livernash of the Harvard Business School. Irving Bluestone, Malcolm Lovell, Charles Myers, Ernest Savoie, Ed Thompson, and Norman Weintraub also provided detailed and instructive feedback on several chapters of the manuscript.

A project of this scope and complexity requires strong and dedicated staff support. Two key individuals helped us through many of the trying stages of this effort. Nancy Mower spent many hours in the field as a research associate and later applied her skills and good spirit to the task of coordinating several of our conferences. Michelle Kamin managed the budget, coordinated travel, processed jumbled ideas, notes, and prose into draft manuscripts and final copy, and generally served as administrative troubleshooter for much of the project. Her abilities and willingness to take on new challenges are well known to us all.

Particular thanks are due to the following individuals and organizations for providing access to several data sets that feature prominently in the chapters that follow. Audrey Freedman of the Conference Board supplied data from the Conference Board's 1978 and 1983 surveys of labor relations practices. Howard Samuel and Richard Prosten from the Industrial Union Department of the AFL-CIO provided access to the union leaders and rank-and-file workers in our studies of worker participation. Thomas Donahue and Charles McDonald of the AFL-CIO provided access to survey data collected by the AFL-CIO's Evolution of Work Committee. Wayne Vroman of the Urban Institute provided a longitudinal data file on collective bargaining settlements that we use to test several hypotheses discussed in chapter 5. And finally, we want to recognize the many companies, unions, and government agencies that allowed us to study their contributions to today's exceedingly interesting and compelling industrial relations scene.

Indeed, the changes underway are so compelling that at times over the past several years we have had time for little else, and we thank our wives and children for their understanding and generosity of spirit.

The Transformation

of American

Industrial Relations

CHAPTER

1

A Strategic Choice Perspective on Industrial Relations

THE EARLY 1980s witnessed a significant change in the U.S. system of collective bargaining and industrial relations. Front-page news stories frequently cited labor concessions in collective bargaining that departed from the pattern of improved wages, fringe benefits, and job security to which the American public in general and union members in particular had become accustomed.[1] Highly regarded business periodicals dwelled on the advent of new forms of labor-management cooperation at the workplace—so much so that some proposed that a "new industrial relations" had overtaken the U.S. economy.[2] But at the same time the cumulative effects of more than twenty years of declining union membership made it apparent that the American labor movement had reached a crisis. Some even suggested that unless new, more successful organizing strategies could be developed, the labor movement could not survive into the next century as a significant economic and social force. Leaders of the labor movement appeared to agree that significant action was needed. In 1985 the American Federation of Labor and Congress of Industrial Organizations (AFL-CIO) took up the challenge; it issued a soul-searching report that reviewed the problems facing unions and outlined a strategy designed to sow the "seeds of a resurgence."[3]

It is not surprising, therefore, that these significant and rather unexpected developments sparked a vigorous debate among professionals from all segments of the industrial relations community over whether the events of the early 1980s represented merely a temporary adjustment to the deep recession of 1981 to 1983 or signaled a fundamental transformation in the industrial relations system, the effects of which would be felt for many years to come.[4]

The purpose of this book is to address this debate. Our view is that an answer to the question of whether recent changes are fundamental or temporary requires a deeper and longer-term historical look at the evolution and dynamics of the U.S. industrial relations system. It is our thesis, developed in the following chapters, that the changes which occurred in the early 1980s reflect deep-seated environmental pressures that had been building up gradually as well as organizational strategies that had been evolving quietly for a number of years. Moreover, we shall argue that to fully understand and interpret current developments requires a fundamental rethinking of industrial relations theories and a broadening of the scope of what managers, union leaders, and government policy makers traditionally envision as the domain of industrial relations professional activity.

We address this debate in the following manner. First, we describe contemporary industrial relations practices as we have observed them among leading union and nonunion firms that we have studied over the past four years. Second, we analyze these practices, and the historical evolution that preceded them, within a revised theory of industrial relations. Third, we draw on both the description of current practices and the revised theoretical framework to assess and interpret the transformations that have occurred and are continuing to unfold in U.S. industrial relations. Finally, we evaluate the degree to which the developments unfolding in the 1980s represent a fundamental departure from the principles and practices put in place in the system that grew out of the New Deal labor legislation of the 1930s and the post–World War II system of collective bargaining.

But our ultimate purpose is not simply to describe and interpret current developments. Instead, we wish to develop a more *strategic* perspective on U.S. industrial relations and thereby demonstrate that future patterns are not unalterably predetermined by economic, technological, or some other forces in the American environment. Our central argument is that industrial relations practices and outcomes are shaped by the interactions of environmental forces *along with* the strategic choices and values of American managers, union leaders, workers, and public policy decision makers. We believe that by better understanding the nature of these interactions, the consequences of alternative strategic choices (and the different values they embody), the parties can gain greater control over the destiny of the organizations and interests that they represent.

The Issues at Stake

American industrial relations has always been characterized by a dynamic interplay or competition between union and nonunion employment systems. Indeed, its history is characterized by long periods of relative stability and incremental change in the role and status of union and nonunion systems, which are interrupted intermittently by periods in which prevailing practices are questioned and new institutional arrangements emerge. Prior to the 1930s, in the absence of any supportive legislation, nonunion practices prevailed for most workers. Unions could manage to organize only a small fraction of the labor force, and union membership rose and fell in direct response to rises and falls in the business cycle.[5]

The labor policies adopted in the 1930s as part of the New Deal were designed to introduce greater stability and order and to lend a degree of permanency to union-management relations. Unions had presumably achieved a position of legitimacy in American society since collective bargaining had been chosen as the preferred mechanism for worker participation and representation in industry. For the next two decades, collective bargaining served as the most significant source of innovation in employee relations.

By the 1960s, however, union membership in the private sector had begun a steady and sustained decline that continues through today. Nonunion employers now took advantage of new market opportunities to experiment and then institutionalize new human resource management practices. The cumulative effects of the decline of unions and the rise of alternative approaches to human resource management by the early 1980s had set the stage once again for an intense debate

5

concerning the role of unions and collective bargaining in American society. Once again, American society in general, and American unions in particular, face fundamental choices with respect to the most basic questions concerning the structure of employment relationships. Is there still a "need" for unions? Is the stated public policy regarding support for collective bargaining in fact working to promote or to suppress this process? Should collective bargaining be promoted, or are new forms of employee participation and representation needed to supplement or substitute for this process? Are fundamentally new strategies for organizing and representing workers needed if the labor movement is to reverse the membership losses of recent years? Can the pace of innovation within American firms that helped to promote expansion of the nonunion sector be maintained in the face of a more intense global competition in product markets and rapidly changing technologies? Can American management maintain the trust and co-operation of the workforce that many believe are necessary and at the same time oppose independent representation of workers through unions? Can the innovations in unionized settings that have begun in the 1980s survive and diffuse to a wider range of union-management relationships, or will the political pressures on those supporting further change and innovation produce a reversion to past patterns? Can labor union leaders envision and then achieve new roles and structures that aid their employers' competitive performance without destroying the solidarity that traditionally gave unions the bargaining power to improve the living standards of their members? How can the basic clash between a democratic society's need for a free labor movement be reconciled with the deep-seated opposition to unions embedded in American managerial ideology?

If, as we believe, we are currently moving through another one of those critical periods of transformation in American industrial relations, then the strategic choices made by leaders of management, labor, and government will shape the answers to these questions. But to adequately frame the issues in this debate, let alone identify the consequences of alternative choices, requires a theoretical framework capable of interpreting our historical experience and contemporary developments. Therefore, we introduce the concept of an industrial relations system that has dominated the analysis of employment issues for the past several decades. We will point out several anomalies in industrial relations practice that this theory cannot adequately explain and then introduce a revised model that will guide our analysis throughout this book.

Anomalies in Industrial Relations Theory and Practice

We use the term industrial relations system to refer to the premises, values, laws, institutions, and practices that govern employment relationships. This term was popularized in 1958 by John Dunlop in his seminal book, *Industrial Relations Systems*.[6]

According to Dunlop's system model, analysis of industrial relations problems should begin by considering the various environmental contexts that affect employment relationships—economic forces, technology, and the broad political, legal, and social forces that determine the power of labor and management in society. Then attention should turn to characteristics of the key actors (labor, management, and the government) and their interactions, and conclude with an explanation of the rules governing employment relationships that evolve out of these interactions. An important assumption in Dunlop's model is that these key actors share an underlying consensus that defines and legitimizes their roles. It is this shared ideology that is expected to lend stability to the system.[7] In a follow-up study of industrial relations systems in various nations, Dunlop and his colleagues Clark Kerr, Frederick Harbison, and Charles Myers further argued that, over time, the logic of industrialization would lead to a convergence toward a common set of formal arrangements and rules.[8]

While this systems framework has not been universally accepted, it did provide an organizing framework that researchers of the 1960s and 1970s used to construct models explaining cross-company and union variations in industrial relations.[9] Indeed, Dunlop's model worked fairly well as long as the environment and the practices of the parties remained stable. It has become increasingly clear, however, that the systems framework, with its emphasis on stability and a shared consensus among the actors concerning their respective roles, has a difficult time explaining the dynamic aspects of industrial relations. It is these dynamic features that need to be understood if we are to interpret the current transformations in industrial relations practice. Several brief examples of anomalies in the theory help illustrate this point.

UNION MEMBERSHIP DECLINES

When in 1935 the National Labor Relations Act (NLRA) established collective bargaining as the preferred method of setting wages, hours, and working conditions, it was assumed that unionism would expand as workers embraced collective bargaining as the best way to advance their common interests. This proved to be the case up through the mid-1950s. Since then, however, the percentage of the unionized labor force has been steadily declining, from a peak of approximately 35 percent of the nonagricultural labor force in the mid-1950s to approximately 19 percent in 1985. The decline in union membership would be even greater if only private-sector workers were considered.[10]

While the magnitude of the decline in union coverage is large, its potential impact on industrial relations is magnified by the differences in the distribution of union and nonunion workers that has resulted from more than two decades in which few new jobs were added to the unionized sector. As we show in more detail in later chapters, the growing and dynamic parts of the economy are today largely unorganized. Union membership is currently concentrated in the older and more mature industries, the older firms in those industries, and the older plants within diversified firms.

This is not an outcome that either the framers of the NLRA or the industrial relations scholars of the post–New Deal period foresaw. Indeed, by the 1960s both researchers and practitioners of collective bargaining seemed to believe that relations between labor and management had matured and stabilized, that management had accommodated to the fact that collective bargaining was here to stay, and that labor unions were a permanent participant in their employment relationships.[11] While there were vigorous debates over the vitality and future of the American labor movement,[12] no one in the 1950s or 1960s foresaw the changes in managerial behavior that would slow and then stop the expansion of collective bargaining and union membership in the private sector of the economy. Changes in the industrial environment as well as demographic and occupational shifts account for some portion of the post-1960 decline in union membership and collective bargaining coverage; but a full understanding of that decline requires a reconceptualization of managerial strategies, structures, and policies that were unfolding, often quietly, during this period.

RETHINKING CONSENSUS ASSUMPTIONS

If managerial values and strategies are an important part of the explanation for the decline in unionization, what does this say about the consensus ideology assumed in conventional industrial relations systems theory? Have managerial values or ideological dispositions really changed in recent years? Did American managers ever accept unions as legitimate and valued actors in industrial relations in a way that could be characterized as a "shared understanding" or a consensus ideology? Or did the majority of industrial relations scholars of the post–New Deal period misinterpret some employers' pragmatic acceptance of unions as philosophical acceptance?

Certainly not since the days of the American plan and company unionism that followed World War I has it been as socially or politically acceptable for U.S. management to embrace publicly a "union-free" preference as it is today. Clearly, the assumption that there is a legitimate conflict of interest in employment relations is not shared by the majority of American managers even though it is built into our public policies. If this is true (and we present data in chapter 3 to demonstrate that it is), it should inform our theoretical assumptions and models in a significant way. In short, a more powerful theory of managerial *values, strategies, and behavior* in industrial relations is needed.

MANAGEMENT AS THE INITIATOR OF CHANGE

Traditional industrial relations theory, particularly as it has been applied in collective bargaining research, treats management as reacting to union demands, pressures, and initiatives. We have reasonably well-developed hypotheses about managerial adjustments to collective bargaining, ranging from Sumner Slichter's early concept of the "shock effects" of unions to more recent empirical studies of the effects of unions on various workplace outcomes and managerial adjustments.[13]

Moreover, we have traditionally studied the spillover effects of unions on unorganized workers and employers, noting, with considerable empirical support, that the threat of becoming organized led many employers to match union wage gains and employment practices.[14] Yet in recent years there have been numerous indications that the causal flow has been reversed. Innovations in human resource management practices that started in nonunion firms are increasingly being carried over into unionized workplaces. A revised framework needs to address this reversal in the source of dynamism.

Rethinking our traditional assumptions about managerial values and behavior opens the door to more intensive analysis of a variety of other managerial initiatives and changes that have profoundly affected the transformation now taking place in U.S. industrial relations. For example, a noticeable shift in the distribution of decision-making power and authority over employment issues has occurred *within* management in recent years. The traditional labor relations professional whose primary responsibility in the past was to achieve stable and peaceful labor relations has lost power both to human resource management professionals and to line managers. In many organizations top executives have demanded greater organizational innovation in managing employees than many traditional labor relations managers could deliver. Recognition of this development, in turn, has led an increasing number of scholars in other countries to stress the need to examine the relationships between broad business strategies and industrial relations practices within the firm.[15]

To the extent that past industrial relations research considered the role of management, it tended to focus on the role of the industrial relations function within the management structure. It has become increasingly clear, however, that the events having significant impact on industrial relations processes and outcomes start well above the functional level of industrial relations within the firm. This development also forces a basic rethinking of our assumptions about the way management's values, strategies, and structures are treated in current industrial relations theory. To consider the dynamics of policy and strategy formulation that often takes place well above both the collective bargaining process and, in some cases, the level of most industrial relations staff, the scope of industrial relations research must be broadened. Previous research has failed to address adequately the strategic decisions that affect workers' basic job security interests but are made far above the traditional reach of workers, their representatives, or the collective bargaining process.

As industrial relations research considers the implications of strategic business decisions, it will benefit by building on existing research on business strategy and policy. Alfred Chandler's classic work on the relationship between strategy and structure has obvious implications for an understanding of the evolution of industrial relations policies and management structures within the firm.[16] The work on strategic planning and the relationship between business policies or strategies and the firm's industrial relations system will form an important part of our analysis. Recent work on the dynamics of industry and business unit or product life cycles and their effects on industrial relations or human resource activities are especially important and will inform our analysis.

We depart from the business policy and strategy research largely on normative rather than on theoretical grounds. The business strategy literature takes the goals of the business as its starting point and builds models primarily to help top managers make and implement strategic decisions that maximize the firm's value. An industrial relations model obviously needs to go beyond management's goals to consider the strategic interactions of other actors and the effects of individual and jointly derived strategic decisions on the goals of workers, labor organizations, and the larger society.

The Revised Theoretical Framework

The broad theoretical framework guiding our analysis of industrial relations is presented in figure 1.1. As we have suggested, our approach draws from the rapidly growing theoretical paradigm that integrates the traditional theories of industrial relations systems with the literature on corporate strategy, structure, and decision making.[17] Although we will elaborate on the propositions underlying this model in later chapters, we will briefly summarize some of them here in order to make explicit the role that the environment, values, business strategies, institutional structures, and history play in the analysis of industrial relations processes and outcomes.

FIGURE 1.1

General Framework for Analyzing Industrial Relations Issues

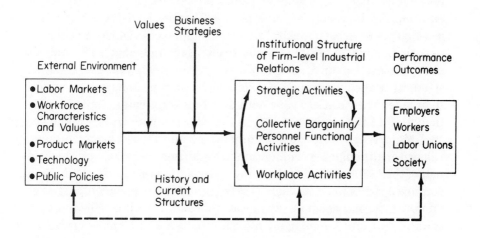

Like traditional industrial relations theory, our model starts with consideration of the relevant forces in the external environment that affect employment relationships. Changes in the external environment induce employers to make adjustments in their competitive business strategies. In making these adjustments, the range of options considered are filtered and constrained so as to be consistent with the values, beliefs, or philosophies engrained in the minds of key decision makers, or, in some organizations, to reflect the norms that have diffused from founders or senior executives to lower levels and succeeding generations of managers.[18] As choices are also embedded in particular historical and institutional structures, the range of feasible options available at any given time is partially constrained by the outcomes of previous organizational decisions and the current distribution of power within the firm and between it and any unions, government agencies, or other external organizations it deals with.[19] Applied to the divergent trends within the industrial relations system, this framework implies that changes in both product and labor markets led to significant economic and organizational restructuring in the period between 1960 and 1980. In choosing how to respond to both new business opportunities and/or the need to lower costs, the deep-seated preference of American employers for operating without a union dominated managerial choices, except where preexisting high levels of unionization constrained this option.

Just as management strategies and values play a more important role in explaining industrial relations outcomes than received theory has recognized, so too do the values and strategies that influence the behavior and policies of unions and government policy. One of the reasons we place management values and strategies at the center of our analysis, however, is that since 1960 union behavior and government policy have been much slower than employers to adapt to changes in their external environment and to changes in managerial strategies and policies. Up until the 1980s most American unions remained steadfast in their traditions of collective bargaining and resisted efforts to broaden their roles to cope with demands for greater employee participation at the workplace and to shifts in markets and technologies that require new strategies for organizing and representing workers. Likewise, although government policies during the 1960s and the first half of the 1970s expanded the array of regulations governing individual employee rights in areas such as safety and health, equal employment opportunity, and pensions, the basic policies governing collective bargaining and union-management relations remained unchanged. The more rapid change in managerial strategies in the face of unchanging labor and government strategies has produced a mismatch in many employment relationships. Many of the changes currently underway in U.S. industrial relations in the 1980s reflect the efforts of one or more of the parties to resolve the tensions that such mismatches produce.

THE ROLE OF THE ENVIRONMENT

Our framework is based on the key premise that industrial relations processes and outcomes are determined by a continuously evolving *interaction* of environmental pressures and organizational responses. The relative importance of either the environment or the parties' responses can vary over time. For example, organizations do not constantly adjust their strategies and policies to changes in the environment. Often considerable pressures must build up before an adaptation occurs. This is one reason why industrial relations systems often go through long periods of relative stability that are interrupted only periodically by major transformations.

Theories of industrial relations have always stressed the importance of environmental forces. This is particularly true in models of union growth, decline, and behavior.[20] We will build on this tradition by exploring in chapter 3 changes in the external labor and product markets that have interacted with employer strategies to account for the union decline during the 1960s and succeeding decades. It should be noted, however, that we are not arguing that labor- and product-market changes have *independent* effects or operate in a unique or deterministic fashion. Rather market forces set in motion a series of employer and union responses. It is the interaction of market forces and the responses of employers, unions, workers, and government policy that together determine the outcomes of cyclical or structural changes. Our major conclusion is that employers adapted to labor- and product-market changes in the post-1960 period in ways that reduced their vulnerability to unionism while unions and government policy remained fixed in the collective bargaining model of the New Deal.

THE ROLE OF CHOICE

A key premise of our framework is that *choice* and discretion on the part of labor, management, and government affect the course and structure of industrial relations systems. Moreover, history plays an extremely important role in shaping the range of feasible strategic adaptations. Although environmental pressures are important and serve as the starting point for discussion of the determinants of an industrial relations system, these pressures do not strictly determine industrial relations outcomes. Thus an understanding of the choices parties make in any given period must be informed by an analysis of the structures and history that constrain those choices. One of the strongest factors impinging on choice is management values toward unions.

An understanding of the transformation that has taken place in industrial relations since 1960 must start with an understanding of the deep-seated resistance toward unions that historically has been embedded in the belief system of U.S. managers. It is through the lens of this value system that managerial decision makers weigh their options for responding to cues from the external environment. Unfortunately, many researchers in industrial relations and the behavioral sciences have been slow or unwilling to acknowledge the existence and the power of this managerial belief system.

During the 1950s and 1960s, the prevailing view in the industrial relations literature was that American managers had accommodated to collective bargaining and accepted unions as legitimate and lasting parties to the employment relationship.[21] Many were convinced that management hostility toward unions was a thing of the past. But the accommodation was only temporary in character and, as we shall see in chapter 3, usually involved only industrial relations specialists and not the key members of management who formulated business strategies and plans. Thus the conclusion that management had adopted and accepted unions as legitimate partners misinterpreted as a change in managerial *preferences* or *ideology* what was actually a *pragmatic* or *strategic* adaptation to the high costs of avoiding or dislodging established unions. Instead, the following statement of Douglas Brown and Charles Myers probably better captured the prevailing ideologies of American managers in the 1950s and 1960s: "It may well be true that if American management, upon retiring one night, were assured that by the next morning the union . . . would have disappeared, more management people than not would experience the happiest sleep of their lives."[22]

This view of management ideology toward unions is consistent with the historical record for managerial behavior, particularly at the level of the firm or individual worksite. Reinhard Bendix makes this point in his classic analysis of managerial ideology by noting that managerial opposition to unions fits into the broader set of American values that stress individual initiative, the centrality of one's right to defend individual property rights, and the desire to maintain managerial control and worker discipline.[23] Howell John Harris developed this argument further in arguing that most American managers historically interpreted unionization as both a personal insult or statement of distrust on the part of their workers and as a black mark on their professional record.[24] Unionization was neither inevitable nor in some way desirable, but rather an indication of managerial failure. It was unnatural, illegitimate, and un-American, and to be resisted, within the law.

Yet while American management remained hostile to unionization in their own firms, there also has been a long tradition—dating at least as far back to the work of the National Civic Federation in the early years of this century—of leading executives of large corporations supporting the legitimacy or even the desirability of a free labor movement as a part of our democratic society.[25] Thus many corporate leaders participate in national labor-management discussion groups or committees as long as they can preserve their ability to also vigorously oppose unionization attempts at their specific places of employment. As such, there has been a curious inconsistency in the dominant management belief or value system: unions are an essential part of the democratic fabric of society, but they are not necessarily desirable or acceptable "in my firm or on my property."

The Three-Tier Institutional Structure

Ever since the pioneering work of John R. Commons in the early years of this century, industrial relations theory has consistently stressed the importance of the institutional structure in which labor-management interactions occur.[26] This view argues that, to explain industrial relations processes and outcomes, it is not enough to simply understand the pressures that economic or other environmental forces place on the employment relationship. Rather the patterns, laws, customs, and structures that build up over time and establish what Commons, Veblen, and other social scientists consider to be the institutional features of the relationship exert an independent effect of their own.[27] This is one of the central features that differentiate industrial relations theory from neoclassical economics and many other general theories in the behavioral and social sciences. These other theories view institutional factors as a black box of random forces that need not be considered in predicting behavior or, in some more recent formulations, as constraints within which choice and individual maximizing behavior occur.[28]

The task of institutional industrial relations theory is to identify the key variables or institutional forces that determine the outcomes of labor-management interactions. Given the central role of collective bargaining in the post–New Deal period, most attention has focused on institutional aspects of this process, such as the formal bargaining structure, the rules and customs governing bargaining behavior and responsibilities, and so forth.[29] Our view is that this is too narrow a conception of the institutional structure and forces that influence industrial relations activity. Indeed, a central theme in our analysis is that the collective bargaining process is being squeezed and pressured to adapt by forces that operate above and below its traditional process and structure. Thus we need to develop a broader conception of the institutional structure within which industrial relations activities occur. The three-tiered framework, to be introduced shortly, plays this role.

Note that here again the introduction of this three-tier institutional structure has more than mere theoretical significance; it represents the broader arena in which industrial relations professionals within management, labor, and government organizations interact and need to have expertise. Yet the narrow focus on collective bargaining that has dominated the training and career progression of these professionals has limited their ability to understand, accept, and deal with issues that cut across all three levels of contemporary industrial relations. An important implication of our analysis, therefore, is that the training and development of current and future industrial relations professionals must change to conform to the broader arenas in which they perform.

Our broader conception of the institutional framework of industrial relations is diagrammed in table 1.1. It divides the activities of management, labor, and government organizations into three tiers: (1) a top tier of strategic decision making, (2) a middle or functional tier of collective bargaining or personnel policy making, and (3) a bottom or workplace-level tier where policies are played out and affect individual workers, supervisors, and union representatives on a day-to-day basis.[30]

In the framework, the middle tier encompasses the most traditional terrain of industrial relations, since it focuses on the practice of col-

TABLE 1.1

Three Levels of Industrial Relations Activity

Level	Employers	Unions	Government
Long-Term Strategy and Policy Making	Business Strategies Investment Strategies Human Resource Strategies	Political Strategies Representation Strategies Organizing Strategies	Macroeconomic and Social Policies
Collective Bargaining and Personnel Policy	Personnel Policies Negotiations Strategies	Collective Bargaining Strategies	Labor Law and Administration
Workplace and Individual/ Organization Relationships	Supervisory Style Worker Participation Job Design and Work Organization	Contract Administration Worker Participation Job Design and Work Organization	Labor Standards Worker Participation Individual Rights

lective bargaining and personnel policy formulation and on the development and administration of the key public policies governing labor-management relations. Indeed, as will be noted in chapter 2, the framers of the NLRA believed that employment outcomes would be determined primarily at this middle level through the engagement of management and labor in joint discussions over the terms and conditions of employment. It should not be surprising, therefore, that this middle tier has been the focus of most of the theory, research, and professional education in industrial relations and personnel management.

Decisions made at the top tier represent an active frontier of practice and research in U.S. industrial relations. Activities and interactions at this level have been more central to many European industrial relations systems where, for example, tripartite negotiations among government, union, and employer representatives occur with more frequency and have greater consequence than is common in the United States. The tradition of business unionism that has dominated the American labor movement has made it appear that few important strategic choices or ideologically driven decisions are being made at this top level of the labor movement. Furthermore, the absence of public policies that encourage worker or union involvement, along with the strong aversion of employers to worker or union participation in basic entrepreneurial decisions, helps explain the lack of theorizing or research regarding this level of strategy formulation. Yet the basic decisions involving such things as what businesses to invest in, where to locate worksites, whether to make or buy various components, and the organizational arrangements used to carry out basic strategies all affect industrial relations at lower levels of the system and therefore are central to an analysis of industrial relations.

Strategic choices that are relevant to the bottom tier are those most directly associated with the organization of work, the structuring of worker rights, the management and motivation of individuals or work groups, and the nature of the workplace environment. This includes such issues as job and work organization design, work rules, worker-supervisor relations, and public policies governing individual rights at the workplace, such as occupational safety and health or equal employment opportunity laws. Since they are part of the ongoing, day-to-day worker-employer relationship, the activities that occur at this level normally are not under the direct control of the collective bargaining process, formal personnel policies, or broad business strategies. Yet they do occur within the context of policies and negotiated agreements decided at higher levels of the system. Thus the effects of higher-level activities in decision making and industrial relations must be considered as explanations of behavior and outcomes at the bottom tier. The model of workplace industrial relations activities developed in chapters 4 and 6 illustrates this argument in more detail.

A great deal of innovation in industrial relations has been underway in the workplace, and has been studied intensively by researchers in the 1950s but largely ignored in much of the subsequent research on collective bargaining.[31] Two specific interrelated developments at the workplace level need to be better understood. First, since the early 1970s there has been a widespread increase in experimentation with new forms of labor-management cooperation and employee involvement in problem-solving activities. Second, there also has been an increase in managerial efforts to introduce greater flexibility in the organization of work and the allocation of human resources. An adequate theory of industrial relations needs to explain why these developments are occurring and, most important, how they relate to the rest of the industrial relations system.

SIGNIFICANCE OF THE THREE-TIER INSTITUTIONAL FRAMEWORK

One of the reasons this three-tier framework is useful is that it helps identify an important development that existing industrial relations systems theory does not specifically address: the apparent inconsistencies and internal contradictions in strategies and practices occurring at different levels of industrial relations within firms. As we illustrate in later chapters, firms that have been actively promoting labor-management cooperation at the workplace level of their unionized worksites often are simultaneously engaged in sophisticated strategies at the highest levels to ensure that any new locations remain union-free. How this situation developed, the conditions that allow it to continue, and its implications for industrial relations are all puzzles that a new theory of industrial relations needs to answer.

While the three-tier framework does not constitute a fully developed new theory of industrial relations, there are several advantages to considering these three tiers and the roles played by environmental pressures and strategic choice. First, this framework recognizes the interrelationships among activities at the different levels of the system and helps explain the origins of any prevailing internal contradictions or inconsistencies among the three levels. Second, this framework considers the effects that various strategic decisions exert on the different actors in the system. For example, it helps us understand how unions have responded to the increased importance of decisions made by employers at the top tier. The framework also facilitates analysis of the effects that increased participation in workplace decisions by individuals and informal work groups have for the labor movement and the industrial relations system. Since activities both above and below the traditional level of collective bargaining and personnel policy making have become increasingly important, industrial relations researchers can no longer isolate the workplace and strategic levels into separate fields of inquiry any more than practitioners or policy makers can segregate them into independent domains.

We also believe that the three-tier framework encourages analysis of the roles that labor, management, and government play in each other's domain and activities. In this way we maintain the broad normative perspective that traditionally characterized industrial relations research, theory, and policy or prescriptive analyses.

In the chapters ahead we use this general framework to describe and analyze the dynamics and current state of U.S. industrial relations. The test of whether our analysis provides a more insightful and useful understanding of the dynamics of industrial relations systems lies in our ability to explain why the U.S. system evolved as it did and to identify the alternative choices the parties face as they shape the future of the system.

Part of the difficulty in resolving whether or not the U.S. industrial relations system is in the midst of a basic change springs from the uneven nature of the country's labor history. As already mentioned, the history of industrial relations in the United States has been marked by periods of stability that intermittently were interrupted by major upheavals during which new principles and practices were established. The 1930s was such a period of turbulence. During that time unions and employers struggled over the birth of industrial unionism and adaptation to the labor legislation of the New Deal.[32] The 1940s served as another period of significant change as the basic principles and practices of collective bargaining were institutionalized through the offices and efforts of the War Labor Board and the major pattern-setting bargains of the postwar years.[33]

The next chapter traces the post–World War II evolution of the U.S. industrial relations system and documents how in this period relative stability dominated collective bargaining in the private sector. It was this long period of stability and incremental change that paved the way for the recent and more fundamental changes in U.S. industrial relations.

2

Historical Evolution of the U.S. Collective Bargaining System

L ABOR and management relations in the post–World War II American economy were shaped by the rise, maturation, and eventual weakening of a system that regulated collective bargaining between the nation's major unions and employers. Even in firms without unions, employment conditions and management actions were influenced heavily by events within the organized sector of the economy. Thus it is important to understand the nature of the union or, as we call it, the "New Deal industrial relations system." One of our main arguments is that recent concession bargaining, workplace innovations, and the rise in the importance of nonunion human resource management systems represent a breakdown of the industrial relations system that was shaped by New Deal labor policies and the early institutionalization of collective bargaining during and immediately after World War II. This thesis provides additional motivation to analyze the key features of the traditional union industrial relations system and the factors that shaped its design.

The New Deal Industrial Relations System

Like any industrial relations system, the operation and features of the New Deal system can be understood by analyzing the three tiers of activity within that system. Such analysis also validates our theoretical framework by illustrating the interactive role played by environmental pressures and the strategic choices of labor and management.

NORMATIVE FOUNDATIONS FOR LABOR POLICY

The passage of the NLRA in 1935 and the various other pieces of New Deal labor legislation designed to protect worker rights represented a shift in the prevailing view of the employment relationship and how to regulate it. Prior to the 1930s public policy was guided by the classical economic theory of the labor market[1]: Labor was viewed as any other economic commodity and appropriately regulated by the outcomes of the marketplace. In this view government policy had the role of promoting and protecting the workings of a free market, the freedom of individuals to enter into contracts, and the property rights of employers to allocate their resources, including their human resources, as they saw fit.[2]

Challenging this classical view of the employment relationship, however, was a more pluralistic model advocated by "institutional" labor economists. The institutionalists argued that a fundamental, but limited, conflict of interest existed between workers and employers and that social regulation was needed to achieve an appropriate balance of power between the parties in order to accommodate these diverse interests. The conflict between labor and management was basic and permanent in the sense that it would not be eliminated either by enlightened management acting in a benevolent fashion toward workers or by an overthrow of the capitalistic system in favor of a socialist system of production.[3] Rather the conflict was embedded in the structure of the employment relationship and the separation between the roles and interests of managers and employees.[4]

In this pluralistic view, employers are responsible for promoting economic efficiency in the use of resources, including human resources. In this sense, labor, like other commodities, is subject to the same pressures of market forces. Yet unlike other commodities, labor is comprised of human beings endowed with economic, physical, psychological, and social needs, who participate as citizens in a democratic society. Thus workers should have a right to participate in the determination of the terms and conditions of employment. Society also has a need for mechanisms to respond to workers' demands for such rights, demands expressed in the protracted labor disputes occurring in the late nineteenth and early twentieth century. Since labor and management also share a common interest in building and maintaining a successful enterprise, means are needed for accommodating their diverse interests without inflicting excessive harm on either party or on the public. This view assigns to government the role of promoting social stability and a fair balance of power between labor and management.[5] It also sees public policy as a means of channeling and institutionalizing labor-management conflicts in ways that foster compromise.

The key point here is that the critical normative premise of classical economics was rejected. No longer was the labor market assumed to operate in a manner that protected the interests of all parties, particularly those workers who lacked the bargaining power associated with labor mobility. A strategy had to be found for protecting worker rights, balancing power, and accommodating diverse interests in ongoing employment relationships.

This view of the employment relationship evolved in the United States out of the research of economists and social reformers such as John R. Commons and his followers and from the efforts of labor leaders such as Samuel Gompers to gain acceptance for "business unionism." These reformers shared a respect for pragmatic solutions. What worked best was what survived the test of trial and error, generated support from and produced results for rank-and-file workers, and was compatible with the prevailing economic and political system. Commons summarized his views as follows:

Once it is realized that there is no such thing as an automatic harmony of economic interests, either under capitalism or future socialism, and that economic conflicts are not merely conflicts between individuals, which can be decided in court after the damage is done or is imminent, but are conflicts between classifications and even classes of individuals, which might be adjusted before a break occurs, then some progress can be made toward approaching not an ultimate ideal of harmony, but merely that series of next steps which will keep the concern from improving day to day.[6]

The institutionalists' view of the labor market eventually came to dominate public policy formulation and helped shape the NLRA. This view was not accepted overnight, nor did all participants in the debates over labor policy and industrial relations practice ever fully accept it. Nor has it been universally accepted by all economists or behavioral science researchers who share an interest in labor, personnel management, or human relations issues.[7] Nevertheless, a major step promoting this view was taken when New Deal legislation endorsed collective bargaining as part of our national policy and as the preferred mechanism to accommodate the partially conflicting and partially shared goals of the parties to the employment relationship. Unions and collective bargaining thereby acquired a degree of stability they were not able to achieve in the absence of such legislation. Moreover, passage of federal legislation in the 1930s as part of the broader economic and social reforms of the New Deal served as notice that the government, as guardian of the larger public interest, also had a stake in the processes and outcomes of the employment relationship.

This view of the employment relationship, and the role for labor policy it implies, leaves to policy makers much discretion regarding the particular institutional mechanisms chosen to regulate and resolve conflicting interests. The choice of collective bargaining as the preferred institutional mechanism reflected not so much the creation of a new idea but the legitimation of a process that had demonstrated its fit with American political values and labor and management practices that were emerging in selected industries in prior years. The NLRA incorporated many of the principles and policies embodied in previous advisory committees, administrative agencies, and statutes such as the industrial commissions of 1880, 1898, 1913, and 1920; the National War Labor Board (WLB) of World War I; and the National Labor Board established in 1933 under the National Industrial Recovery Act. As the first annual report of the NLRB noted "the National Labor Relations Board was created not as a completely new experiment in the field of labor relations, but as a result of the cumulative experiences of many years during which various ways to deal with labor relations have been tried by the Federal Government."[8]

The form of collective bargaining that was chosen also fit nicely with the American political and social ethos favoring limited government intervention in substantive decision making, the protection of private property rights, and the freedom to contract. The NLRA did not dictate the terms and conditions of employment but rather endorsed a process by which the parties could shape their own substantive contract terms. Senator David Walsh, chairman of the Senate Labor

Committee, stated his interpretation of the NLRA's philosophy as follows:

When employees have chosen their organization, when they have selected their representative, all the Bill proposes to do is to escort them to the door of the employer and say, "here they are, the legal representative of your employees." What happens behind those doors is not inquired into, and the bill does not seek to inquire into it.[9]

COLLECTIVE BARGAINING AS THE CORNERSTONE

While the design of the NLRA was shaped in part by its historical precursors and private practices, by no means should it be construed as the only possible institutional structure for regulating labor-management relations. A number of choices shaped the growth and development of the New Deal industrial relations system. The key choice, however, was that collective bargaining would serve as the cornerstone of labor-management interactions. Enactment of the NLRA and the subsequent mass organizing of major industries by industrial unions was expected to increase the influence of collective bargaining as unions grew via employment expansion in organized firms and through union representation election victories in new establishments.[10] Union security clauses would serve to stabilize union membership and produce a ready expansion within a bargaining unit. Once unions were recognized, the employer's continuous duty to bargain in good faith was expected to preserve collective bargaining through future recessions in ways that many craft unions failed to do prior to the Great Depression. Thus it was believed that unions and collective bargaining would develop a more permanent place at the workplace than craft unions had acquired when operating without supportive legislation.

The New Deal system was *not* premised on the expectation that management would abandon its philosophic opposition to unionism, an attitude earlier revealed in the American plan and other employer campaigns to operate on a nonunion basis. However, the NLRA was expected to give *employees* the freedom to choose whether or not they wanted to be unionized; it was assumed that in such an open environment unions would be highly successful in recruiting new members. Management *was* expected to adapt to union organizing efforts in a pragmatic fashion consistent with the rules of conduct specified in the law.[11] Where unions were successful in their organizing efforts, the proponents of the act believed that more stable and efficient operations would allow management to recoup any increased labor costs associated with collective bargaining.[12] Election procedures and institutionalized collective bargaining therefore were to replace earlier episodes of conflict and violence.

Keynesian macroeconomic theory also helped provide acceptance for the New Deal industrial relations system. This theory can be traced to the underconsumptionist view of the Great Depression.[13] In brief, this view held that the Depression was caused by insufficient aggregate demand and a failure of purchasing power to keep pace with the productive capacity of the growing mass-production industries. This was to be cured initially by Keynesian fiscal policies and government demand for war material and, after World War II, by the expansion in consumer purchasing power spurred by the reconstruction of western economies. The fact that many managers endorsed this view is illustrated by the following statement made by H. M. Robertson, General Counsel to Brown and Williamson Tobacco.

It became obvious to the management of our company that no mass production could long be carried on unless there was increased purchasing power by the great masses of people. To us this meant there must be increases in wages and shortening of hours. This became the very fixed conviction of our management. The more difficult question was as to how this should be accomplished, and we arrived at the conclusion that collective bargaining by employer and employee . . . was the only means by which, under our system, any adjustment in the equitable distribution of income could be accomplished.[14]

Union policies that increased wages through collective bargaining were compatible with this strategy as long as markets continued to expand and productivity continued to increase.

An important microeconomic theoretical argument of the institutional economists, underlying their support for collective bargaining, was that the expansion of product markets had eroded the ability of local unions to achieve wage standardization. Stability in collective bargaining could be achieved only as long as unions were successful in organizing a sufficient part of the market and spread a standard wage across the market so as to take wages out of competition.[15] Wage standardization was promoted during World War II by the WLB's encouragement of industry comparisons as a central wage criterion and after the war by the extension of the wage formula—3 percent plus cost-of-living annual (COLA) wage increases—which was first adopted in the automobile industry.[16] The centralization of bargaining structures and the adoption of pattern bargaining within and across industries would help to spread union-negotiated wage levels. Consistency with macroeconomic goals would be provided by the fact that the spread and emulation of the 3 percent-plus-COLA formula ensured that national purchasing power expanded at about the same rate as productive capacity, which throughout the 1950s and 1960s also was growing at 3 percent per year.

THE STRATEGIC LEVEL OF THE NEW DEAL SYSTEM

The expectation that management would pragmatically accommodate to collective bargaining was one feature of the strategic level of the New Deal industrial relations system. Another feature was the principle that in return for acceptance of a union role in setting wages, hours, and working conditions, management would retain the initiative with respect to strategic and entrepreneurial decisions and shop-floor actions. Formalization of this principle came when grievance arbitrators adopted and enforced the doctrine that "management acts, and workers and their unions grieve."[17]

Underpinning this principle was the philosophy that management had the right to manage, while workers and their union representatives had the right to negotiate the impacts of those management decisions on employment conditions. Since strategic decision making was left exclusively to managerial control—the middle tier of the industrial relations system—the negotiation and implementation of collectively bargained agreements became the dominant forum for labor-management interactions.

Leaving the strategic level of business decision making to the discretion of management was also consistent with the American labor movement's business unionism philosophy. Business unionists rejected the view that effective representation of worker interests required that they eventually wrest away from employers control over the enterprise. Moreover, for internal political reasons American union leaders have generally preferred to avoid participation in managerial decisions for fear of getting coopted in ways that might limit their independence and their ability to pursue their members' interests. Thus focusing on negotiation of a formal contract through collective bargaining that specified workers' rights and management's obligations fit the dominant values and strategic preferences of the labor movement.

The lack of a role for unions at the strategic level of the New Deal industrial relations system was also consistent with the moderate political role labor chose to play in American society. The labor movement staunchly defended the principles underlying the free enterprise system and rejected, as it had historically, a fundamental transformation of that system.[18] Unions—especially the industrial unions and the AFL-CIO more generally after their merger in 1955—also actively lobbied for labor and social legislation that benefited both organized and unorganized workers.[19] Labor's political program included support for social security, minimum wages, safety and health, national health insurance—issues that not only extended beyond the narrow scope of collective bargaining but also created a floor of social benefits and thereby narrowed the gap between the labor costs of union and nonunion firms.

Thus the particular industrial relations system that was put in place in the 1930s and began to spread more widely throughout the economy during the war years was a product both of explicit management and labor choices and of the economic and political environment of the time. The narrow scope of bargaining was particularly attractive to managers who were fearful of unions' and workers' potential intrusion into issues deemed to be managerial prerogatives. At the same time this system was attractive to labor because it meshed well with American labor's business union and voluntarist traditions. The business union traditions led labor to favor a limited involvement in entrepreneurial decisions. And limited reliance on political activity and political solutions was a principle that voluntarist AFL unions had long promoted.[20]

JOB CONTROL UNIONISM AT THE WORKPLACE

At the workplace level, a form of "job control" unionism made up another of the basic principles of the New Deal industrial relations system. Job control unionism entails highly formalized contracts and a quasi-judicial grievance procedure to adjudicate disputes during the term of those contracts. In this system workers' rights and obligations are linked to highly articulated and sharply delineated jobs. For example, what a worker is expected to do on the job is outlined in a job description and a job ladder typically is included in a plant's local collective bargaining agreement. Strict lines of demarcation separate jobs within the bargaining unit from work performed by supervisors or work belonging to members of some other bargaining unit. Workers' income is determined by attaching a particular wage rate to each specific job. Unions control career income by seniority rules governing the allocation of internal job vacancies among candidates for promotion. Job security is maintained by a set of rules that specify who gets laid off (after *management* decides a layoff is to occur) and how the remaining work is allocated among the workforce.

In this system of job-control unionism, industrial democracy is reduced to a particular form of industrial jurisprudence in which work and disciplinary standards are clearly defined and fairly administered and disputes over the application of rules and customs are impartially adjudicated through the grievance procedure. Administration of the labor contract, with its detailed written rules, becomes the central task for management and union leaders during the term of the agreement.

The workings of this system require that jobs are unambiguously defined and changes in job definitions and work assignments are sharply delineated. If such is not the case, it is impossible to attach specific wages and employment rights to each job, and the governing rules and customs become too ambiguous to be administered effectively through the grievance procedure.

This system of work organization predates the rise of industrial unionism and can best be understood as an adaptation to the technology and procedures American management had developed for the mass production of standardized goods.[21] Previously industrial engineers, following scientific management practices and guidelines, had broken down work into a discrete set of well-defined jobs; wages already had been linked to these specified jobs through time-motion studies and job evaluation; and many of the work standards, disciplinary, and appeals procedures already had been codified and formalized in management's attempts to assert control over supervisors and workers. Thus unions found many of these procedures already in place. Union and worker support for the establishment of detailed job classifications and contractual rights also was provided by their interest in substituting adherence to established principles and due process as an alternative to managerial caprice and favoritism.

The Evolution of the New Deal System 1935–1980

At least until the emergence of more sophisticated managerial opposition to unions in the 1960s, in broad terms many of the goals of the New Deal system were achieved. Throughout the postwar period, collective bargaining developed in many firms and industries as a means for peacefully resolving labor-management disputes. Meanwhile, as labor negotiated wage increases and other improvements in employment conditions, management took a number of steps to professionalize the administration of personnel and other managerial functions so as to recoup the costs of improvements in employment conditions through improved economic efficiency.[22]

Furthermore, although unions were never able to gain representation rights for all blue-collar workers and were even less successful in their efforts to organize white-collar workers, collective bargaining did come to exert substantial influence on employment conditions throughout the American economy. Through collective bargaining, wages and other employment conditions were set directly for the majority of blue-collar workers in a number of key industries. And in firms where unions were absent, the threat of unionization limited managers' discretion and induced them to provide wages and other benefits so as to deflect demands for unionization.

The industrial relations system just outlined did not develop instantaneously; nor were labor-management relations, once initiated, completely resistant to further modification. In broad terms it is possible to identify a series of eras that characterized U.S. labor-management relations and shaped its central features over the post–New Deal period.[23] As these eras are described, it is important to keep in mind two facts. First, the changes that occurred in collective bargaining until recently tended to be incremental and did not involve fundamental alterations in the structure of the dominant collective bargaining model just outlined. Changes and innovations did occur within collective bargaining, but in ways that did not challenge the viability of the whole system. Second, although it is possible to identify broad patterns in labor-management relations, there were always numerous exceptions to these patterns.[24] We present not a detailed historical account of the rich array of different patterns found in various firms or industries but rather a broad overview of the common patterns of development and evolution.

THE 1940s: THE INSTITUTIONALIZATION OF
COLLECTIVE BARGAINING

The war years brought the creation of institutions and procedures that introduced regularity and stability to collective bargaining. Encouraged by the election procedures established by the NLRA, unions spread their jurisdiction across a number of key industries, including automobiles, steel, clothing, textiles, and rubber. Unions benefited particularly from the WLB's encouragement of bargaining and were protected by the board's support for maintenance of membership policies that made it difficult for workers disaffected by unions' adherence to no-strike pledges and wage guidelines to give up their union membership. From 1940 to 1945 the percentage of employees in nonagricultural establishments who were union members grew from 26.9 to 35.5. (See figure 2.1.) Meanwhile, the absolute number of union mem-

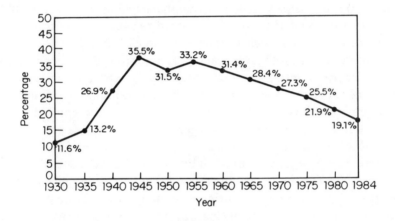

FIGURE 2.1

Union Membership as a Percentage of the Nonagricultural Labor Force 1930–84

NOTE: The September 1984 figure is the percent of employed wage and salary workers (in all) industries, private and public who were union members. In 1980, this figure was 23.0 percent. The 1984 figure is reported in Larry T. Adams, "Changing Employment Patterns of Organized Workers," *Monthly Labor Review,* 108 (February 1985): table 1.
SOURCE: The 1930–80 figures are from the *Handbook of Labor Statistics,* Washington, D.C.: Bureau of Labor Statistics.

bers grew in those years from 8,717,000 to 14,322,000. Along with increasing membership, unions were able to spread their influence into an expanding array of working conditions. Negotiated agreements grew in length and complexity and thereby codified the detailed regulations governing the expanding array of provisions on wages, fringe benefits, and other working conditions.

The federal government continued to play an active role in shaping and institutionalizing industrial relations practice during the 1940s. For example, the NLRB clarified the scope of issues over which collective bargaining would occur by making distinctions among mandatory, permissive, and illegal subjects for negotiation.[25] During World

War II, the WLB helped to institutionalize this particular form of unionism at a critical stage in the system's development. It encouraged a sometimes reluctant management to accept collective bargaining in exchange for the stability provided through the adoption of no-strike agreements and grievance procedures.[26] Furthermore, as part of its mediation role during the war, the War Labor Board recommended the introduction of narrow bounds to grievance procedures so as to keep basic business decisions outside the purview of arbitrators and collective bargaining.[27] The board's tripartite structure and weak enforcement powers helped induce it to emphasize compromise and build on the practices that had already emerged in industries with longer histories of bargaining, such as railroads and clothing.[28]

The board served another critical function for the postwar operation of the industrial relations system: as a training ground for many of the key individuals who were to later serve critical roles as mediators, arbitrators, and advisors to labor, management, and government leaders. These individuals were deeply committed to collective bargaining and in their activities helped to promote practices that were consistent with the principles just outlined. Thus while NLRB decisions and doctrines helped promote a stable arena for collective bargaining, the WLB helped diffuse and institutionalize many of the principles that guided labor-management relations within that arena in the postwar period.

Although union membership grew steadily during the war, the end of the war and the lifting of the WLB's wage and other regulatory controls helped to produce an unsettled period within labor-management relations. A number of long strikes occurred in key industries such as automobiles, steel, meatpacking, and coal. In 1946 the percentage of total working time in the economy idle due to strikes reached an unprecedented level.[29] This period represented a critical point within labor-management relations. Freed from the moderating influence of the War Labor Board, management could have opted to return to the more aggressive opposition to unions characteristic of the Depression and earlier periods.[30] But, given the provisions of the NLRA that provided continuity to the union-management relationship, management could not simply do so. Thus management was forced to attempt to repeal the law or change it in ways that would strengthen employers' hands in collective bargaining. As we will see, employers and their political allies took both approaches.

The legislative initiatives of employers and conservatives in Congress did not result in repeal of the national policy favoring collective bargaining but rather in the passage of the Taft-Hartley amendments to the NLRA, amendments that sought to limit the power of unions and to articulate a new set of principles concerning the rights of individual workers in union-management relationships. While as James Gross has noted, some of the Taft-Hartley principles are inconsistent with the original principles underlying the Wagner act,[31] for our purposes the key point concerning the Taft-Hartley act is that it did not alter in any significant fashion the basic NLRA principles governing industrial relations activity. Thus while it undoubtedly produced a shift in bargaining power from unions to employers, Taft-Hartley allowed the basic features of the New Deal industrial relations system to continue to evolve along the path envisioned by the original framers of the system and reinforced by the War Labor Board.[32]

After the war, labor also faced choices regarding how far it was going to try to intrude into managerial decisions. In the auto industry, in a long strike against General Motors (GM), President of the United Auto Workers (UAW) Walter Reuther demanded that GM "open the books" so as to allow consideration of profits and prices during evaluation of the appropriateness of the union's wage demands. Many leaders of other major unions, however, argued that these demands went too far. As head of the CIO, Philip Murray put pressure on Reuther to abandon his more far-reaching demands and conform to the wage settlement negotiated in the steel industry.[33] Inside unions there were also battles underway pitching left and right groups against one another for leadership positions and in the debate regarding labor's agenda.[34] The outcomes of these internal union debates and political conflicts served to reinforce the basic features of collective bargaining. Reuther failed to extend his union's influence into management perogatives concerning pricing, employment, or investments. Left-wing and communist leaders of unions were either purged or lost influence within unions.[35]

The GM-UAW agreement negotiated in 1948 emerged as the model for others that followed in many industries. This agreement, which lasted two years, instituted cost-of-living and annual improvement-factor wage increases; included grievance and arbitration procedures; provided an array of fringe benefits, including pension, health, and insurance benefits; and was followed in 1950 by a five-year agreement that included these clauses as well as union security (union shop) and dues check-off procedures. A series of multiyear agreements followed, providing steady and substantial improvements in wages and fringe benefits.[36]

Similar multiyear agreements and contract gains were won in a number of industries, including steel, coal, rubber, and trucking. Union contract advances in these industries were facilitated by their extensive unionization and by the limited penetration of imports into the American market.

These contractual advances were accompanied by changes in internal union affairs. Centralization of power increased within the union hierarchies of strong industrial unions in the auto, steel, and coal industries. The national union in these industries played key roles in the negotiation of wages and fringe benefits, in overseeing strikes and the administration of the grievance procedure, and in maintaining a high degree of standardization through pattern bargaining in wages and employment conditions across plants and firms.

Collective bargaining in many other industries, such as paper, meatpacking, and auto parts, also provided substantial improvements in employment conditions but operated in a more decentralized fashion. In these industries the distribution of power was tilted relatively more in favor of local unions. Comparatively more decentralized bargaining also prevailed in industries dominated by craft unions, such as construction and electrical products. At the same time, pattern bargaining across and within those industries with more decentralized bargaining structures helped stabilize collective bargaining and standardize employment conditions. Furthermore, many of the more decentralized unions imitated the pay and other contractual advances negotiated by either the UAW or other relatively centralized national unions.

Management's response to unions in this period was by no means passive. Where unions won organizing campaigns, management worked hard to negotiate agreements that limited the scope of union and worker influence and, in particular, to prevent union influence from extending into strategic investment or entrepreneurial decisions. Furthermore, a number of firms, such as Thompson Products (later called TRW) and Du Pont, successfully worked to ensure that the unions that eventually did organize parts of their workforces were independent, not affiliated with either the AFL or CIO.[37] Still other companies struggled to avoid union organization completely. The strategies used by these nonunion firms were early versions of the tactics that became of major importance to the evolution of the U.S. industrial relations system and are discussed more fully in the next chapter. For now it is important to note that overall in this period, unions were fairly successful in spreading their influence across blue-collar workers in the nation's key industries. As figure 2.1 shows, by 1954 union membership had climbed to 17,022,000 (34.7 percent of the workforce).

Union influence on the economy was even wider than this number implies, given the leadership role and threat effects unions exerted on unorganized workers. Firms without unions felt compelled to pay wages and benefits that came at least close to union advances and adopt many of the formal layoff, promotion, and discipline procedures being developed within organized firms. As Sanford M. Jacoby notes, "The continuing irony in personnel management was that it best served the purpose of thwarting unionism by introducing the same reforms unions sought."[38]

Professionalizing Management of Industrial Relations. Central to the evolution of the U.S. industrial relations system in the 1940s was the transformation that began occurring in managerial staffs responsible for industrial relations and personnel. World War II and the rise of industrial unionism brought a new kind of environmental pressure to management. The increased demand for wartime production was accompanied by labor shortages and a drop in immigration. The pressure of labor-market shortages and rising production costs induced management to create specialized employment departments to administer relations with the workforce, a response encouraged by the War Labor Board. These new employment departments in turn led to greater centralization in hiring and disciplinary decisions and spurred the development of formal testing and assessment procedures.

Unions brought additional pressure to bear on management. The payroll costs associated with union demands were an obvious pressure, but far more important was the potential instability created by the possibility of disputes. Personnel departments moved to combat this pressure at first by pursuing aggressive antiunion tactics, including organized violence and industrial espionage. However, when the NLRA was upheld as constitutional in 1937, and as unions continued to win recognition, these efforts decreased.

Throughout World War II unions and the WLB helped encourage the adoption of formal and bureaucratic personnel procedures. Personnel practices that became more widely used during this time included job analysis and evaluation, seniority provisions, employment testing, and performance rating systems. The development of such procedures in turn spurred the formation of personnel departments that had a vested interest in the preservation and expansion of these procedures and the staffs that managed them.[39]

Management thus responded to all these pressures by adopting more formal policies and creating departments to administer them. Jacoby documents how ". . . decisions in a number of areas—hiring, promotions, wage determination, dismissals—were centralized or made subject to strict rules and procedures."[40] John T. Dunlop and Charles A. Myers point out how the ability of unions to turn grievances into organizing issues forced management to make personnel policies explicit and to centralize policy making so as to prevent unions from exploiting differences in treatment.[41] With collective bargaining came the need for management specialists to administer and interpret the technical aspects of labor agreements and the growing number of rules concerning work.

As their experience with unions and worker unrest increased, management came to realize that strong unions and union leaders could control their membership and bring stability to industrial relations—albeit for a price. The more management came to see unions as inevitable, the more it saw the advantages of cooperation with union leaders and a stabilization of bargaining relationships. By taking this position, of course, industrial relations specialists were also working to secure their own position within the management hierarchy. By stabilizing union functions and the position of union leaders, labor relations managers ensured the need for their own expert help and role. Thus a symbiotic relationship developed between union leaders and industrial relations professional staffs.

In practice, this new relationship brought the creation of new institutions for handling conflict and new rules governing employment policies, such as grievance and arbitration procedures. The introduction of dues check-off procedures, other forms of union security, and the central role played by seniority arrangements also served to increase the influence that union organizations and leaders had over workers, and in this way further stabilized labor relations. As the larger firms in the nation's key industries came under the influence of collective bargaining and the growing CIO- or AFL-affiliated unions, the union model came to be imitated by other, often smaller, firms. As Baron, Dobbin, and Jennings state, "the bureaucratic system of control that started to congeal by the end of World War II apparently persisted in older, dominant firms through inertia and diffused to newer, smaller firms through organizational modeling."[42]

The search for stability and the regularization of relationships spurred an expansion in corporate-level labor relations and central-level union activities and staffs. For example, at International Harvester in the late 1940s and early 1950s, labor relations managers along with their union counterparts struggled to eliminate wildcat strikes, handle grievances in an orderly manner, and administer the master national company contract uniformly across the company's many plants.[43]

A number of statistics reveal the power and position of industrial relations professionals due to these developments. In 1952 a Bureau of National Affairs survey found that in roughly 70 percent of surveyed large firms, the personnel/industrial relations function was thought to be as important to the firm as production, marketing, or finance.[44] In over 80 percent of the surveyed firms, contract negotiations were viewed as one of the most important personnel functions, if not *the* most important. Annual surveys of managerial practice found that corporate staff titles reflected the growing influence and importance of labor relations as the titles of "personnel director" were changed to "industrial relations director."[45] Just as the rise of manpower issues during World War I had brought forth personnel journals and training programs, the rise of labor-management conflict and the search for new ways to achieve industrial peace in the 1940s led to the founding of schools and centers of industrial relations and to major journals and professional societies.[46]

For those of us who know only secondhand about the turmoil and conflict that prevailed in shop-floor labor-management relations during the 1930s, it is hard to appreciate how strongly those events committed management to a search for stability and order. The professionalization of industrial relations that accompanied the gradual institutionalizing of collective bargaining procedures during the 1940s reflects the seriousness of that search.

THE 1950s: MANAGEMENT'S HARD-LINE RESPONSE

Management's efforts to limit the influence of unions heightened in collective bargaining throughout the 1950s and led some observers to conclude that a "hard line" had returned.[47] At General Electric (GE), for example, management developed a set of policies often labeled Boulwarism, after Lemuel R. Boulware, the vice-president of industrial relations and chief architect of the policies.[48] In this approach, GE sought to acquire the initiative by directly polling workers regarding their interests and complaints and then fashioning final bargaining positions that reflected the company's financial status, external conditions, and workers' priorities. A long series of court cases debated whether these procedures satisfied the company's obligation to bargain in good faith. But the important point is that this policy reflected the emergence of more widespread efforts by management to constrain union influence.

When recessionary economic conditions weakened labor's strike threat and bargaining power, management's efforts to gain greater control over work rules and other employment terms intensified. During the 1958–59 national recession, U.S. Steel led such an effort, which resulted in a 116-day strike, although the final settlement in fact included no major work-rule amendments. In industries such as electrical products, airlines, and railroads, management was somewhat more successful in reversing or at least slowing the expansion of labor's earlier gains.[49]

This did not prevent the further institutionalization of collective bargaining where unions had gained a foothold. Reflecting on developments in the 1950s, Slichter, Healy, and Livernash concluded that "day-to-day contract administration reflects growing accommodation."[50] Unions also continued to negotiate multiyear agreements and extend the terms of those agreements to a wider array of fringe benefits.[51] Examples of the expanding list of fringe benefits won by unions include supplementary unemployment benefits, created to provide income security to laid-off workers, and improved pension and health benefits. The repeated negotiation of national agreements that set wage patterns within and across industries produced identifiable wage rounds, wage contours, and "orbits of coercive comparison" across firms.[52] The merger of the AFL and CIO in 1955 gave the union movement even more stability by establishing procedures for resolving the disputes that arose between unions competing for the same prospective members.

Noteworthy government activity in this period included occasional use of Taft-Hartley emergency dispute resolution procedures and emergency boards created under Railway Labor Act guidelines. Some expanded government influence resulted from the McClellan hearings in the U.S. Senate on internal union corruption and the eventual passage of the Labor-Management Reporting and Disclosure Act in 1959, regulating internal union affairs and finances. Nevertheless, compared with earlier and later periods, the government played a relatively inactive role in labor relations at this time.

THE 1960s: THE RISE OF SHOP-FLOOR MILITANCE

The civil rights movement, urban riots, war in Vietnam, and campus protests created an environment of social turmoil and unrest in the

1960s. This environment combined with the strong economic growth that followed President Kennedy's tax cuts and the Vietnam buildup to produce tighter labor markets and increased worker power and militance on the shop floor. The rate of contract rejections in union ratification processes reached a record high of 14 percent in 1967 (compared to a range of 8 to 12 percent in prior and subsequent years.[53] The incidence of contractual and unofficial (wildcat) work stoppages also rose dramatically.[54] In some industries unrest on the shop floor was revealed by a rise in grievance rates and the emergence of local issues that prolonged contract negotiation processes.

For example, in the auto industry the percentage of total working time lost in work stoppages varied between 0.21 and 0.28 in those years between 1951 and 1959 when a new national contract was not being negotiated. By 1968 and 1969 (also noncontract years) the percentage of days lost had risen, respectively, to 0.74 and 0.94.[55] At General Motors, the number of written grievances per one hundred blue-collar workers rose from 50.4 in 1960 to 71.9 in 1973.[56] The number of issues raised in local contract negotiations at GM also rose: from 11,600 in 1958, to 19,000 in 1961, 24,000 in 1964, 27,000 in 1967, and 39,000 in 1970. In addition to reflecting the general unrest of the 1960s, the problem of local issues reflected the inability of the master national contract and central dealings between labor and management to attend to the myriad of problems that arose across the more than one hundred GM plants. The parties had not found means for addressing these local issues—quality of working life programs and greater worker participation at the plant level were still to come. In addition, managers were sometimes faced with the fact that the union leaders with whom they had forged close working relationships were unable to control their rank and file or to ensure the smooth operation of the institutions created in the previous decade.

Meanwhile, union organization in the public sector increased dramatically; this helped mask the initial signs of the movement's stagnation and declining ability to organize new firms and workers in the private sector. At the same time, given that unions were increasingly unable to organize new industries such as high technology in the 1960s, the percent of employees in nonagricultural establishments that belonged to unions declined from 31.4 to 27.0 over the decade. (See figure 2.1.)

This era also was characterized by government's increasing and more direct involvement in collective bargaining and in the direct regulation of employment conditions. For example, the Taft-Hartley emergency procedures were more frequently applied in industries such as long-shoring. More direct government intervention into the substantive outcomes of collective bargaining also came through federal pay guidelines that, though technically voluntary, were often promoted through the "jawboning" practiced by Presidents Kennedy and Johnson. As a consequence of the passage of civil rights legislation, which tried to ensure equal pay for equal work, government's role in the regulation of employment conditions also increased.

STABILITY AND ATROPHY IN THE 1970s

In the 1970s the unionized sector of the economy began to feel the effects of more direct competition from abroad, sharp pressure to respond to large employment declines during the deep recessions of 1970–71 and 1974–75, the effects of deregulation, and heightened competition from the growing nonunion sector. In industries such as meatpacking and garments, these pressures led to sharp declines in union membership and moderation in negotiated contract terms. In general, however, although the parties involved in collective bargaining perceived changing environmental pressures on their relationship, during the 1970s they continued to behave much as they had in the last decade. Management and labor's major preoccupation continued to be the maintenance of stability and continuity in the bargaining process.

Events in the steel and auto industries illustrate this pattern. In steel, the Experimental Negotiating Agreement (adopted in 1970) provided automatic wage-rate escalation in exchange for the steelworkers' giving up the right to strike during contract renegotiation. GM, in turn, initially set out in a strike in 1970 to get away from the use of an uncapped cost-of-living escalator. After a sixty-six day strike, management gave up on those efforts and consolidated its relationship with Leonard Woodcock, the new president of the UAW, agreeing to a contract that preserved the traditional wage formulas (the COLA and 3 percent-per-year annual improvement factor wage increases).[57] The terms of other private-sector contract settlements reflected this status quo orientation. The use of cost-of-living formulas grew during this period in response to high inflation, and fringe benefits continued to expand. In 1970, only about one-quarter of workers under major agreements (those covering more than 1,000 workers) had COLA protection. By 1977, COLAs were included in 61 percent of all major agreements.[58]

Concurrently, the number of new labor-market entrants, including females, teenagers, and the baby-boom cohort, increased markedly. Along with high inflation, this increase of workers produced a fall in real earnings for many unorganized workers and especially in the earnings of unskilled workers. Given that many organized workers continued to receive hefty wage increases, including COLAs, the gap widened between the earnings of organized and unorganized workers and differentials narrowed between low and high skilled workers within the same firm. The union/nonunion wage differential rose from 19 percent in the late 1960s to 30 percent by the late 1970s.[59] For the period between 1971 and 1981, total effective wage-rate changes of union workers averaged 9.4 percent per year compared to 8.5 percent per year for nonunion workers.

The steady economic gains unions negotiated during this period were met with a status quo orientation within the ranks of industrial relations management. The general approach of these professionals was to maintain continuity in established relationships and avoid anything other than incremental adjustment of the existing labor-management relationship even though various pressures were emerging that could have led to greater changes. The status quo orientation of industrial relations departments in the 1970s is revealed in a survey of labor relations executives conducted by the Conference Board in 1978.[60] The survey found that the labor relations function had become highly centralized. Ninety-two percent of all firms placed primary responsibility for developing union policies at the corporate level—in the hands of either the top labor relations executives (60 percent) or the company's chief executive officer (32 percent).

In another part of the Conference Board survey, corporate industrial relations executives were asked to assess the effectiveness of various aspects of the industrial relations function in their firm. The respondents gave the highest effectiveness ratings to the aspects of their work that reduced conflict: the ability to avoid "unnecessary" strikes, the avoidance of legal maneuvering, and the ability to coordinate labor policies within management and to cooperate with the union. Lower effectiveness ratings were assigned to specific bargaining outcomes (such as the ability to achieve management goals) or to their ability to introduce change. The lowest level of effectiveness was reported for aspects of the employment relationship that concern individual workers—such as attitudes and productivity issues. Not surprisingly, elsewhere in the survey few efforts were reported underway to address problems associated with employee attitudes and productivity.

The survey also asked questions about bargaining goals. These responses further substantiate that the primary objective of industrial relations staffs in the 1970s was to maintain the status quo and the stability of their relationship with unions and to seek change only in an incremental manner. The wage criterion given the greatest weight in the survey was comparisons, either with industry patterns or other competitors. A similar orientation dominated management's nonwage goals. The only issue in which management strongly sought to tighten existing provisions concerned the flexibility in the assignment of employees.

The resistance that industrial relations professionals evidenced in the early 1970s to worker participation experiments was another indication of their opposition to major changes in collective bargaining. Indeed, industrial relations managers were often cited as the major opponents of work innovation programs, an opposition that sprung from the fact that these programs threatened the relationships that had developed between industrial relations staffs and union leaders. Perhaps the best example of this resistance was found in GM and their efforts to develop Quality of Worklife (QWL) programs. As Bert Spector notes:

GM's traditional-minded labor negotiator, George B. Morris, Vice President for Labor Relations, saw QWL as a surrender of management powers. . . . As a concession to both Bluestone [the union Vice-President who supported the program] and Stephen Fuller [the Vice President of Personnel], Morris agreed to a letter of understanding with the UAW. In it, he recognized the "desirability of mutual effort to improve the quality of work life," and agreed to a joint Committee to Improve the Quality of Work Life with responsibility for reviewing and evaluating all QWL programs. The Committee met only occasionally in the first years of its existence. The failure of the Committee to pursue actively any QWL programs was due to the suspicion with which Morris viewed the notion of QWL.[61]

While industrial relations professionals were pursuing stability in collective bargaining, after 1960 the power and importance of the personnel functions outside of industrial relations were gradually expanding in most corporations. The most important pressure inducing this change was increasing government regulation. In a 1977 Conference Board survey two-thirds of the responding personnel executives cited government regulation as "a major or primary influence for change in their company's personnel management over the past ten years."[62] Dunlop estimates that between 1960 and 1975, the number of regulations administered by the U.S. Department of Labor tripled—

from 43 to 134.[63] Failure to comply with these regulations raised the possibility of costly litigation, penalties, and the loss of government contracts.

Employers responded with a number of changes in their organizations and policies, changes that often included the establishment of groups responsible for monitoring compliance with these regulations. Typically, these new groups were placed within the personnel staff function. The 1977 Conference Board survey found that 97 percent of the surveyed firms had an equal employment opportunity unit and 95 percent of these firms assigned that unit to the personnel function.[64]

Meeting government mandates and establishing programs of affirmative action required analysis of human resource flows and policies. This led to the collection of information regarding personnel levels and movements, a trend also spurred by the availability of low-cost data information and processing services. Meshing these personnel flows with general business plans in turn helped lay the foundation for new human resource planning techniques and staffs. Significantly, these new staffs also were placed within the expanding personnel department.

The power and influence of personnel staffs also grew because they had the skills to respond to problems associated with the growth in the number of technical, managerial, and professional employees. Since performance on these jobs was heavily dependent on the individual worker, previous systems of personnel administration based on collective approaches were inappropriate. Instead, personnel policies geared toward individual motivation and career goals rose in importance. Personnel staffs with training in psychology and the behavioral sciences were more suited to these policies and problems than were industrial relations staffs. Reflecting this transition, these specialists were called human resource rather than personnel specialists.[65]

While other aspects of personnel/industrial relations were finding new influence and undergoing growth, the influence of labor relations staffs began to undergo significant decline in the 1970s. In addition to the fact that they were being left out of the expanding areas of human resource management, their importance was declining because the share of the workforce represented by unions was declining. Union representation as a percent of the labor force declined to 21.9 percent by 1980. The newest industries, the newest firms in existing markets, and the newest plants in existing firms increasingly tended to be nonunion. In other words, no longer were unions an inevitable fact of life and no longer was it necessary for management to accept their existence. Firms were successfully pursuing nonunion options. The next chapter traces where and how the nonunion strategy developed and succeeded. At this point it is sufficient to note that the development of personnel policies geared toward union avoidance also tended to occur within personnel staffs and not within traditional labor relations staffs, thus contributing to the decline in the influence within corporations of those individuals tied to labor relations.

During this period the labor movement also generally rejected worker participation efforts and other programs that might have led to fundamental alterations in collective bargaining. In the aftermath of the well-publicized strike at GM's Lordstown (Ohio) plant and also partly in response to shop-floor unrest, a number of workplace experiments were initiated in the early 1970s. But with only a few exceptions, such as Irving Bluestone in the UAW's GM Department, most unionists were skeptical of these efforts and opposed their expansion, seeing them as antiunion ploys designed to undermine the role of the union and the sanctity of the collective bargaining agreement. The fact that initial management support for these programs came from those outside the traditional industrial relations function reinforced unions' suspicion of the experimental programs.[66]

At the same time, the labor movement was frustrated in its efforts to modify the nation's basic labor laws. The impetus for labor-law reform arose partially from labor's frustration with the existing regulation of representation election campaigns and the emergence of new employer tactics that served to delay and defeat unions in these elections. Congressional debate in 1977 produced a labor-law reform bill that had the support of President Carter and an apparent majority in Congress. But to the dismay of the labor movement, the bill died in a Senate filibuster.[67]

The failure of labor-law reform represented a more general stalemate that prevailed regarding labor policy; neither labor nor management had the power unilaterally to initiate major changes in the nation's labor laws or override the other group's veto power. Simultaneously and incrementally the government was increasing its substantive regulation of employment conditions in a manner that was not linked to collective bargaining. For example, the federal push for increased health and safety regulation was largely unassociated with union efforts to negotiate contract terms concerning health and safety, in the workplace or with the aid of existing health and safety committees.

Thus as the 1980s approached, the pressures on the New Deal industrial relations system were building to a crisis point. In retrospect, the crisis can be seen as inevitable, given an industrial relations system that for the most part was holding to the status quo while the environment was changing more and more.

Summary

The New Deal model of industrial relations emerged as the dominant form of collective bargaining after World War II and until the 1970s set the pattern for human resource management even where unions had not won representation rights. This system worked well in the post–World War II years because it provided stability while also satisfying other basic economic and organizational needs of labor and management. Another key to the success of this model was that it produced outcomes that were consistent with the economic environment. The push by industrial relations managers and labor leaders for continuity and stability in their relations was encouraged by the long-run growth underway in the U.S. economy. Thus stability in industrial relations was central to the business strategies of growing firms and industries. Moreover, the professionalization and upgrading of industrial relations staffs and functions after World War II reflected management's pragmatic adaptation to the perceived inevitability of unionization.

A critical aspect of the operation of the New Deal system was the long history of incremental change and resistance to more fundamental modification. This incremental adjustment orientation was apparent in government policy, managerial practice, and union bargaining objectives. While the scope of collective bargaining expanded over the years, it did so gradually and in a fashion that left intact the basic principles of the New Deal system.

Management's hard line in collective bargaining in the 1950s revealed that economic recessions would weaken union's power, but more importantly demonstrated that unions would not be so easily broken as had occurred in the pre–New Deal days. To many observers and practitioners, collective bargaining looked like a system that by 1960 had developed a set of permanently institutionalized practices in the nation's core industries. In light of this apparent growing accommodation between labor and management, many observers expected collective bargaining to spread to other industries as those industries matured.[68]

What was not foreseen were the emerging economic pressures and alternative business and human resource management strategies. These new developments led to the subsequent decline in the prominence of the New Deal collective bargaining system. In fact, by the mid–1950s, the system had already reached its pinnacle. In the 1960s and early 1970s, pressures that challenged the traditional system began to build up. These pressures included changes in the economic environment, but even more important was the development of a nonunion industrial relations system as an alternative to the traditional model. Before we can understand the eventual response of the union sector to all these pressures, it is important to understand the nonunion system and the managerial strategies that shaped its development.

3

The Emergence of the Nonunion Industrial Relations System

AT the same time that collective bargaining was developing and maturing, an alternate nonunion system of industrial relations was steadily emerging in the same companies and industries—first, slowly and quietly and then, by the 1970s, more rapidly and visibly. Between 1960 and 1980 the growth and diffusion of this nonunion human resource management system took place across a broad enough array of industries and firms to cause major changes to be introduced in unionized relationships during the 1980s. In this chapter we explore the relationships among the external environment, the values and business strategies guiding top executive decision making, and the management of industrial relations since 1960 that are central to understanding this evolution.

Our analysis of the growth and diffusion of the nonunion sector will apply the theoretical framework outlined in chapter 1. In doing so we will demonstrate how much of what traditionally has been defined as industrial relations at the middle and bottom tiers of our three-tier framework is shaped by environmental forces and strategic decisions made well above these levels. This, in turn, will demonstrate why we see management policies and actions as the driving force in American industrial relations in recent decades.

The Magnitude and Scope of Union Decline

Perhaps the best way to make our point is to briefly summarize the magnitude and scope of the decline in unionization that has occurred in the private sector of the U.S. economy since 1960. The overall magnitude of the decline in unionization was highlighted in figure 2.1; figure 3.1 summarizes its distribution across broad industry classifications.

It is not possible to provide a single precise measure of growth and decline in unionization since World War II because no single historical data series is available to track union membership changes over this period. Piecing together several different data sources does, however, provide a reasonably clear pattern. Estimates obtained by the Bureau of Labor Statistics (BLS) from surveys of national unions indicate that the peak levels of union membership (measured as a percentage of the nonagricultural labor force organized) occurred in the mid-1950s, at around 35 percent. In 1960 approximately 31 percent of the non-agricultural labor force was unionized.[1] Estimates shown in figure 3.1 suggest that this percentage declined slowly during the 1960s and then more rapidly in the 1970s and 1980s. By 1984 the BLS estimated union membership among employed wage and salaried workers had fallen to approximately 19 percent.[2] The 1984 estimate most comparable to the earlier BLS measures obtained from surveys of national unions puts the figure slightly lower, at about 18 percent.[3] The declines were particularly strong between 1980 and 1984 since the most highly unionized industries were hit hardest by the effects of the 1981–82 recession, the declining competitiveness of U.S. manufactured goods on world markets, and the economic and organizational restructuring underway within these industries.

While these overall numbers demonstrate the seriousness of the decline in unionization, they mask an even more important characteristic of the current pattern of unionization that was identified in the various case studies we conducted. Over the two decades of the 1960s and the 1970s, a significant nonunion sector emerged in virtually every situation that we examined. For some industries such as petroleum refining, where union membership had declined from approximately 90 percent of all blue-collar workers in the early 1960s to approximately 60 percent in the 1980s, the change is not surprising, given the tradition of independent unions, decentralized bargaining, and elaborate personnel policies that bear the imprint of dominant founders. The decline has also been dramatic, however, in three industries that have historically been viewed as strongholds of unionism: mining, construction, and trucking.

In underground bituminous coal mining, the nonunion sector has grown from virtually zero to approximately 20 percent of the industry. Major companies have opened nonunion mines, often in the heartland of United Mineworkers territory, such as Kentucky and West Virginia. In construction, the penetration of nonunion activity has occurred even in large commercial construction. During the 1950s and 1960s, open-shop construction companies moved into residential and light commercial construction but unionized companies continued to dominate the important, heavy construction sector. However, starting in the 1970s, the situation changed; increasingly, major office buildings and large industrial sites are being put up on a nonunion basis. Overall, between 1975 and 1984 nonunion activity has increased from approximately 50 percent to 75 percent of all construction work.[4] Over-the-road trucking presents a similar picture. Since deregulation in 1980, the industry has experienced a sharp transformation. Approximately 20 percent of the large, unionized carriers went into bankruptcy and were replaced by smaller, independent, and generally nonunion companies.[5]

At the company level, data from a number of highly visible firms further illustrate this general trend. In the early sixties, General Electric had thirty to forty nonunion plants. By the mid-eighties, this number roughly doubled as a result of the nonunion status of the new plants that went into operation in the 1960s and the 1970s. The drop in percentage of workers organized has not been as great as these figures suggest since the newer plants are smaller (often dedicated to a particular component) and usually have about five hundred to one thousand employees. Companies such as Monsanto and 3M have seen a drop in the representation rate for production and maintenance

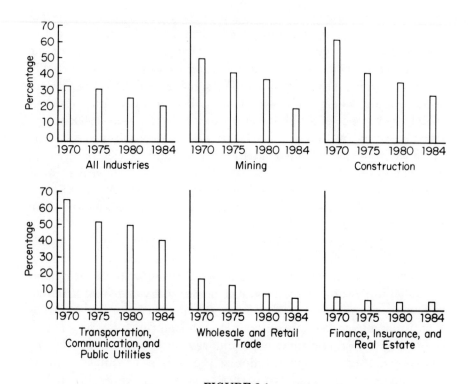

FIGURE 3.1

*Union Membership as a Percentage of Wage and Salary Workers
in Selected Industries, 1970–84*

SOURCE: Richard B. Freeman and James L. Medoff, "New Estimates of Private Sector Unionization in the United States," *Industrial and Labor Relations Review* 32 (January 1969): 143–74; and Larry T. Adams, "Changing Employment Patterns of Organized Workers," *Monthly Labor Review,* 107 (February 1985): 25–31.

workers from approximately 80 percent to 40 percent or less. Similarly, some of the major companies in the auto parts field, such as Dana, Bendix, and Eaton, have developed sizable nonunion sectors. The most complete transformation has occurred at Eaton, where as of the early 1980s, the only unionized operation to remain is at its main facility in Cleveland. The other union plants have been closed down and all the new plants that have been opened have remained nonunion.[6]

In short, the decline in union membership is both steep and broad. Yet it varies in degree, timing, and, as we will see, cause. We now need to turn to data to explain this pattern and variation in the decline of union membership and the rise of the nonunion human resource management system.

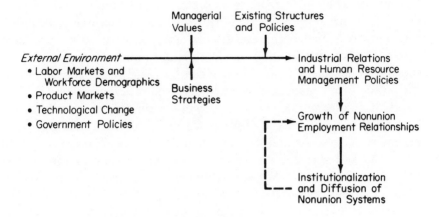

FIGURE 3.2

Emergence of Nonunion Employment Relationships

The Theoretical Framework

Figure 3.2 summarizes the way in which we see the key causal forces interacting to produce the growth and diffusion of the nonunion sector since 1960. Implicit in this model and in the analysis to follow is the view that there is no single causal explanation but rather a set of interdependent factors whose relative importance can be inferred only by piecing together a variety of case study, survey, and demographic data.

Shifts in the structure of the economy and the occupational distribution provide the starting point for the analysis and explain a portion of the decline in union membership. However, these external shifts do not act independent of the behavior of unions and employers. To understand why structural change has resulted in a decline in unionization in the United States but not in Canada or in most other highly industrialized democracies,[7] we need to analyze the key values and business strategies followed by U.S. firms and the historical and structural constraints specific firms faced in responding to new opportunities and pressures posed by environmental changes.

Because values, strategies, and structures do not change easily, major redirections of organizational strategies do not evolve in a smooth,

51

continuous fashion. Instead, most organizations tend to make incremental adjustments to existing strategies and structures until environmental pressures become so intense or new opportunities pose such significant potential gains that they can no longer be ignored.[8] The speed of adjustment is also influenced by the distribution of power within the firm's management and industrial relations system. Major efforts to challenge this perceived power distribution are feasible only in the face of significant environmental changes. Thus, during periods of environmental stability or incremental change, organizational strategies and structures tend to solidify and become more deeply embedded. Because models and strategies of successful organizations diffuse to other organizations through professional networks, organizations tend to become more alike.[9] In periods of significant strategic adjustment, however, a wider variety of choices and experiments emerge. Both strategies and structural arrangements become more variable until successful models are identified, the pace of environmental change slows, and the dominant values or beliefs that constrain strategies and internal structures and policies are clarified. Thus we will discuss the role played by two structural features of industrial relations: the degree of centralization in the structure of bargaining and the power of industrial relations staff specialists within the management decision-making structure.

The history of union organizing prior to the 1960s is particularly important to an understanding of the alternative paths and timing the decline in unionization has taken in different firms and industries. Throughout the analysis that follows we will illustrate these different paths and timeframes by distinguishing among the behavior of those firms and industries that: (1) were never unionized, (2) came out of World War II with an existing nonunion sector or the ability to develop such a sector via expansion, and (3) were totally or almost totally unionized prior to 1960 and where unions possessed the ability to organize new employment. In this third case the development of a nonunion sector usually came about through the arrival of new companies in the industry.

The final portion of our analysis focuses on the dynamics by which this alternative human resource management system diffused from one firm and industry to another. Implicit in this model is the notion that some firms, particularly a number of well-known firms that were never unionized, took the lead in experimenting with new human-resource management strategies, achieved initial success, and served as visible examples for other firms to emulate and improve upon. By the end of the 1970s the new nonunion model had been clarified sufficiently to support its more systematic use by firms in most sectors of the economy.

Empirical Evidence on Causal Forces

To summarize the evidence on the roles played by these causal forces, we will draw on a number of studies we and other researchers have conducted in recent years. Unfortunately, no single data base exists that allows us to partition the decline in unionization into unique or independent components. Thus, after presenting the evidence from various studies, we will provide our own interpretative summary of the relative importance of the different forces. Our analysis starts with the most obvious explanation for the decline: structural changes in the economy and labor force.

LABOR-MARKET CHANGES

The growth in the demand for and supply of white-collar workers, the expansion of the service sector of the economy, the relative growth in employment in the South, and the increase in the labor-force participation rate of women all have had the effect of expanding employment opportunities in occupations, regions, and industries where unions had not penetrated extensively by 1960. Given the fact that management had historically been even more adamantly committed to avoiding unionization of white-collar, professional, and midmanagement employees than for blue-collar employees, we would expect that the relative expansion of these jobs would contribute to the growth of the nonunion sector. The question is: How much of the decline experienced since 1960 can be attributed to these structural changes?

Our best estimate of the proportion of the decline in unionization due to structural changes in the economy and the labor force is summarized in table 3.1. Using a regression equation, Henry Farber derived estimates of the percentage of the labor force that would have been organized in 1977, *if* there had been no change from the demographic, occupational, regional, and sectoral mix of jobs that existed in 1953.[10] His estimates suggest that, taken together, these structural changes account for approximately 40 percent (3.9 of the 9.4 percentage points) of the decline in the labor force unionized between the mid-1950s and late 1970s. More specifically, his estimates suggest that the greatest portions of this decline are due to shifts from blue- to white-collar occupations, from the North to the South, and from manufacturing to the service sector. Each of these changes accounts for about 1.0 to 1.2 percentage points of the decline. The growth in the proportion of women in the labor force, on the other hand, accounts for only about 0.5 percentage points of the decline.[11]

TABLE 3.1

Decomposition of Decline in Unionization,
mid-1950s–1978

Dimension	Percentage-point drop	
	Regression Estimate	*Simple Estimate*
Away from Manufacturing	1.0	1.7
Toward the South	1.2	1.2
Toward White Collar	1.2	2.1
Toward Female	0.5	2.4
Total Accounted For	3.9	7.4

NOTE: The regression estimate is computed as the decline in the proportion of the workforce with a given characteristic multiplied by the appropriate regression coefficient contained in an equation that estimates the probability of being a union member in 1977 as a function of industry, region, occupation, and gender. The simple estimate is computed based on the decline in the proportion of the workforce with a given characteristic using the proportion of that workforce with that characteristic organized in the mid-1950s. The actual decline in unionization over this period was 9.4 percentage points.

SOURCE: Henry S. Farber, "The Extent of Unionization in the United States," in Thomas A. Kochan, ed., *Challenges and Choices Facing American Labor* (Cambridge, Mass.: MIT Press, 1985), table 2.5, p. 22. Copyright MIT Press.

It would be incorrect to infer, however, that the union declines that resulted from these structural shifts occurred independent from management or union influence. Clearly the shift in employment to the

South reflected, in part, management's seeking out the region's lower labor costs compared with those prevailing in the more highly unionized North and its feeling that the social and political climate of the South reduced vulnerability to unionization. Similarly, the shift of employment to services did not lead to a corresponding strategic response by unions in the allocation of organizing resources to the service sector. For example, Charles McDonald, director of the AFL-CIO Department of Organization, noted recently that:

While employer behavior and the shifts in the economy have important impacts, we also recognize that our organizing strategies have not always been well targeted. Up until 1974 [before the Health Care Amendments to the National Labor Relations Act], only 8% of our elections took place in the service sector. Since 1974, service-sector elections have increased to approximately 22%, but this is still well below where it should be, given the movement of jobs toward this sector of the economy. We believe we should be holding 70 to 80% of our elections in the service sector.[12]

The failure of unions to organize white-collar workers in the private sector also reflected the opposition of employers to encroachments across the blue-collar line and the exclusion of supervisors from coverage under the Taft-Hartley act.

Thus while changes in the structure and composition of the economy explain an important part of the decline in unionization, a more complete account requires an examination of the interactions of external economic changes and organizational policies. These interactions are most clearly illustrated by exploring the interplay among changes in product markets, business strategies, and management values.

MANAGERIAL VALUES TOWARD UNIONS

Underlying Farber's analysis is the assumption that if employment shifted to a sector previously unorganized, that sector would continue to be unorganized. We will expand on this premise by examining the various ways in which firms shifted employment away from unionized plants to new unorganized plants in the same sector, such as to a satellite plant one hundred miles away.

As noted in chapter 1, we see managerial values acting as a lens through which environmental pressures or opportunities pass in the process of producing organizational responses. Options that are inconsistent with accepted values are rejected, discounted as being outside the range of acceptable alternatives, or not even consciously considered. The deep-seated opposition to unions embedded in the ideology of American management and the culture of many American firms serves as the relevant value in explaining the rise of the nonunion human resource management system in American industry.

Throughout the following section we draw on the statistical results of a quantitative analysis of declines in union membership in a sample of two hundred large firms surveyed by the Conference Board in 1977 and again in 1983.[13] Our analysis of these data, along with the regression equations on which the estimates discussed in this chapter are based, is presented elsewhere.[14]

The role of management values can be seen most clearly in those firms that were never organized even though they had sizable operations during the 1940s and 1950s in industries that were otherwise highly unionized. While these companies represented a very small minority, they served as models for other companies that later sought to transform themselves from predominantly unionized to predominantly unorganized in their employment relations with production and maintenance workers. An understanding of how companies such as IBM, Motorola, Delta Airlines, Grumman Aircraft, and Burlington Mills avoided unions, especially during the critical organizing decades of the 1930s and 1940s, requires an analysis of the imprint of the founder, the centrality of personnel policies to the firm's business planning, and the industrial relations strategy of matching or exceeding improvements in wages, fringe benefits, and working conditions in similar unionized companies. In the 1950s these companies carefully copied the personnel policies and matched the compensation patterns established through collective bargaining in unionized firms.[15] Indeed, by the mid-1960s and 1970s the personnel policies of some of these companies had advanced beyond those of their unionized competitors. By then the human resource policies of the older, never-organized companies combined with newer advances in human resource policies and practices of the emerging high-technology firms of the 1970s in ways that added to the pressures on the unionized sector to respond.[16] A profile of the stages in the evolution of industrial relations and personnel practices of one such firm is presented in the following boxed display.

In other cases the implementation of management's underlying

Evolution of Union-Avoidance Strategies
of a Large Nonunion Firm

1950s–1960s

This is a large consumer and durable-goods manufacturing firm with corporate headquarters in a highly industrialized area of the Midwest. The company successfully resisted union organizing efforts throughout the 1940s and 1950s and has never had one of its major manufacturing facilities organized. In the 1950s the firm developed a reputation for being strongly antiunion. All efforts to organize its production facilities were defeated during those years.

During the 1960s the company diversified its product mix and opened a new manufacturing division in the western part of the country.

1970s

By the end of the decade this new division employed approximately 35,000 people. Ninety percent of its direct labor force is female. The cornerstone of the company's human resource management policy is an employee participation program. The company describes the program in an internal publication as follows:

> The program is a system of management—a change in culture if you will—that invites and requires the participation and involvement of each of us in managing our affairs in the company ... The program is based on the assumption that every employee wants to work in an atmosphere where practices, procedures and rules make sense and are reasonable ... The employee participation program encourages every employee to regularly attend meetings during which all matters relating to their work environment and their jobs are discussed.

The participation program contains a gain-sharing feature that can pay out up to 41 percent of direct wages. The actual payout in 1981 was 10 percent of base pay. The company has also been a leader in introducing work sharing as an alternative to layoffs during temporary periods of slack demand. The firm also employs a variety of communications programs, including an individual suggestion system, a "Speakout" program in which an employee can submit a written statement or question and get a response from a senior executive, and periodic attitude surveys. A company manager described the employee participation program as "a real defensive strategy against the prospect of union organization." No significant union organizing efforts have occurred in this division since its startup.

preference for doing without unions moved through several early phases of encouraging "cooperative unions." Thus when it was not feasible to avoid unions per se, the strategy was to encourage organization by former AFL affiliates or independent unions rather than CIO unions, which were perceived to be more militant. During the late 1940s and early 1950s, for example, Westinghouse established new plants in Vicksburg, Mississippi; Upper Sandusky, Ohio; and Reform, Alabama. These plants were organized by the International Brotherhood of Electrical Workers (IBEW)—a more pragmatic union than the International Union of Electrical Workers/United Electrical Workers (IUE/ UE), with whom the company had unsatisfactory past dealings. Westinghouse chose remote, rural locations in order to tap available labor and also to enable it to pay lower wage rates, assuming it could key its compensation to the local labor market. The arrival of the IBEW in these sites indicated that the company accepted the fact that during that period some union would organize its employees.

The strategy of encouraging the formation of local independent unions was especially prevelant in the oil and chemical industries in the 1950s. Consider the following statement of a large oil company's philosophy provided during our field interviews:

Employees have a right to choose whether to be represented by a third-party bargaining unit. The company does not feel that a third-party bargaining unit is necessary and will deal with employees directly pursuant to the [our] human relations' philosophy. However, if the employees feel that a bargaining unit is necessary, then an independent employee association is preferable to an international union which may have interests other than those directly related to the company and its subsidiary employees. If an international union is the legitimate and totally free choice of the employees involved, the company will bargain in good faith with that representative union and work to establish a positive relationship so that the best interests of the company and the employees may be met.

By the 1960s and 1970s, when they no longer perceived national unions as a serious threat, most firms (including the firm just quoted) abandoned this policy of encouraging independent or less militant unions and switched to a strategy of avoiding any and all unions. The boxed display (p. 59) profiles this evolution in the policy of one such firm.

Evolution of Union-Avoidance Strategy:
From Independent Unions to a Union-Free Strategy

This is a large diversified firm operating in all regions of the United States.

1900–1940s

Top executive develops strong view that unions are unnecessary and undesirable. Company philosophy of paternalistic management takes hold.

1940s–1960s

Independent unions were first accepted into the firm after a number of organizing efforts were made by AFL- and CIO-affiliated unions. In the 1950s several international unions organize existing plants, and other unionized plants are acquired.

In mid-1950s initial plant is set up on a nonunion basis after relations with existing unions began to deteriorate. A manager who participated in the design and management of this nonunion plant described the company's strategy as follows:

1. A plant manager was selected who was human-relations–oriented.
2. A strong personnel department was set up to serve as a representative of the people on the shop floor.
3. The company pledged to meet community wage standards and working conditions.
4. A nonunion "problem" or grievance procedure was established.
5. A wide range of social and recreational programs were provided.
6. A seniority system was created to handle layoffs if they occurred.
7. Employees from the previous (unionized) plant that had been shut down by the previous owner were screened out during the selection process.
8. Local political leaders welcomed the company into town since the plant had been closed by the prior owner.

1970s–1980s

All new plants of the firm opened on a nonunion basis. Plant managers are encouraged to follow innovative work designs. All but one new plant remained unorganized. The one new plant that was organized has been sold.

THE CONSTRAINTS OF HISTORY AND BARGAINING STRUCTURE

Given these managerial preferences, what kept all firms from taking steps to reduce unionization or seeking unions to their liking? This is the point in our model where the effects of history and the institutional structure and distribution of power in the firm's industrial relations system must be considered. In both the 1977 and the 1983 Conference Board surveys, the best predictor of whether a firm assigned a high priority to union avoidance was the extent of the firm's labor force unionized at the time. That is, the higher the proportion of the firm's labor force that was already organized, the lower the probability that management would put a high priority on union avoidance. In 1977 this correlation was −0.43; in 1983 it was −0.57.[17] Basically this correlation indicates that firms with high levels of unionization cannot feasibly pursue nonunion options because to do so would risk jeopardizing their current relationship with their unions and unionized workforces. This is especially true in centralized bargaining structures or where a single union represents enough of the firm's employees to give it the ability to interact informally with top executives. High levels of interaction and centralization give union leaders greater access to the strategic level of management decision making and provide them with a forum for pointing out the consequences a union-avoidance strategy would have for the union-management relationship. Several examples from our case files will illustrate this point.

The clearest example of this may be General Motors. GM's effort to develop a nonunion sector in the early and mid-1970s is well known. The steady expansion of the auto industry during that period created the need to build new plants. In the early 1970s GM constructed a series of plants in the deep South in such locations as Fitzgerald, Georgia, and in Clinton and Brookhaven, Mississippi. The first plants were set up on a paternalistic basis; but as the company gained experience, the next wave of new plants were modeled on the newly emerging work-organization concepts such as the use of teams and pay for knowledge.

However, the UAW forced GM to abandon its southern strategy in the mid-1970s in return for the union's continued cooperation in promoting quality-of-work-life programs at the workplace. The UAW first achieved a neutrality pledge from GM, then recognition based on a card check, and eventually accretion (automatic recognition) for new plants. The UAW was able to do this because it (1) represented all other production and maintenance employees of GM and GM's domestic competitors, (2) bargained centrally with the company, and (3) was able to force GM to make its overall corporate labor relations strategy consistent with its strategy of union-management cooperation in improving the performance of existing plants.

The chief executive officer of a large retail business that is also 100 percent unionized described to us his pragmatic adaptation as follows:

We have over two thousand stores in the United States and all of them are unionized. Our philosophy is to work with the union because if we were to go the nonunion route, it would take us twenty years to have any significant impact on the bottom line. Opening one nonunion store somewhere would have no impact on our bottom line but it would run the risk of increasing the hostility in our relationships with the union and could have a big impact on us. . . .

Another executive in this industry in a similar situation stated said: "We are 100 percent unionized and while we would prefer to be nonunion, it is a fact of life that we are not going to be doing anything about it." Few union leaders, however, were in the UAW or the retail food union situation.

As mentioned earlier, it is important to note in analyzing the attitudes of management toward unions that even during the 1940s and 1950s companies remained unalterably opposed to the organization of their white-collar workers. In fact, the first sector in which companies sought to roll back the perimeter of unionization was in those areas where there had been spillovers of organizing efforts from blue-collar into supervisory, professional, and technical occupations. Thus, for example, by the late 1940s almost 10 percent of all professional engineers were in unions. By the late 1960s, this number had dropped to approximately 3 or 4 percent.[18] The same story can be told for other white-collar areas. Companies such as General Motors and Ford that learned to live with unions in the factory drew the line when it came to their offices and laboratories and indicated in very explicit ways that they would (and did) oppose the UAW vigorously in its efforts to organize white-collar employees.

The Conference Board survey data demonstrated the power of both union-avoidance values and the ability to implement such a strategy because of an existing low rate of unionization and/or a decentralized bargaining structure and absence of a dominant union in the firm. Regression analysis of the probability that new plants opened by firms would be unionized showed that other things being equal, firms that gave high priority to union avoidance reduced the probability that their new plants would be organized by about 20 percentage points. Moreover, the absence of a single dominant union in the firm and the use of decentralized bargaining structures reduced the probability of unionization of new plants by an additional 37 percentage points.

INTERNAL MANAGEMENT DYNAMICS OF POLICY SHIFTS

Within most firms the motivation to actively pursue nonunion alternatives was felt first by line managers and high-level corporate executives, not by the industrial relations specialists responsible for dealing with union leaders. After all, as noted in chapter 2, industrial relations professionals had risen to power within the management hierarchy in the post–World War II period by achieving peaceful, predictable settlements in collective bargaining. Thus, if line managers or top executives were to translate their preferences for a nonunion option into an active organizational strategy, they needed to (1) assert influence over those industrial relations decisions that would influence the future degree of dependence on unionization in the firm and (2) enlist the aid of staff specialists who shared their union-avoidance values and had the technical expertise to design effective work systems that would be difficult for unions to organize. The rise of behavioral science–trained human resource management specialists in the 1960s provided this staff support and expertise. Thus, as we suggested earlier, decision-making power shifted back to line management and from the industrial relations to the human resource staff specialists.

One reason for the staff power shift is that human resource, behavioral science training did not pay any attention to collective bargaining and unions. Instead behavioral scientists' training focused on innovative work systems that stressed flexibility in work design, high commitment to the goals of the firm, and participation by individual workers and work groups. Thus those specialists were both willing and able to design innovative work systems (which we will discuss in detail in chapter 4) that effectively reduced the incentives of employees to organize.

Table 3.2 demonstrates that this shift in decision-making power occurred in a large sample of partially unionized firms in the United States. The data are drawn from the 1983 Conference Board survey and show that (1) the power and centrality of labor relations professionals has declined relative to human resource management profes-

TABLE 3.2
Line and Staff Responsibilities for Human Resource Management Activities

N = 504	Line Executive		Human Resource Executive		Labor Relations Executive		Chief Executive		Line Role Is Increasing (%)
	R + A[a] (%)	Primary[b] (%)	R + A (%)	Primary (%)	R + A (%)	Primary (%)	R + A (%)	Primary (%)	
Human Resources Planning	24.4	20.3	17.4	67.5	10.3	8.6	71.4	4.4	55.6
Development and Training	34.2	18.6	15.4	70.7	8.8	8.6	50.4	2.4	53.8
Salary Budget Decision	19.3	16.1	19.6	58.4	8.6	5.1	66.5	21.3	23.4
Introduce Employee Participation Programs	34.7	27.1	22.0	51.8	14.9	18.1	37.4	2.7	55.7
Strategies vs. Government Regulation	31.8	5.9	10.8	70.4	12.2	24.7	53.3	1.2	24.9
Developing Wage and Benefit Goals	28.6	7.6	13.2	64.8	14.2	25.9	73.3	9.0	27.1
Set Wage Bargaining Limits	26.4	18.1	22.5	26.9	16.6	40.6	57.0	17.1	21.5
Set Policy Toward Unions	28.1	6.1	22.5	37.9	10.0	48.4	60.9	11.5	23.9
Directing Union Avoidance	32.3	9.5	22.0	35.9	8.1	49.6	43.3	1.0	30.4

NOTE: [a]R + A means authority to review and/or approve policies.
[b]Primary means the primary responsibility for developing and implementing policy.

SOURCE: Conference Board 1984 survey of employee relations practices of major U.S. firms. See Audrey Freedman, *The New Look in Wage Policy and Employee Relations* (New York: The Conference Board, 1985).

sionals; (2) line managers are taking a more active role in human-resource management and industrial relations issues so that power has been shifting away from *both* labor relations and human resource management professionals toward line managers; and (3) top executives are taking a greater interest and getting more involved in the human resource and industrial relations issues of the firm. For example, the last column of the table reports that the role of line managers is increasing in more than 50 percent of the firms on major human resource policy and planning issues, employee and management development and training, and the introduction of employee participation programs. The interest of chief executive officers in human resource issues is also suggested by the fact that they review and approve most of these policies in most of these firms.[19] Regression analysis of these data also showed that the power of line managers is increasing more in those firms that give a high priority to union avoidance.[20] This finding is consistent with the notion that it is the line managers more than the industrial relations or human resource management professionals who serve as the driving force in union-avoidance efforts.

Further analysis of these survey data indicated that the strategic shift toward a human resource model of workplace design and the realignment of decision-making power proved to be very effective. For example, we found that the more control line managers asserted over human resource and industrial relations policies, the more innovation in work organization and design and practices (autonomous work teams, pay for knowledge, flexible work hours) resulted. In turn, the use of these innovations significantly reduced the probability that a firm's new plants would be organized and thus contributed significantly to the reduction in number of the firm's unionized employees. Moreover, these effects were quite large. Specifically, firms that implemented the average amount of these innovations (compared to those not using any of the innovations) reduced the probability that a new plant would be organized by approximately 17 percentage points.

We further estimate that from the mid-1970s to the early 1980s, union membership declined by approximately 1,133 workers in firms employing the average amount of innovation in their nonunion plants compared to firms with no workplace innovations. Since only about 20 percent of these new plants were organized, these estimates confirm what our case-study data suggested: wherever plants were designed and run on the new human resource management model, they were essentially immune to unionization in the 1970s.

In short, both case-study and survey data demonstrate the validity and practical significance of our central hypothesis concerning the role of managerial values in the transformation of U.S. industrial relations in the period from 1960 to 1980. The first preference of managers was to avoid unionization. Firms chose strategies that were consistent with this preference wherever feasible. As we shall see, changes in the environment since 1960 served to gradually increase both the opportunities and the economic incentives for firms to act on these preferences.

PRODUCT MARKETS AND BUSINESS STRATEGIES

The sequence of strategic business decisions set in motion by increases in product market competition is illustrated in figure 3.3. When competition increases, the initial decision a firm must make is whether it wants to remain active in that line of business and compete in the new environment or withdraw and reallocate its capital resources to other opportunities. If the firm decides to remain in the market, the next decision it must make is whether to compete on the basis of low prices (costs) and high volume or to seek out more specialized market niches that will support a price premium.[21]

The central industrial relations effect of this increased sensitivity to prices and costs is that firms shift their priorities away from maintaining labor peace to controlling labor costs, streamlining work rules (so as to increase manufacturing efficiency), and promoting productivity. The pressure to control or lower costs is especially intense if a firm attempts to compete across all segments of its product market on the basis of low prices and high volume.

Changes in product-market structure and in intensity of competition also encourage firms to rearrange their capital in ways consistent with what Joseph A. Schumpeter described as the process of "creative destruction."[22] Since this process involves a change in production technology, it affects the mix of job skills and workforce requirements. Often, however, the changes in technology and/or workforce requirements are great enough to introduce another strategic choice that has significant implications for industrial relations: the choice of whether to reinvest in an existing site or to direct new investment to a new location. As we shall demonstrate, this choice and the speed of the capital reallocation and disinvestment process have a highly significant effect on the number of union members who survive these processes.

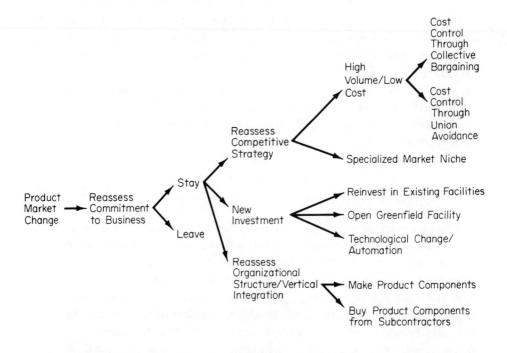

FIGURE 3.3

Sequence of Business Strategy Decisions Affected by Product Market Changes

Finally, as product markets mature and technological innovations diffuse to a wider range of firms, the economics of vertical and horizontal integration often changes, opening up a host of new choices about whether to make or buy different components of the firm's products and services. New lower-cost entrants, who can use state-of-the-art technology to supply product components or specialized services that earlier had been produced internally, can be expected to enter mature markets. Thus again the incentive for the firm is to reallocate work and employment to these outside contractors as part of its cost-reduction strategy.

CHOICES OF PLANT LOCATION AND THEIR EFFECTS

One of the key choices that surfaces as firms adjust to changing markets is whether to expand and modify existing facilities or open new "greenfield" sites. The outcome of these choices exerted a profound effect on the level of unionization in partially organized firms in the 1960s and 1970s. A review of the findings of a major study of plant location decisions conducted by Roger Schmenner and by data from our own research will demonstrate this effect. Schmenner noted that: "Most companies, when confronted with a need to expand capacity, think first about expanding onsite—a very natural tendency, because onsite expansion is often low cost and not too disruptive of the existing management controls."[23] However, another consideration works in a reverse direction. According to Schmenner, "A second informal decision rule that some corporations follow is that no plant which is unionized will be expanded onsite."[24]

How do these two contrasting tendencies balance out? Schmenner surveyed large companies that had approximately 9,500 plants in place throughout the 1970s. Of these, 18 percent expanded onsite, for a total of 1,700 plant expansions. By comparison, these companies opened slightly over 1,600 new plants during the same period. Thus it is clear that both strategies were pursued. Further analysis showed that those firms most likely to expand existing plants (1) were dependent on the existing site because of fixed capital costs; (2) needed to remain in an existing location for marketing reasons; or (3) were nonunion at the existing site. In contrast, those firms most likely to open a new plant were sensitive to labor costs or needed to locate in new areas for marketing reasons.[25]

Further evidence for the effects of union-avoidance considerations in plant-location decisions can be found in the Conference Board data introduced earlier. Controlling for differences in employment growth, those firms giving union avoidance a high priority opened approximately 1.5 more new plants than sampled firms that assigned a lower priority to this objective. Since the average firm opened only three plants during the eight years covered by the study, the 1.5 estimate represents a 50 percent increase in the likelihood that a firm that puts a high priority on union avoidance will choose to invest in a new plant rather than reinvest in an existing facility in the face of similar employment expansion or contraction opportunities or requirements. Moreover, further analyses showed that, consistent with Schmenner's data, only about 15 percent of the new plants opened by these firms between 1975 and 1983 are unionized, and organization for the majority of these plants is the result of voluntary or automatic recognition, not National Labor Relations Board (NLRB) elections. Indeed, our analysis suggests that on average, each new plant opened resulted in the loss of approximately 117 union members in the firm as work was shifted from the older unionized to the newer nonunion plants.

The relationship between a management preference for nonunion operations and business strategy decisions can be seen most clearly in the plant-location decisions of companies that have never been unionized. IBM, for example, has many centers in the United States where employment concentrations are very large. For example, the Poughkeepsie, New York, area has about 25,000 IBM employees and the Endicott, New York, area has about 15,000 employees. The expansion of employment, if not physically at the base site, occurs nearby in the general community. Over time, companies like IBM have come to be known as good places to work; such companies can capitalize on the returns of a good corporate image. In some instances, local community leaders have opposed unionization because they know that should the company that provides the base of employment in their area become organized, it would expand elsewhere.

Clearly, there are limits to the concentration of employment that even a nonunion firm would allow to develop in a given community or region. Most companies set upper limits so as not to exert too large an effect on the economic health of a particular region. Nevertheless, these limits appear to be much higher for nonunion companies than for heavily organized ones. Thus, during the 1950s, 1960s, and 1970s, when most unionized companies were dispersing employment, unbundling some of their large concentrations, and opening small plants, many never-unionized companies were expanding employment in already established areas.

DIFFUSION TO PARTIALLY ORGANIZED FIRMS

It is difficult to detect any generalized expansion of the nonunion sector within manufacturing firms that were wholly or partially organized prior to the 1960s. Nevertheless, in the 1950s a handful of companies had begun to learn from the policies of firms that were never organized and began to adapt their policies. Consider the experience of Du Pont.[26] During World War II the company constructed and operated a number of nonunion munitions plants. In light of this experience, in 1946 the company adopted a policy that all new plants would be started up and maintained on a nonunion basis. At that time,

94 percent of Du Pont's blue-collar workers were represented by independent or national unions. A total of fifty-one current sites were started up after 1946, and only three are organized (despite 78 representation elections at these sites). Today about 35 percent of Du Pont's blue-collar workers are represented by unions; independent unions have representation rights at 24 sites and national unions rights at eleven sites. The personnel policies put in place by Du Pont resemble those used by the companies that were never unionized and include an emphasis on individual treatment, pay in the upper bracket of the local area, and enhanced employment security with length of service.

Procter and Gamble (P&G) is another company that adapted the nonunion model quite early, perfected the strategy, and in turn served as a model for other firms. During the 1950s and 1960s P&G expanded steadily. The plants that were constructed during this period usually were organized, often by an independent union, or in some cases by a local of one of the major unions in the chemical field, such as the Oil, Chemical and Atomic Workers (OCAW) or the International Chemical Workers (ICW). Most production facilities were located close to major urban centers. Starting in the mid-1960s, however, P&G entered into a very ambitious program of expansion and thereafter opened a new plant approximately every fifteen months. Many of these plants were located in outlying areas (in the case of the Charmin Paper Division, to secure adequate supplies of water) and for the most part, they have been kept nonunion.

At first the company's approach was experimental. In the case of its Augusta plant the company installed a gain-sharing system (a modified Scanlon plan). As more plants were opened to support the expansion of the Charmin Paper Division, the company moved beyond elementary concepts of participation and gain-sharing into full-fledged teams and the absence of traditional management—what has come to be called the "technician system." All of this experimentation took place in their nonunion plants.

For both the Du Pont and P&G–type companies, the selection of sites for expansion was of critical importance. The approach appeared to be one of differentiating the union-free experiment as much as possible from the core operations that were presumably unionized. Geography often provided this separation. For example, Goodyear chose to build its nonunion plant in Oklahoma rather than in the Akron, Ohio, area, where its headquarters are located.

The decision by a company to enter a line of business that could be differentiated from that of the core areas also provided, in a number of instances, the opportunity to pursue the nonunion alternative. For example, when Alcoa entered the magnesium field it built its plant in Addy, Washington, near a source of raw materials. The combination of a distant location, different product, and innovative organizational and managerial concepts have made it possible for Alcoa to keep this facility nonunion.

One of the best guarantees for keeping a plant unorganized was to locate it in a southern state. It was not the right-to-work legislation found in most of these states per se that made a difference, but rather the area's generally antiunion social and political climate as well as lower labor costs that made the location attractive. One company that we studied opened twenty-six new plants between 1960 and 1982. Of these, eleven were located in the Southeast and seven were located in the Southwest.

Our case files contain many examples of other companies that have followed the route of opening greenfield site plants and keeping them nonunion. Table 3.3 summarizes some of the major examples.

INCREASED INCENTIVES TO AVOID UNIONS

An important reason why so many firms accelerated the move to new plants in the 1970s was that the opportunity arose at the same time when the economic incentives to do so were increasing. For example, in chapter 2 we noted briefly that union/nonunion wage differentials were increasing over the course of the 1970s, thus making the opening of new nonunion plants more attractive to management. While the efficiency benefits of the shock effect of unionization may have been enough to offset the 10 to 15 percent wage premium in union facilities in the 1950s and 1960s, few managers could find productivity improvements to offset the 20 to 30 percent wage and fringe-benefit differentials many of them faced in the mid- to late 1970s. Moreover, in chapter 4 we shall present specific data to document that these differentials do in fact apply to union and nonunion plants *within* the same firm even after controlling for difference in industry, skill mix, and age of the plant. Thus in the 1970s many firms were in a position to choose between investing in and expanding employment in a high-cost union plant versus opening a new lower-cost plant that in all probability could be operated successfully on a nonunion basis. Finally,

TABLE 3.3
Development of the Nonunion Sector via New Plants

Company	
General Mills	A new plant was opened in Iowa on a nonunion basis. The company continues to operate existing facilities (all unionized) in Chicago, Buffalo, and on the West Coast.
Pepsi Cola	Over the past decade, this company has opened a number of distribution centers and warehouses on a nonunion basis, with the bottling plants remaining unionized.
Paper companies such as Mead, Champion International, International Paper, Union Camp, and Weyerhauser	All of these companies have opened new paper mills and kept them nonunion. This is in addition to fabricating plants, which have traditionally been less unionized and are becoming increasingly less unionized.
Mobil Oil	In the early 1970s, the company opened a new refinery at Joliet, Illinois, which has remained nonunion.
Tire companies such as Goodyear, Firestone, General, and Uniroyal	All of these companies have opened major new tire plants, often in the Oklahoma/Tennessee region, and these plants have been kept unorganized.
Corning Glass	Despite the fact that all of the plants in Corning, New York, and the expansion plants opened during the 1950s and 60s were unionized—often by the company voluntarily recognizing the union—when a new medical products plant was opened in Medfield, Massachusetts, the decision was made to keep it union-free.
Cummins Engine	New plants opened during the 1970s in Jamestown, New York, and Charleston, South Carolina, have remained nonunion. The core facilities in Columbus, Indiana, are unionized by an independent union.
Pratt & Whitney	Satellite nonunion plants (to the Hartford, Connecticut, base) have been opened in Maine and Georgia.
ACF Industries	In the early 1980s the company closed a key carburetor plant in St. Louis and opened a replacement facility on a joint-venture basis with a European automobile company. This latter plant, located in North Carolina, has operated on a nonunion basis.
Piper Aircraft	This company opened a new facility in Florida. This plant, which produces many of the same models of aircraft as those produced at the home plant in Lock Haven, Pennsylvania, has remained nonunion.
Electric Boat Division of General Dynamics	A new major facility opened in Providence, Rhode Island, employing over four thousand workers, has remained nonunion despite the state's supportive union atmosphere and a number of organizing drives by the Craft Council that represents the workers at the home base in Groton, Connecticut.

the newer work-organization designs emerging in the most innovative nonunion plants offered relief from what many managers had become convinced were outmoded, restrictive, and costly work rules.[27] We shall address the factual data on this issue in the next chapter.

THE SPEED OF DISINVESTMENT

While our analysis thus far has emphasized the common pattern by which companies created a nonunion sector by directing expansion to greenfield sites, a great deal of diversity exists in the speed and nature of the redeployment and disinvestment process. This certainly was the case during the 1960s and early 1970s; it intensified by the end of the 1970s as competitive pressures mounted and the labor-cost gap between union and nonunion alternatives expanded. Several examples will illustrate this diversity.

The Case of Slow Disinvestment. The first case we will consider involves a large conglomerate employing more than 94,000 workers in 300 locations in the United States and other countries. The company manufactures a wide range of industrial products. Although serious organizing efforts had begun in the early 1940s, the firm remained unorganized until late in that decade. During much of this period, a high-profile company president pursued a nonunion/"pro-employee" policy.

When, in the late 1940s, unionization was seen as inevitable, the company sponsored the formation of independent unions. In the 1960s several international unions came into the company as a result of plant acquisitions. By the 1970s the company had developed a strategy to open new plants and maintain their nonunion status. No attempt, however, was made either to dislodge existing unions through decertification drives or to rapidly divest or close unionized plants, and no appreciable quantities of production have been moved away from union plants to nonunion ones.

However, evidence on capital investments in the firm's union and nonunion sectors demonstrates management's inclination to prefer nonunion over union plants. This can be seen from data we collected from five nonunion and three union plants. Year-to-year expenditures on plant and machinery document the gradual shift from union to nonunion plants. Table 3.4 shows the capital expenditure per employee over the years 1971 to 1981. Expenditures in union plants are consis-

TABLE 3.4

Expenditures on Plant and Machinery by Union Status and Age
(in 1965 dollars per employee)

Year	Union	Nonunion	Old Nonunion	New Nonunion
1971	713	1230	1230	—
1972	266	992	992	—
1973	551	993	993	—
1974	212	3679	3679	—
1975	504	603	603	—
1976	405	916	916	—
1977	521	1203	1203	—
1978	408	1230	489	2711
1979	474	1239	1129	1461
1980	842	1216	1072	1505
1981	1020	1814	1120	3202
Average	538	1374	1220	2220

SOURCE: Based on data from Anil Verma, Union and Nonunion Industrial Relations Systems at the Plant Level, Unpublished Ph.D. Dissertation, Sloan School of Management, MIT, 1983.

tently lower both overall and in each of the eleven years. It was not possible to collect detailed data on the value of output per employee and other relevant data needed to control for variation in the value of products made or processes used in the plants. It was possible, however, to examine the age of the plant to see if that variable could explain the differences in capital expenditure. To examine the effect of age, these data were broken down three ways into union, old nonunion, and new nonunion plants. The results are reported in the last two columns of table 3.4. As before, capital expenditures in union plants were lower than in the old nonunion plants. Expenditures in new nonunion plants were high. A large portion of these expenditures may be attributed to start-up investments. But the differences in expenditures between the union and the old nonunion plants cannot be attributed to age.

Planned Disinvestment. A number of firms took a more aggressive approach to the disinvestment of union operations. Planned disinvestment describes companies that directed any expansion in capacity to new plants but, more importantly, shifted capacity from old union plants to new plants. Companies such as Cooper Industries and Emerson Electric are examples of this approach, as the following quotations suggest:

Approximately 50 percent of Cooper's workforce is unionized but the percentage has been declining as Cooper has relocated facilities from high-to-low labor cost areas. Cooper strives to provide wage rates that are competitive in the community in which the plant is located, but their rates must also be competitive within the industry. Where the latter criterion is not possible and the union is unaccommodating, Cooper will relocate the plant. In the past 15 years, 18 plants have been relocated from high-to-low labor costs areas, with another six moves in progress. Of the 18 plants already relocated, 15 of the newly opened plants are nonunion.[28]

Emerson's culture has its roots in the twenty-year reign ... of W. R. ("Buck") Persons who transformed Emerson from a high cost manufacturer into a cost-driven, diversified business.... he pioneered the company's "southern strategy," pushing its manufacturing out of highly unionized St. Louis into small plants scattered across the South. Today, most of the company's 116 plants are located in the mid-South. The company, which ties 10% of its division managers' bonuses to keeping plants union-free, has gotten unusually adept at this practice. It has lost just one of thirty-four organizing campaigns over the past decade.[29]

Quite often, instead of abruptly shutting plants down, a company following planned disinvestment would gradually shift products or components from the union plants to new sister or satellite operations. Our research uncovered the following example of a large company that over time "unbundled" its operations in a large unionized plant. As a result, employment fell from a peak of 13,000 in the 1940s to approximately 1,200 in 1985, with substantial gains in employment in the new nonunion operations.

A Case Study of Rapid Disinvestment.[30] This case study follows one major division of a large firm engaged in the production of industrial goods. This division began operations in 1918 at a site in the Northeast. The plant remained nonunion until the late 1930s, when it was organized by an international union. By the early 1940s the plant employed 13,000 workers, many of whom lived in company-built housing near the site. After the war, employment declined and held steady at about 8,500 beginning in the late 1950s. Meanwhile, labor-management relations deteriorated. In the decade following 1948, management and union conducted two long and bitter strikes over incentive rates.

Beginning in the 1960s, an accelerated disinvestment strategy began to take shape within the company. In 1963 some operations were moved to a nonunion facility, resulting in a loss of 400 jobs. This process continued over the next twenty years. By 1982 a total of 2,340 jobs were moved out of the plant to nonunion facilities. Between 1983 and 1985 more jobs were scheduled to leave the site. Besides moving existing work to new locations, the company has also directed new investments to its nonunion plants. Three new plants were opened in the Southeast between 1967 and 1972 to add capacity in product lines already covered by the union plant. As a result, the nonunion sector has grown rapidly since the 1960s. In 1960 the original—and only—union plant employed 8,500 workers. By 1983 the nonunion units employed 3,700 workers compared to 2,100 in the original union plant, with plans to further reduce employment in the union location to 1,200. With even modest growth rates, employment in the nonunion sector should rise to 4,500, which would make the union sector's share of total production and maintenance employment about 21 percent, down from 100 percent twenty years earlier.

Between 1965 and 1970, when the nonunion sector was taking shape, gross assets grew by 77 percent (in 1972 dollars) in the union plant. However, this growth rate slowed to 59 percent between 1970 and 1975 and 47 percent between 1975 and 1980. Since 1980 this rate has been still lower. In contrast, between 1970 and 1975 the real growth in the assets of the nonunion plants was 177 percent. As expected, this extremely high growth rate slowed down between 1975 and 1980 but at 72 percent it was considerably greater than the growth rate in the union plant. Similarly, between 1970 and 1975 net fixed assets increased 19 percent in real terms in the union plant while those of the nonunion operations grew by 137 percent. Between 1975 and 1980 the union plant's assets declined 2 percent, compared to an increase of 32 percent for the nonunion plants.

ACCELERATION OF THE TRANSFORMATION IN THE 1980s

During the 1980s a number of companies have followed an even more aggressive strategy of cutting back and shutting down their older, unionized operations more extensively than their newer, nonunion operations. A dramatic example of this was Florida Steel, which decided during the early 1980s (and after a comparison of costs between its unionized and unorganized plants) to consolidate all of its operations in its nonunion plants.[31] A recent newsletter of Dana Corporation indicated that due to business conditions between spring of 1979 and December of 1982, employment in the five largest plants (all unionized) had been cut in half, whereas employment for the remainder of the plants (smaller and many of them unorganized) had dropped by only

20 percent.[32] Such cutbacks often become permanent because as volume picks up, the additional activity can be handled by the newer nonunion plants and the unionized workers remain laid off, thereby accelerating the attrition rate of union membership.

Another firm that followed this pattern in the 1980s is Ingersoll-Rand. As a 1985 *Wall Street Journal* report noted:

> In the past few years, Ingersoll-Rand has moved production from union plants in the North to nonunion plants in the South. It has withdrawn from businesses, including some that were heavily unionized. And, where it has had the chance, it has encouraged workers to reject their unions. The result: 30 percent of Ingersoll-Rand's U.S. production workers now are represented by unions, down from 60 percent at the end of 1981.[33]

Thus Ingersoll-Rand serves as a prime example of how the gradual strategy of opening small nonunion expansion plants in the 1970s laid the foundation for a more abrupt shift of operations from union to nonunion plants during the period of excess capacity caused by the recession of the early 1980s.

CERTIFICATION AND DECERTIFICATION

Throughout this chapter we have examined the various avenues by which companies were able to expand the relative importance of the nonunion sector. Basically, the key step in this process was a shift of assets and employment to new plants or to operations that had never been unionized. The second step that was necessary for this strategy to be successful was the ability to avoid representation elections, and if they were held, to avoid union victories. Thus we need to understand what happened to the union's ability to organize new workers in recent years. A growing body of empirical evidence suggests that unions have had increasing difficulty recruiting new members via organizing campaigns. Therefore, we need to briefly summarize this evidence and note how it relates to the explanations for the declines in union coverage emphasized in our analysis.

The managerial strategies discussed in this chapter are likely to affect union organizing through representation elections in two ways. First, in settings where management introduces innovations at the workplace and responds to employees' needs in new and unorganized facilities, workers have less incentive to initiate an organizing drive. Second, where organizing drives are initiated, the probability of a union winning an election should be lower, especially in those firms that attach a high priority to union avoidance. Some of the lowered probability of a union win is due to the lower incentives to unionize and some to the more intensive legal and illegal management tactics used to defeat unions in elections. Data from national studies of union-organizing activities and outcomes and some of the data from the Conference Board survey discussed earlier suggest both of these effects have been operating since 1960.

The results of an analysis of overall trends in union election activity since 1950 performed by Richard Freeman showed that between 1960 and 1980, the number of elections held as a percentage of the labor force, the number of workers included in these elections, and the union's win rate in the elections held all declined.[34] The result of these declines in election activity and in union win rates meant that the percentage of eligible workers in the labor force that were newly organized per year fell from about 1 percent in 1955 to about 0.2 percent in 1980. This rate of new union organizing produces less than half the number of new members that are needed just to offset the rate of attrition experienced annually during the 1970s.

A more recent analysis of the effects of the declining returns to representation election procedures further helps place these numbers in perspective. William Dickens and Jonathan Leonard compared the relative importance of changes in the economic environment and organizational policies to the net effects of changes in the number of elections held and the union success rates in those elections. They concluded that "even if unions had continued to win representation rights for the same percentage of voters in certification elections as they did in 1950–54, their share of employment would still have fallen over this period [1960–80] nearly as much as it actually did."[35] They further noted that union coverage would still have fallen if unions had won 100 percent of the elections held since 1950. Moreover, even though the rise in union decertification elections has received much publicity, Dickens and Leonard showed that decertifications account for less than 2 percent of the union decline over this period. Therefore, besides the declining win rate of unions in representation elections, some broader set of factors is responsible for the decline in unionization during this time.

Analysis of the effects of election activity on union membership trends in the sample of firms included in the Conference Board survey further supports these national data. Of the firms that opened new plants, only 78 percent had one or more union representation elections within the past five years. Although we cannot tell from these data, the percentage of newly opened plants that had an election was undoubtedly even lower. Thus a significant number of firms were not subject to any serious organizing effort. Furthermore, of those elections held, unions won only 20 percent. Union win rates were particularly low in those firms that assigned a high priority to union avoidance. Specifically, unions won only 17.6 percent of the elections held in firms that place a high priority on union avoidance, compared to a union win rate twice as large, or 37.9 percent, in other firms. Thus a corporate strategy of union avoidance has a significant effect on the results of union-organizing efforts in a given plant or location. Moreover, regression analysis of changes in union membership in these firms showed that even if the union win rate doubled or tripled, the new members gained would not have offset the losses incurred due to the previously discussed broader environmental and organizational forces leading to declining membership. Thus these data reconfirm what the national trends suggest: not only are unions faring poorly in the elections that are being held, but changing the outcomes of these elections would still not be enough to reverse the pattern of declining membership that has been occurring over the past two decades.

We do not discount the growing body of evidence that documents serious problems with union representation election processes. Legal scholars and empirical researchers have clearly demonstrated that (1) illegal activity by employers during representation elections has increased markedly since 1960; (2) time delay in completing elections has increased; and (3) about 40 percent of union election wins fail to produce lasting bargaining relationships because of failure to negotiate first contracts. The combination of illegal employer behavior during the election and initial bargaining and time delays significantly lower the probability of a successful bargaining relationship being established.[36] All these results are evidence of significant problems in the current labor law that need to be remedied. Yet, taken together, the effects of these problems with the law and its administration have been small compared to the larger forces affecting union membership declines. Reversing union membership trends will take more than labor law reforms.

Summary

The central argument in this chapter is that the emergence of a large nonunion sector in the United States since 1960 was a function of a changing environment, deep-seated managerial values opposed to unions, and increased opportunities and incentives to avoid unions resulting from changing competitive and cost conditions. Management responded by shifting power away from its staff experts most deeply committed to working within the union-management relationship. Line and staff managers who were willing and able to introduce innovative new systems of human resource management gained power and were successful in helping to develop and stabilize a new nonunion system.

Thus our explanation for the decline of unionism and the growth of the alternate nonunion system emphasizes the larger environmental changes and fundamental values and strategies more than management's specific tactics in opposing unions in certification and decertification elections. Indeed, we see collective bargaining in the mass-production industries as a type of asset that was put in place as a result of the social and economic crises and public policy innovations of the 1930s and 1940s. By the early 1950s the institutional arrangements for collective bargaining were well established. Then the slow process of erosion began. The small sector that had remained unorganized throughout the postwar period served as a model for partially unionized companies and for those firms that began operations after 1960.

This is not to deny the fact that management opposition and illegal behavior in election campaigns increased over this period and reduced the probability of unions winning elections and establishing successful collective bargaining relationships. Our point is that this illegal or more aggressive employer behavior is only the tip of the iceberg.

Meanwhile, in industries and firms where union coverage was nearly or actually 100 percent by 1960, additional capacity was often brought under master agreements voluntarily by management or as a result of clauses negotiated into collective bargaining agreements as a matter of course. Unions in the most highly organized industries remained protected from the nonunion model until a crisis in labor costs developed in the late 1970s or early 1980s. Companies found their ability to pursue a nonunion strategy limited by the power of their unions to counter with pressure at the bargaining table and to insist on neutrality clauses. Thus, in these industries nonunion operations emerged only through the entry of new firms.

The extent of unionization within a given firm or industry does not, however, fully explain developments in the heavily unionized sector, since many companies that started the 1960s with all of their plants organized were able to evolve a substantial nonunion sector. Rather, a more complex explanation lies in the degree to which bargaining was centralized and whether or not union leaders perceived the implications of the growth of nonunion competition and stopped it by engaging top executives in strategy discussions.

In many ways the development of the new nonunion model followed a pattern of diffusion observed in other areas of organizational innovation. A few companies experimented and refined the concepts involved early on (carrying them over from the companies that were never unionized). Slowly, these ideas became the standard beliefs and norms for management professionals, and the process of emulation ensued. In the next chapter we shall examine in more detail the nature and performance of these alternative systems at the workplace level of industrial relations.

CHAPTER

4

Industrial Relations Systems at the Workplace

AS SHOWN in the last chapter, a critical element in the expansion of the nonunion sector since 1960 was the development of a sophisticated nonunion model of industrial relations. This chapter describes in more detail the central workplace features of this nonunion system and then evaluates whether this system yields higher organizational performance than the traditional union system. To understand the challenges posed by the new nonunion system, however, it is first necessary to describe and evaluate the performance of the workplace features of the union industrial relations system that this newer model is trying to replace.

The workplace level of an industrial relations system includes the day-to-day interactions of workers with other workers, supervisors, and, in unionized settings, local union representatives. This is also the environment in which individuals experience the effects of higher-level decisions and strategies. An important proposition in our strategic choice theory is that innovations in the workplace create pressures for

81

change at the middle and strategic levels of industrial relations activity, just as changes at higher levels influence workplace policies, practices, and industrial relations outcomes. Therefore, analysis of the workplace level cannot be isolated from these higher levels.

All workplace industrial relations systems perform certain generic functions. In the following sections we describe these functions and their interrelationships. We also describe how union and nonunion workplace systems have competed with each other over time and, in the process, traded places as the innovative leader and follower. We then compare the contemporary performance of both systems, a comparison that reveals the current relative success of the newer nonunion system. This sets the stage for the next two chapters, which examine how through changes at the workplace and collective bargaining level some unions and unionized employers are responding to various pressures, in part in an effort to close the competitive gap with innovative nonunion workplace systems.

Generic Features of Workplace Systems

Figure 4.1 diagrams our model of workplace industrial relations systems. The model rests on two basic propositions. First, workplace systems perform three interrelated generic functions: (1) the management of conflict and the delivery of due process, (2) the design and modification of work rules and work organization, and (3) the motivation

FIGURE 4.1

Generic Features of Workplace Industrial Relations Systems

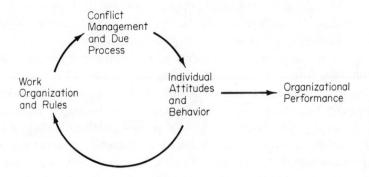

and supervision of individual employees and work groups. Second, the performance of these three generic functions affects the firm's organizational performance.

CONFLICT MANAGEMENT/DUE-PROCESS SYSTEMS

It has always been recognized that the periodic formation of personnel policies or the negotiation of labor contracts by employer and worker representatives can neither resolve nor anticipate all the problems that occur on a day-to-day basis at the workplace. Moreover, many issues that arise between employees and supervisors, or among different employee groups, lie beyond the scope of written policies. Therefore, means are needed for managing conflicts and ensuring procedural adjudication of individual rights at the workplace.

In the union sector, grievance and arbitration procedures perform this function.[1] Traditionally, in nonunion workplaces complaints were resolved informally through direct communication between workers and supervisors. In the more sophisticated nonunion systems, however, increasingly formal complaint mechanisms, such as speak-up programs or ombudspersons, perform this role.[2] Indeed, an increasing number of nonunion firms have adopted grievance and appeal procedures, some of which are modeled after those developed in unionized settings.[3]

Although the need for procedures that manage conflict and provide due process is common to all employment relationships, the effectiveness of these procedures varies widely across organizational settings and over time within a given setting. Furthermore, more effective conflict management and due process leads to better organizational performance and improvements in employees' working environment. There are several reasons for this connection between the performance of conflict management systems and organizational effectiveness. First, administration of formal grievance or other due-process procedures requires considerable time, people, and resources. Thus the sheer volume of grievance or disciplinary activity will affect administrative and production costs. Moreover, to the extent that management and worker or union resources (time and people) are devoted to managing these procedures, fewer resources are available for training, problem solving, communications, and other human resource development activities. Thus poorly performing conflict management/due-process systems consume management, worker, and union resources (what can be termed a displacement effect).

Second, the volume of grievances and disciplinary actions is symp-

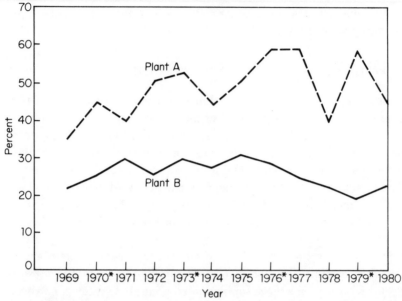

FIGURE 4.2

*Percentage of Grievances Advanced to Third Step of the Grievance Procedure
in Two Plants, 1969–1980*

SOURCE: Nancy Russell Mower, "The Labor-Management Relationship and Its Effects on
Quality of Work Life: A Comparative Case Study." Masters Thesis, MIT Sloan School of
Management, 1982.

tomatic of the parties' inability to communicate effectively or of their
inability to resolve differences on a more informal basis. Thus a large
number of grievances or disciplinary actions signals deep-seated problems in an organization's conflict-management system.

Third, because complaint procedures are, in part, adversarial, they
entail some of the political posturing, gamesmanship, bluffing, and
commitment-building tactics that are part of any distributive bargaining process.[4] In addition, in unionized settings grievance procedures are an extension of the collective bargaining process and therefore
are affected by and, over time, reinforce the degree of conflict and
political posturing that occurs in the formal negotiations process.[5]

This difference in grievance activity and the effectiveness of conflict
management is illustrated by the data presented in figure 4.2. These
data compare the percentages of grievances settled at the first, second,

and third steps of a grievance procedure from 1969 to 1980. They are drawn from two plants of the same large auto manufacturing firm. Plant A had a highly adversarial relationship prior to and throughout this period, while plant B had a relatively cooperative relationship. The actual number of grievances filed in plant B did not differ markedly over these years, and the dynamics of settlement followed a rather consistent pattern. In contrast, in plant A unresolved grievances built up and stockpiled during times of contract negotiations, reflecting a highly politicized process. Specifically, throughout the 1970s plant B resolved a higher percentage of its grievances at the first and second steps than did plant A. Moreover, plant A shows peaks in the percentage of grievances appealed to step 3 in each of the years that the parties negotiated new collective bargaining agreements, namely 1970, 1973, 1976, and 1979. No similar systematic variation in the stockpiling of grievances is apparent in plant B.

More detailed analysis of the grievance activity in these plants shows that the peaks in grievance activity in bargaining years in plant A were due to an increase in the filing of contractual grievances (grievances filed by local union officials alleging contract violations rather than those filed by an individual employee) precisely during the months that bargaining over a local contract was underway. Thus in the adversarial plant the parties consistently used the grievance procedure for tactical purposes and carried over conflicts from negotiations to it, while in the more cooperative plant the parties isolated the resolution of grievances from the conflicts that occurred over negotiations of new national and local collective bargaining agreements.

The data from plant A presented in the figure, therefore, represent the type of high-conflict/low-trust pattern that can develop when political or distributive bargaining tactics carry over in time or spread across the entire range of issues with which the parties deal. That is, the parties get caught in a cycle whereby conflicts involving some issues drive out the potential for cooperation and problem solving on issues where the parties share common interests.[6] It is this high-conflict/ low-trust syndrome that most observers have in mind when criticizing the traditional American industrial relations system for being too "adversarial."[7]

WORK RULES AND ORGANIZATION

The substantive rules and practices governing the organization of work, the compensation system, and the adaptability of work practices serve as a second important channel through which the workplace level influences economic performance and worker goals. Work rules and their administration historically have been recognized as important factors influencing labor costs and productivity.[8] These rules and practices develop over time, both explicitly through collective bargaining provisions and implicitly through informal customs and traditions in both union and nonunion settings.[9] Rules are necessary to assure stability, predictability, and uniformity in the administration of the employment relationship and to protect workers' and employers' rights.

Over time, however, work practices and rules can accumulate and become outmoded because of changes in technology, product or job design, or plant layout. Yet they are often hard to change; change can alter individual workers' status, employment security, and promotion opportunities either by affecting the scope of job responsibilities or by altering such things as worker seniority and transfer rights. Discussions aimed at modifying work practices, therefore, are generally mixed-motive in nature—all parties share some interest in eliminating inefficient practices, yet changes may threaten the rights and interests of some workers. Thus it is not the existence of work practices or rules governing work organization per se that jeopardizes economic performance or worker interests. Rather the critical factor is the flexibility by which rules and practices can be adjusted when circumstances change. The ability to adapt seems to be a function not just of whether a union is present but also of the age of the employment relationship.

INDIVIDUAL AND WORK GROUP ATTITUDES AND BEHAVIOR

While the conflict management and work-organization policies reflect the *institutional* features of the workplace level of an industrial relations system, it is clear that the motivation, attitudes, and behavior of individual employees and informal work groups also affect organizational performance.

Organizational psychologists have long debated the causal relationships between individual attitudes and behaviors at the workplace and performance. On the one hand, empirical research has failed to demonstrate a consistent causal relationship between individual worker job satisfaction and performance. On the other hand, almost all psychological theories of individual behavior at the workplace agree that interest in and motivation to perform one's jobs should somehow affect job performance and satisfaction.[10] Thus if workers can be motivated and given the opportunity to participate in the search for improved methods of job performance, and if this motivation and participation can be maintained over time, job performance should improve.[11]

All these intuitively reasonable hypotheses have been developed over the years by psychologists and put into practice by organizational development and change specialists within firms. However, despite their intuitive appeal to managers, there is a paradox that is yet to be resolved satisfactorily. That is, there is little empirical support to demonstrate that improving individual attitudes and/or motivation produces lasting economic benefits to organizations. From the Hawthorne experiments in the 1930s to the quality-of-work-life projects of the 1970s, it has been shown that improving attitudes and trust between workers and supervisors normally leads to short-run or temporary performance improvements.[12] But maintenance of the changed climate and its organizational benefits has proven to be a more formidable challenge.

We believe the paradox stems from the failure to relate these individual attributes to the other features of workplace industrial relations systems or to higher levels of management and, where present, to union policy making and interactions. What is often overlooked in organizational psychology's focus on the individual level is that for improvements in individual worker or work group performance to be translated into significant improvements in organizational performance, improved attitudes and motivation must diffuse across the organization. The organizational change literature is replete with examples of "success stories"—changes that have occurred within an "experimental" group or work unit—that then get isolated from the rest of the organization, the benefits get encapsulated in that group, and diffusion does not occur.[13] For lasting organizational benefits to result, therefore, a diffusion and an institutionalization process needs to occur.

Thus, if participation in workplace problem solving diffuses across a sufficiently large proportion of the workforce, then organizational effectiveness should also improve. High levels of trust, commitment, and participation likely can be maintained over time and across large numbers of workers, however, only if they are reinforced by higher-level business and collective bargaining strategies. For example, if management's strategic decisions or collective bargaining demands threaten workers' job security, trust will quickly erode.[14] Thus the individual dimension of a workplace industrial relations system is interrelated in a mutually reinforcing cycle with the system's conflict management and work-organization aspects, and all three workplace dimensions are affected by management and labor interactions at higher levels of the employment relationship.

THE EVOLUTION AND BEHAVIOR OF UNION WORKPLACE SYSTEMS

While both union and nonunion workplace systems perform these generic functions, they do so in quite different ways and vary in the emphasis they place on the different functions. In this section we draw on several of our studies that highlight these differences. We start with the union system since its development predates the newer nonunion system.

The Shock-Effect Era. As noted in chapter 2, the rise and diffusion of industrial unionism in the nation's core manufacturing industries made the job-control unionism model, featuring grievance arbitration and detailed contracts, the dominant mode of workplace industrial relations in the 1940s and 1950s. The War Labor Board's support for this model served to diffuse and institutionalize this approach. Job-control unionism worked well at this time because it was well suited to the economic environment and to the needs of the parties. It provided management with the stability and labor peace it needed to take advantage of expanding markets, while for labor the emerging principles of joint contract administration overcame the arbitrariness of prior foreman-driven discipline and workplace administration.

This system of work regulation arose during the spread of mass production and other large-batch technologies that were designed to serve and cultivate the expansion of mass markets for standardized products.[15] The system was well suited to those economic and technological contexts. This form of work organization also was consistent with the professional standards of the staff experts (industrial engineers) who played the dominant role in job design, and it was responsive to workers' and unions' demands for fairness.

Collective bargaining contracts were gradually transformed from simple documents specifying the economic terms of the employment bargain to detailed and enforceable manuals guiding workplace practices. The emphasis on equity and the formal specification of the rights and responsibilities of workers and employers enforceable through the grievance procedure led to what Slichter, Healy, and Livernash and others have described as one of the significant contributions of collective bargaining to the management process: the codification of personnel practices and procedures and the reduction in the variability in administration associated with the foreman-driven management system.[16]

This system of work organization grew out of the principles of supervision, job design, and motivation embedded within scientific management and industrial engineering. Workers were assumed to be motivated primarily by the economic compensation received for job performance, and efficiency was to be maximized by dividing work into simple and narrow tasks. Decisions regarding how work was to be done were to be made by supervisors or engineers, while employees were left to execute their assigned tasks. Job evaluation procedures attached specific wage rates to each job, and seniority became the bedrock principle governing the allocation of scarce job opportunities.

The emphasis on uniformity in this workplace system left little room for concern with individual employee differences in motivation and talent. Indeed, the specification of collective rules was a reaction to the distrust workers and unions had for the way foremen and other managers previously had handled their discretionary power. More than anything else, the new nonunion model can be differentiated from the traditional union system by the attention it pays to individual employee concerns and its effort to provide employees with more discretion through the design of broader jobs. As discussed below, the models of job design that developed in the 1960s and 1970s focused on the individual and psychological aspects of the worker-employer relationship.

AN EMPIRICAL ILLUSTRATION

Data collected from twenty-five auto plants in one GM division for the years 1970 through 1980 illustrate the interdependent nature of workplace features of this unionized industrial relations system.[17] Correlations of measures of conflict management performance and the individual dimensions of the workplace systems operating in these plants are shown in table 4.1. Strong correlations exist between indicators of the amount of conflict as measured by the number of grievances per one hundred workers (Grievance); number of discipline cases per one hundred workers (Discipline); and measures of individual attitudes and behavior as measured by average scores on an organizational climate survey (Attitude), the rate of absenteeism in the plant (Absentee), the number of suggestions per employee filed in the plant suggestion system (Sugperem), and the percentage of the plant's employees participating in the suggestion system (Sugpct). For example, the higher the grievance rate, the poorer the attitudes ($r = -0.47$), the higher the absenteeism rate ($r = 0.26$), the fewer suggestions ($r = -0.15$), and the fewer employees participating in the suggestion system ($r = -0.20$).

A similar pattern of correlations exists for the volume of disciplinary activity in these plants. The amount of conflict in local contract negotiations as measured by the number of demands introduced (Demands) and number of days required to reach a local agreement (Negtime) is positively correlated with the number of grievance and disciplinary cases and negatively correlated with the attitudinal climate.

Unfortunately data are not available that allow us to statistically test for the relationships between work-rule complexity or adaptability and the industrial relations performance indicators found in table 4.1. However, descriptions of the reality of workplace life provided by workers and managers as well as our own observations give strong evidence that the intensity of conflict, the adaptability of work rules, and individual attitudes and behavior at the workplace in these plants are closely interrelated in a pattern that fits the high-conflict/low-trust syndrome. In turn, these workplace patterns are related to the amount of conflict occurring at higher levels of the worker-manager relationship in formal collective bargaining negotiations. Note, however, that the existence of these interrelationships does not mean *all* unionized relations are characterized by high conflict and low trust. The correlations also imply that high trust and low conflict relationships are also found in some of these workplaces.

Indeed, there is tremendous variability among plants in the various indicators reported in the table. For example, in 1980 the rate of grievances among these plants ranged from a low of five per one hundred workers to a high of 120 per one hundred workers. Thus the generic dimensions of a workplace industrial relations system appear to be interrelated in a reinforcing cycle so that if trust at the workplace is broken, a high rate of conflict and resistance to change can be expected, which in turn reinforces the low-trust climate. In the next section we discuss the negative effects this high conflict/low trust cycle can exert on economic performance.

The Effects of the Union System. What evidence do we have that the performance of workplace industrial relations systems significantly influences organizational performance? Since the theoretical model we have outlined is still quite new, it has not yet been subjected to a

TABLE 4.1

Interrelationships among Industrial Relations Performance Variables as Measured by Simple Correlations Coefficients[a]

	Grievance	Absentee	Discipline	Demands	Negtime	Attitude	Sugperem	Sugpct
Grievance	1.00							
Absentee	0.26***	1.00						
Discipline	0.34***	0.32***	1.00					
Demands	0.22**	0.08	0.33**	1.00				
Negtime	0.38***	−0.01	0.30***	0.34***	1.00			
Attitude	−0.47***	−0.51***	−0.25**	−0.22	0.02	1.00		
Sugperem	−0.15*	−0.12	0.15*	0.09	0.24*	0.43***	1.00	
Sugpct	−0.20**	−0.10	0.11	0.11	0.22	0.43***	0.91***	1.00

NOTE: [a] The number of observations for correlations involving: measures of grievance and discipline rates is 275; the absentee rate is 250; participation in the suggestion program is 125; and attitudes, the number of contract demands, and negotiating time is 100.

* Significant at 0.10 level.
** Significant at 0.05 level.
*** Significant at 0.01 level.

SOURCE: Harry C. Katz, Thomas A. Kochan, and Mark Weber, "Assessing the Effects of Industrial Relations Systems and Efforts to Improve Quality of Working Life on Organizational Effectiveness," *Academy of Management Journal*, 28 (1985):509–26. Numbers presented in this table differ slightly from those in the article due to differences in sample sizes.

large number of empirical tests. We can, however, document the power of the model with several studies from our own research and from that of our colleagues. The first two sets of studies to be discussed are part of the same research reported in table 4.1. The data are annual observations for the years 1970 to 1980 from plants in two divisions of General Motors. The correlations presented in table 4.2 show that plants with relatively good industrial relations performance also have relatively higher labor efficiency (productivity) and product quality.

TABLE 4.2

Correlations Between Industrial Relations Performance and Organizational Performance[a]

	Labor Efficiency		Product Quality	
	Study 1	*Study 2*	*Study 1*	*Study 2*
Grievance	−0.49***	−0.41***	−0.27***	−0.30***
Discipline	−0.35***	−0.22***	−0.20**	0.07
Demands	−0.32**	0.01	−0.20*	0.05
Negtime	−0.40***	−0.34***	−0.39***	−0.13
Absentee	−0.38***	−0.22***	0.13	0.07
Attitude	0.44***	0.40***	0.44***	0.48***
Sugperem	NA	0.31**	NA	0.53***
Sugpct	NA	0.22**	NA	0.53***

NOTE: [a]The sample size for the correlations involving the direct labor variable ranged from 225 to 100 and involving the quality variable ranged from 150 to 100.
  * Significant at 0.10 level.
 ** Significant at 0.05 level.
*** Significant at 0.01 level.
NA Not available.

SOURCE: Study 1: From Harry C. Katz, Thomas A. Kochan, and Kenneth Gobeille, "Industrial Relations Performance, Economic Performance and QWL Programs: An Interplant Analysis," *Industrial and Labor Relations Review*, 37, no. 1 (1983):3–17. © Cornell University. All rights reserved. Study 2: Harry C. Katz, Thomas A. Kochan, and Mark Weber, "Assessing the Effects of Industrial Relations Systems and Efforts to Improve Quality of Working Life on Organizational Effectiveness," *Academy of Management Journal*, 28 (1985): 509–26.

The correlations show that higher rates of grievances and a higher degree of trust in the organizational climate (as measured by the attitude surveys) are associated with higher rates of labor efficiency and higher product quality. Regression analysis further showed that the overall variations in industrial relations performance across these plants explains a significant portion of the variance in both labor efficiency and product quality after controlling for the size of the plant and other plant specific characteristics. Moreover, J. R. Norsworthy and Craig Zabala found a similar pattern of effects for indicators of industrial relations performance using aggregate industry-level data. They went a step further than we did by converting their results into estimates of the economic losses experienced in the auto industry due to poor labor relations performance. They estimated that a 10 percent improvement in worker attitudes and behavior would have translated into a 3 to 5 percent reduction in the annual unit costs of production. In turn, this would have produced between $2.2 and $5.5 billion annual savings in production costs between 1959 and 1976.[18] Thus it is clear that the performance of both the conflict management and the individual dimension of workplace industrial relations can have substantial effects on plant economic performance.

Casey Ichniowski's analysis of variations in the productivity of a set of eleven highly capital-intensive paper mills shows similar effects from variations in grievance and accident rates.[19] After controlling for the various capital-, material-, and energy-related factors that affect productivity in these plants, he found that compared to plants with zero grievances, plants experiencing the average number of grievances had 1.2 percent lower productivity. Plants with average injury rates had 1.3 percent lower productivity than would have been attained at a zero injury rate. Further analysis showed that the output losses associated with high grievance and injury rates have substantial effects on profits. Moving from zero grievances to the average level of grievances was estimated to reduce profits in a mill by approximately 15 percent. Moving to the average rate from a zero rate of injuries was estimated to lead to 17 percent lower profits. Thus even in highly capital-intensive settings, plant-level industrial relations performance has substantial effects on organizational performance.

THE RISE OF THE NEW NONUNION WORKPLACE MODEL

Individual Attitudes and Behavior. Whereas the union system reflected the need to overcome the abuses of individual rights associated with the foreman-driven system prior to the 1930s, a more flexible nonunion model started to evolve in the 1960s to overcome the rigidities and legalistic patterns of contract administration that had built up over the years in many union systems. While the traditional union system stresses contractual rules and uniformity, the new nonunion model stresses individual motivation and differences in abilities and work performance.[20] It is this new model that we shall describe in detail. The reader should keep in mind, however, that not all nonunion firms follow this sophisticated model. Some follow a modern variant of the old system centered around low wages and unchallenged managerial authority. In these firms, management's aggressive actions during representation elections and more open antiunion tactics are central features of personnel administration.

The new and more sophisticated nonunion workplace system is based on theories of motivation that were emerging in the early 1960s. Individuals are assumed to be intrinsically driven to work hard, have strong psychological growth needs, and to be highly committed to the goals of the firm.[21] By this time behavioral science theories of job enlargement and enrichment were also gaining the attention of management educators and a small group of innovative companies and thus began to play key roles in the design of the new workplace. These new theories fostered the development of techniques for introducing greater variety, challenge, and personal growth into individual work assignments.[22] Eventually students of job design concluded that a good job was one that provided a high degree of feedback, task variety, challenge, autonomy, and opportunity to learn new skills. Sociotechnical theorists added their support to this school of thought and went on to recommend organizing work around groups or teams rather than individual task assignments and job descriptions.[23]

These new models of job design and work organization also favor a participatory management style and a high level of employee involvement in task-related problem solving. Decision making is more decentralized. In the face of this decentralization, substantial worker trust and commitment are required since, in their absence, the shift away from job-control unionism would bring costly instability and unpredictability (remember that avoiding such an eventuality was one of the prime motivations for the development of job-control unionism).

New work-system concepts are difficult to incorporate into existing union (and nonunion) plants since they depart so dramatically from established patterns and assumptions. Moreover, the consent and acceptance of workers, supervisors, and middle managers is needed before such major changes can be implemented in an existing facility. On the other hand, management can act unilaterally in designing the initial work system in a new worksite.[24] Consequently, the earliest experiments with these innovations in the 1960s and 1970s were largely confined to new nonunion greenfield facilities.[25]

Nonunion Conflict-Management Processes. The behavioral science theories that gave rise to the new nonunion systems generally viewed organizations as cooperative systems and downplayed or completely ignored the existence of conflicts of interests between employees and employers. Instead, the implicit assumption in most of these theories was (and still is) that effective management can integrate the goals of employees with those of the firm. Conflicts that do occur are viewed not as inevitable byproducts of the structure of the employment relationship but as arising out of normal interpersonal tensions or misunderstandings. Thus these models tend to downplay formal grievance systems for resolving conflicts over individual rights. In their place, however, have grown up a variety of informal and formal communications, appeals, and management review procedures, some of which are modeled after union grievance procedures.

One way to illustrate the nature of conflict management in these settings is to briefly summarize the various communication and appeals procedures employed by IBM, a company that is often cited as one of the leaders in this area of human resource management. Consistent with the individual orientation of the nonunion model, the philosophy underlying IBM's personnel policies stresses "respect for the dignity of the individual." To make this policy operational, the company has developed five different communication and conflict-management programs: (1) a standardized opinion survey that provides comparative data on employees' attitudes toward their job, their supervisor, and the company, and which is used by managers, supervisors, and workers to develop action plans for addressing problem areas; (2) a resident manager program in which a senior manager is assigned responsibility for hearing complaints and discussing issues of concern to employees in a given area; (3) a "skip-level" interview program in which employees have the opportunity to meet with managers one level above their immediate supervisor; (4) a "speak-up" program in which employees can submit written questions or comments to senior managers on an anonymous basis; and (5) an "open-door" program in which an employee may ask managers up to and including the chief executive to review unfavorable personnel-related decisions made at lower levels.[26]

Other organizations have established the role of ombudsman to help manage and facilitate the resolution of organizational conflicts.[27] In selected nonunion settings a variety of less formal systems have been introduced for performing these generic industrial relations activities of managing workplace conflicts and providing due process. None, however, give as much prominence to this dimension of workplace industrial relations as does the union grievance system with third-party arbitration.

95

Work Rules and Work Organization. Although these newer theories of job design were first presented as strategies for meeting individual worker needs, by the 1980s the desire for flexibility in work organization more than the psychological or motivational benefits of broader job designs accounted for the tremendous interest of managers, particularly line managers, in these new work systems. Advances in computer-based manufacturing and information-processing technology now make it technologically feasible to adapt production processes more readily to more specialized markets and shorter production runs, provided that the system of work organization and human resource management is also flexible and adaptable. Flexibility is designed into the new systems by having a small number of broad job classifications, few rules governing specific job assignments, less restrictions on the work supervisors can perform, and more limited weight given to seniority in promotion and transfer decisions. In its most complete form, this model replaces individual job assignments and pay structures with team or group forms of work organization and compensation. Since these team work systems are not yet well understood, we shall draw on one of our case studies to briefly describe a particular plant that was designed with these principles in mind.

A TEAM-CONCEPT PLANT

This team-concept plant was opened in 1977 by TRW, Inc., a large multidivisional and highly diversified manufacturing firm.[28] It is located in a small community in the Midwest and primarily produces electric cables for use in various pumping and drilling operations. In 1983 it employed 150 workers, all of whom are salaried. A pay-for-knowledge system of compensation also is used—that is, worker's pay is set according to skill level rather than according to the amount of work produced on any specific job on a given day. Workers work in teams rather than on specific individual jobs.

The plant is divided into four production, one maintenance, and one administrative team, and several teams that serve as resources to production. Team sizes vary considerably but normally range between eight and fifteen workers. In some cases the teams function as autonomous work groups; in other cases they are semi-autonomous, with a "team manager" assigned to oversee several teams. In most cases the managers are former team members who have been promoted. The role of the manager is to act as a group facilitator in helping teams make day-to-day decisions. Aside from these team managers, there are no first-line supervisors in the plant.

The plant has nine job levels for classifying workers. Workers may start at level 1 and work their way up to level 9. Upward movement, in principle, is contingent upon learning extra skills. Workers must learn to operate, set, or maintain another machine to move up a skill level. Each of the nine levels is ten points apart, and all skills in the plant are calibrated in terms of points. A new hire must learn any one of the skills worth ten points within the first thirty days to qualify as a level-1 worker. After being promoted to the next level, a worker must wait four months before learning another skill. The plant manager described the system as follows:

Our philosophy here has been to let the evolutionary process mold our systems rather than adhere sharply to defined work rules. For example, when we started the plant, we wanted to train all workers on all jobs. Soon we discovered that we were spending too much time on training and not enough on production. So we moved to a system where workers primarily concentrate on learning other jobs within their own teams. Also, we created two paths along which workers could move up. One of them of course is by learning an extra operation and the other is by improving proficiency on the same job. A number of proficiency levels have been defined for each job in the plant by the team members themselves.

The responsibility for training initially was left to the current job operator. That is, all operators were expected to act as trainers. It was discovered, however, that some individuals made better trainers than others. Thus a trainer classification was established with a wage higher than a level 9. By 1983, six years after plant startup, about 70 percent of the plant's workers had attained the highest level (i.e., level 9). The other 30 percent were distributed over levels 5 through 8.

The underlying principle in the plant design is to decentralize decision making at the shop-floor level. Workers participate in the scheduling of production, assigning work to team members, monitoring production and scrap levels, determining overtime requirements, providing feedback to other teams, and making hiring and promotion decisions. At the beginning of each month, each team makes its own projections of how much work will be done and the resources needed. These calculations start with such things as the number of standard hours, overtime hours, manpower requirements, support services, and go on to estimate total labor costs, percent of labor utilization, and other productivity measures.

Promotion decisions are made by the team in a highly programmed manner. Individuals have to meet predetermined skill and performance levels. Skill must be demonstrated both in output quality and quantity and in a number of functional areas such as teamwork, problem solving, and housekeeping.

In many of these decisions, a blending of management inputs and team decisions appears to be the norm. In the plant manager's words:

Recently members of a team went through the exercise of deciding who moves to another job that came open in another team. At first, asked to make the decision themselves, they picked the worst performer in the team. Since we did not perceive this to be in the best interests of the plant, we intervened. My reasons for intervention were that I wanted them to deal with the problem themselves rather than to unload it on some other team. They reacted to my intervention by trying to unload the decision on the management. That too was unacceptable because it was a sort of abdication. Next they wanted to draw lots to make the decision. Two managers worked together with this team over two weeks. Over time, they began to explore the implications of the move in terms of opportunities, etc. Finally, the position of "what if I move" was developed for each member of the team. This was in contrast to the earlier position they took by way of "let's see who will be asked to leave." Once a self-examination note was struck, we immediately had a volunteer for the move.

Performance on the job is appraised and tested through skills tests developed by the team members every four to six months. Evaluators are drawn from team peers as well as management. When promotions are being considered, the team rates the candidates based on attendance records, indicators of proficiency, and performance on a written test. The plant manager describes the role of seniority in promotion decisions as follows:

When speaking of promotion, one needs to distinguish between the employee-initiated movement from levels 1 through 9 as different from the personnel needs of other teams which require promotion from production teams to maintenance team or management to other resource teams. Movement through the levels [1 to 9] are initiated by the employee. The only constraint on movement is time. Once an employee moves to a new level, he or she must stay with the newly acquired skill at least for four months before moving on to learn newer skills. These upward movements may be strongly correlated with seniority simply for the reason that the employee with more seniority has been in the plant that much longer to learn new skills. The other kind of promotion, i.e., from production to maintenance or management, would have a much lower correlation with seniority because promotions are based entirely on ability.

Wages are comparable to those paid by other area employers. The entry-level wage rate is relatively low ($4.15 per hour in March 1982);

however, the average wages of workers in the plant tend to be higher since the pay-for-knowledge system allows workers to progress up the point and pay levels more rapidly than in a traditional system. Thus the average wage rates in the plant were in the upper half of the wage distribution among comparable firms and occupations in the area. These rates, however, are lower by approximately 15 to 20 percent than the average wages paid comparable unionized workers in other plants of this firm.

Voluntary turnover at the plant has been low (about 5 percent) recently although about 40 percent of the first hires quit their jobs in the first year of the plant's operation. This illustrates another common characteristic of these team-concept organizations—only a select group of the American workforce seems to perform well in them. Even though organizations using these systems are usually very selective in their hiring, they still experience an initial sorting-out process. The personnel manager of this plant described the start-up as a process of sorting for the "right kind" of worker:

There were some with high absence records. Others found it difficult to handle all the freedom they had on the job. We had several very young people who didn't have enough work experience and hadn't as a result developed the work ethic. Now our recruitment is more selective and our teams participate heavily in the recruitment process.

Diffusion of the New Nonunion Model. The Conference Board survey data discussed in chapter 3 provide a general indication of how widely these practices are used in nonunion settings. Table 4.3 lists the percentage of partially unionized firms that report encouraging use of these workplace practices in their new *nonunion* facilities.

The data indicate that the vast majority—73 percent—of the firms encourage establishment of formal complaint or grievance procedures for nonunion employees. An almost equally strong majority—72 percent—encourage use of employee participation programs. One-third of these nonunion firms also report encouraging use of all salaried pay plans, profit-sharing and work-sharing practices, while between 20 and 30 percent of the firms encourage use of three practices that are part of the more flexibly designed work organization systems, namely flexible work schedules, pay-for-knowledge compensation schemes, and autonomous work groups.

These data suggest that the due-process and employee-participation dimensions of these new systems have diffused to over three-fourths

TABLE 4.3

Workplace Innovations in Nonunion Establishments

Question: Does Your Company Encourage Managers to Set Up Any of the Following for Nonunion Groups?	% Yes
Formal Complaint or Grievance Systems	72.9
Employee Participation Programs	71.9
All Salaried Compensation Systems	34.2
Profit Sharing Plans	33.3
Work Sharing	31.8
Flexible Work Schedules	29.3
Payment for Knowledge	19.8
Autonomous Work Teams	19.3

SOURCE: 1984 Conference Board Survey of employee relations practices of major U.S. firms. Further survey results are presented in Audrey Freedman, *The New Look in Wage Bargaining* (New York: The Conference Board, 1985).

of the nonunion worksites of the large firms surveyed by the Conference Board. The flexible work-system concepts, which are newer, seem to be limited to a minority—approximately 15 to 20 percent—of nonunion workplaces in the firms surveyed. Interestingly, further analysis of these data indicate that partially organized firms make even greater use of these more recent work-organization innovations than do totally unorganized firms. This suggests that where potential unionism is still a threat, there is a spur to experiment with more advanced human-resource management systems.

PERFORMANCE OF UNION AND NONUNION WORKPLACE SYSTEMS

Do nonunion workplace systems on average outperform union systems? This is an extremely important yet extremely difficult question to answer. Some of the difficulty arises because such a high proportion of new plants opened since 1960 are unorganized. Thus there is a strong correlation between plant age and union status—nonunion plants tend to be younger. Furthermore, as a plant ages work rules tend to become more rigid and cause a reduction in plant economic performance. Given the association between nonunion status and plant age and the fact that both exert independent effects on plant economic performance, it is difficult to separate the effects of each of these factors on plant economic performance.

Since union plants are on average considerably older than nonunion plants, union plants are more likely to display less flexible systems of work organization. Clearly, given the nature of traditional union workplace systems, relatively more rules and rights governing specific jobs exist in union settings. Moreover, some of the informal customs and practices that build up at the workplace become enforceable as past practices through grievance arbitration, further rigidifying work organization in union plants. The question that remains, however, is how much this inflexibility in work organization is a generic union effect and how much is due to the age of the plant. To address this question Anil Verma conducted an intensive comparison of eight plants in the same multidivisional manufacturing firm discussed earlier.

In the early 1960s this company began experimenting with the use of behavioral science concepts in the design and management of its professional, managerial, and hourly workforce. Almost all of its efforts to introduce these concepts to hourly workers were concentrated in nonunion plants. At one point the company did try to experiment with some of these concepts in a union plant, but it abandoned the effort when it failed to gain the support of local union leaders. Since the 1960s a number of new plants were designed with some or all of the systems described in the case study.

TABLE 4.4

Comparison of Work Practices in Union and Nonunion Plants of the Same Firm

	Type of Plant		
Work Practices	New Nonunion (N = 3)	Old Nonunion (N = 2)	Union (N = 3)
Number of Job Classifications	6	65	96
Number of Wage Grades	7	11	14
Number of Maintenance Job Classifications	1	10	11
Percent Maintenance Workers in a "General Maintenance" Classification	75%	20%	1%
Supervisors Prohibited from Doing Subordinates' Work	No	No	Yes
Subcontracting Occurs Only after Meeting with Union/Employees	100%	0%	0%

SOURCE: Anil Verma, "Union and Nonunion Industrial Relations at the Plant Level." Ph.D. Dissertation, Sloan School of Management, MIT, 1983.

Table 4.4 summarizes some of the differences in the workplace industrial relations systems found across these eight plants in 1982. Of the eight plants, five are nonunion. Two were opened in the 1970s, one in the 1960s, one in the 1950s, and the other was opened in the 1930s. All three union plants were opened prior to 1960. In the analysis that follows the three plants opened after 1960 are treated as "new nonunion" plants since case-study evidence indicates that 1960 was the approximate time when the firm began experimenting with more flexible forms of work organization.

As expected, the new nonunion plants are smaller than both the union and the old nonunion plants. Keeping new plants small was an important design feature in the firm's overall strategy.

As the data in the table show, in contrast to both the union and the older nonunion plants, the newer nonunion plants make greater use of all salaried compensation policies and pay-for-knowledge systems and less use of cost-of-living escalator payment systems. Thus these innovations in compensation systems appear to have more to do with the concepts in compensation system design prevailing at the time the plant was opened than with the facility's union status.

Similarly, four measures of the structure of jobs and work practices in the older nonunion plants are closer to the union than to the new nonunion plants. Union and old nonunion plants report an average of ninety-six and sixty-five job classifications respectively, compared to six in the new nonunion plants. Likewise, the number of wage grades was fourteen in the union plants, eleven in the old nonunion plants, and seven in the new nonunion plants. New nonunion plants had only one job classification for maintenance workers, compared to ten and eleven in the old nonunion and union plants respectively. Furthermore, 75 percent of the maintenance workers in the new nonunion plants were classified as "general maintenance workers," compared to 20 percent in the old nonunion plants and only 1 percent in the union plants.

On the other hand, on a number of issues, both old and new nonunion plants report fewer constraints on managerial flexibility to allocate workers than do union plants. Issues that fit this pattern include restrictions on subcontracting and the rights of supervisors to fill-in or do the work of their subordinates.

While these comparisons draw on a very limited sample of observations and crude measures, a consistent pattern emerges that places the practices found in old nonunion plants between the practices of older union and newer nonunion plants. We observed the same patterns in the workplace practices of a number of other firms that include both union and nonunion plants. This suggests that both the union status and the age of a plant exert independent effects on the design and operation of workplace industrial relations systems.

Labor Costs. Do these other factors produce net labor-cost differences between union and nonunion plants? An extensive body of econometric research documents the existence of union/nonunion wage differentials across otherwise comparable *individuals.*[29] Our analysis of the differences in wages and fringe benefits across eighty-five union and nonunion plants of the large conglomerate discussed earlier reinforces and extends these findings to union and nonunion *plants* within the same firm. If firms making the choice of how to allocate new investment dollars confront a labor-cost differential between union and nonunion options, we can generally expect investment and employment to favor the nonunion alternatives. Table 4.5 reports the wage- and fringe-benefit premiums found in this firm's union plants. These estimates are derived from regression equations that control for differences in plant size and age, industry group, region, and, in the 1983 analysis, the skill mix in the plant. Several patterns are reflected in these results. First, across all three years of data, union plants pay significantly higher entry-level wages, have higher fringe-benefit and total labor costs, and have a smaller differential between the wage rate paid to the most highly skilled workers and the wage paid to entry-level workers. Second, no significant differences exist in any year between the wage rates paid the most highly skilled workers in the union and nonunion plants. Third, although the magnitude of the estimates in the wage and cost differentials vary somewhat from year to year, the differentials appear to be quite persistent over the course of the business cycle in the period between 1979 and 1983.

The persistence of these cost differentials suggests that union plants either have some offsetting productivity advantages that help them recoup their higher costs or that they operate at lower levels of profitability compared to their nonunion counterparts. If the union plants are unable to recoup their higher costs, then they are likely to experience continual shrinkage and low rates of reinvestment as the corporation reallocates its resources to more profitable options. Indeed, as the data in table 4.6 demonstrate, this is exactly what has been happening in this corporation. The number of union plants and employees per plant has been slowly but steadily declining, while the number of nonunion plants and total nonunion employment has been slowly expanding. Indeed, this is simply another example of the longer-term disinvestment trends described in chapter 3.

Thus, while we have no direct evidence to reject the hypothesis that this firm's union plants have higher productivity rates that can offset their higher costs, our case-study data show that the union plants are

TABLE 4.5

*Percentage Union Labor Cost Differentials
Across Union and Nonunion Plants
of the Same Firm, 1979–83*[a]

	1979	1982	1983
Top Wage Rate	5	1	6
Bottom Wage Rate	28	24	34
Average Wage Rate	6	12	20
Total Benefit Costs	24	23	30
Total Labor Costs	11	15	23
Wage Differential	−39	−42	NA

NOTE: [a]All numbers are approximate percentage wage differentials based on regression equations that include control variables for plant age, size, region of the country, and industry. The 1983 equations also control for skill-mix differences across the plants. Sample size varies between 80 and 85 for the different years.

SOURCE: Unpublished data from our field research for 1983. Data for 1979 and 1982 are reported in Anil Verma and Thomas A. Kochan, "The Growth and Nature of the Nonunion Sector Within a Firm," in Thomas A. Kochan, ed., *Challenges and Choices Facing American Labor* (Cambridge, MIT Press, 1985), 89–118.

on average considerably older than their nonunion counterparts, have less flexible work-organization systems, receive fewer investment dollars, and are shrinking in size. Moreover, although previous studies have demonstrated that the lower turnover rates often found in union establishments may provide advantages that offset higher labor costs, analysis of the turnover patterns in these plants found no significant union-nonunion differences. All of this suggests that higher union costs are not being offset by other productivity advantages. Even if some offsetting advantages exist for union plants, the corporate executives who control resource allocations in this firm do not appear to be acting in a way that would maintain these productivity advantages and support the high wages and more costly fringe benefit systems that exist in the union plants.

Work Rules and Economic Performance. The most difficult issue to assess through quantitative research is the effect of work rules or alternative forms of work organization on organizational performance. It is nearly impossible to collapse into a quantitative measure the complex array of differences between the traditional and newer work sys-

TABLE 4.6
Production and Maintenance Worker Employment in Union and Nonunion Plants, 1979–83

	1979		1980		1981		1982		1983	
	Union	Nonunion	Union	Nonunion	Union	Nonunion	Union	Nonunion	Union	Nonunion
Number of plants	27	44	27	44	27	49	28	54	28	56
Average workers per plant	612	256	563	252	503	266	406	215	360	197
Total employment	15,902	10,741	14,637	10,844	13,576	13,060	11,365	11,597	10,089	11,017
Total	26,643		25,481		26,636		22,962		21,106	

SOURCE: Unpublished data from field research.

tems described in this chapter, even if such systematic data were available from a large sample of workplaces. While researchers in the future may solve this problem, for now we must rely on perceptions of managers working in various plants.

The results of a survey of forty-four managers in a diverse sample of manufacturing plants show that, as argued earlier, both age and union status of a plant are associated with more reports of work rules acting as significant productivity restraints.[30] The managers in these plants were asked what they viewed as the most significant barriers to productivity and productivity improvement in their establishments.

Table 4.7 presents some descriptive characteristics of these plants. For the purposes of comparison, the plants are divided into three categories: new nonunion, old union, and new union. As before, we use 1960 as the dividing line between new and old (only one old nonunion plant was in this sample and therefore this category could not be included in the analysis). The characteristics of the plants in the three categories are consistent with the patterns described throughout this chapter. The new nonunion plants are smaller than plants in the other groups; however, even the new union plants are smaller than older union plants. The new nonunion plants are also more highly concentrated in the South than the union plants. While six of the eighteen new plants are organized, these plants did not become unionized through a contested representation election process but rather as part of industry- or corporate-level agreements with international unions to extend representation rights to new plants as they are opened. All the new plants opened on a nonunion basis have remained nonunion.

The range of productivity restraints reported by the managers of these plants are categorized into the work-rule restrictions; resistance of employees or supervisors to technical change; motivation problems; government regulations; insufficient training and other investments in the human resources of the plant; and insufficient investment in the plant.

The limitations of sample size and the exploratory nature of this research require us to be cautious in drawing firm conclusions from these data. The responses do suggest, however, that managers in the old union plants experience more work-rule problems than do managers of newer union or newer nonunion plants. New union plants again appear to lie between older union and newer nonunion plants on measures of work rules, resistance to change, and employee motivation. However, there is no clear pattern across the union and nonunion groups on questions pertaining to government regulations, human-

TABLE 4.7

Productivity Restraints as Perceived by Managers

	Old Union	New Union	New Nonunion
Average Plant Age	50	15	11
Average Number of Employees	2,921	2,121	695
Percent of Plants in the South	16	17	42
Percentage Reporting Problems with			
Work Rules in General	88	67	33
Resistance to Technical Change	96	50	58
Motivation of the Workforce	84	67	50
Government Regulations	48	67	42
Inadequate Human Resource			
Investments/Training	4	33	8
Insufficient Capital Investment	20	67	17

SOURCE: Unpublished data. For a summary of the implications of these data see Robert B. McKersie and Janice Klein, "Productivity: The Industrial Relations Connection," in *Productivity Growth and U.S. Competitiveness,* ed. William J. Baumol and Kenneth McLennan (New York: Oxford University Press, 1985), 119–59.

resource investments, or capital investment. Thus, again, both age and union status appear to exert an effect on the buildup of work rules that can affect productivity. We should note, however, that very limited data are available on this issue. Remedying this gap should be an important priority in future research.

Summary

Although this chapter has drawn on a wide variety of different samples and studies, the evidence can be pieced together to form a consistent pattern. First, there are clear differences in the ways the generic functions of workplace industrial relations systems are carried out in traditional union systems and newer nonunion systems. The design of new nonunion systems offers greater flexibility in the management and allocation of human resources. Second, nonunion systems, on average, have lower labor costs and appear to retain their wage and fringe-benefit cost advantage over time. While union plants may have some offsetting productivity advantages that our research has failed to identify, the magnitude of the observed cost differentials appears to be large enough to make the union plants less profitable. Furthermore, the investment behavior of corporate executives appears to be consistent with this interpretation. Third, the performance of workplace industrial relations systems, as measured by such things as the amount of conflict, the degree of trust in the relationship between workers and managers, and the complexity of work rules, exerts significant effects on organizational performance. This suggests that there is considerable variability in the performance of union systems and, therefore, an opportunity to introduce changes that narrow the gap between their performance and that of newer nonunion systems.

The data reviewed in this chapter demonstrate that the historical competition between union and nonunion workplace systems exists and is likely to continue into the foreseeable future. Currently, the newer nonunion systems appear to have some cost, flexibility, and other strategic (i.e., they help keep establishments nonunion) advantages for management and also appear to satisfy the motivational and developmental interests of a significant proportion of the workforce. Moreover, because these workplace systems are easier to introduce in new worksites than in existing facilities, they benefit from the most up-to-date technology. Consequently, the traditional workplace systems operating in older unionized facilities are experiencing severe pressures to change. The next two chapters explore the responses to these pressures that have been occurring at the collective bargaining and workplace levels in unionized settings.

CHAPTER

5

The Process and Results of Negotiations

I

N the early 1980s union industrial relations systems began to respond more extensively to accumulating environmental pressures through major and, in some cases, what we will argue are fundamental structural changes in the process and outcomes of collective bargaining. These changes involved significant departures from the roles that management and union leaders had developed over the post–World War II period and from the trends in bargaining outcomes of the 1960s and 1970s, including a number of pay freezes and cuts and alterations in work rules. Some of these contractual changes were linked to workplace changes that introduced increased worker and union participation in production decision making, more flexibility in the allocation of workers, and greater employment security. Others expanded union influence into strategic business issues. In still other cases, however, contractual changes were associated with a harder bargaining stance by management that included threatened or actual plant closings, the hiring of strikebreakers, bargaining to impasse, and/or union decertification. Meanwhile, in firms and industries facing less severe environmental pressures or those following business strategies for which concessions or other changes in bargaining would have little value for the firm or its employees, more of the traditional bargaining processes and outcomes continued.

This chapter examines these changes in the process and outcomes of collective bargaining. In doing so, we will demonstrate why the 1980s stand out as a period of fundamental and structural change. By this we mean that the roles of labor and management have departed from traditional patterns in ways that not only alter in a nonincremental manner the process and results of negotiations, but also change the roles and strategies of the parties at higher and lower levels of industrial relations as well. In short, fundamental changes are ones that alter the entire institutional structure of industrial relations and that will continue to alter the system's performance in the years ahead.

The Issues in Question

One might expect a general consensus among industrial relations researchers and practitioners that something new has happened in the early 1980s that should alter their theories and approach in the future. But this is not the case. In any period of social, political, or economic transition, there is great uncertainty and debate over the meaning of unfolding events. Some believe that what is occurring is simply a short-run deviation or response to a temporary crisis and that old and familiar patterns will return when the crisis eases. Others interpret the new developments as the dawning of a new day of fundamental and lasting changes. This type of debate has recently arisen among academic researchers in both labor economics and industrial relations[1] and among management and labor practitioners.[2]

Having an accurate interpretation of the events of collective bargaining in the 1980s is important to researchers' ability both to accurately forecast outcomes of future bargaining and, more important, to develop a richer understanding of the mix of economic and institutional forces that influence the full range of labor-management relations processes and outcomes. Such an understanding is especially important for those who wish to go beyond description or prediction to offer policy prescriptions.[3] Practitioners have even higher stakes in an accurate reading of experience in the 1980s; interpretations of these events will influence the extent to which they return to traditional bargaining practices or take advantage of changes in the environment and in the institutional structures of bargaining to forge new strategies. Thus it is not an overstatement to suggest that an accurate interpretation of the changes to be discussed in this chapter will have an important bearing on the future course of collective bargaining.

Before citing the full range of evidence and detailed examples from our research, we shall sketch the essence of this debate and our overall interpretation. The debate centers on three questions.

Question 1: Have wage outcomes negotiated under collective bargaining in the early 1980s systematically deviated from the trends established in the post–World War II period? While much econometric work is yet to be done on this issue, there is little doubt that the answer to this question is yes. For example, preliminary results from our analysis of a large sample of collective bargaining contracts compiled by Wayne Vroman of the Urban Institute indicate that a model that accurately predicted wage settlements negotiated between 1958 and 1979 *overpredicts* the actual wage settlements negotiated between 1980 and 1984 by, on average, about 1 percentage point per year. Moreover, the model overpredicts wages by the largest amount in those bargaining structures that were highly centralized and in those relationships that relied on regional or industry pattern-bargaining prior to 1980. In the more centralized structures and in those that relied on pattern bargaining our estimates suggest that wage increases were as much as 3 percentage points lower in the post–1980 period compared to what they would have been if the wage determination model from the previous period had not changed.[4] These findings provide initial support for a hypothesis discussed in more detail later in this chapter, namely, that the changes in bargaining outcomes were most dramatic in those relationships that had been most highly centralized and/or characterized by pattern bargaining prior to the 1980s.

Even some of those who originally took the position that the lower rates of wages negotiated in the early 1980s were only a temporary response to the deep recession of 1981–1982 have now agreed that "wage norms" have shifted downward and stayed depressed longer than they expected.[5] For example, in a similar analysis Daniel Mitchell estimated that a wage model he used to successfully predict negotiated wage changes from 1960 to 1980 overpredicts actual wage changes between 1980 and 1984 by between 1 and 3 percentage points annually.[6] Thus, there is a growing body of econometric evidence that something has changed in the forces that influence wage behavior.

Question 2: What has changed? Here the debate turns on the question of what should go into a useful model of the determination of wages and other bargaining outcomes under collective bargaining. The answer we will develop is consistent with our overall approach; namely, one needs to consider the interactions among changes in the external environment and the institutional structures and practices that the parties to collective bargaining have built up over the past several decades. We believe that the deep, nonincremental intensification of economic pressures of the 1980s, along with the change in the political environment that coincided with the 1981–82 recession, produced equally nonincremental bargaining responses by management and labor.

More specifically, management became more aggressive in requesting early contract openings, argued for a decentralization of the structure of bargaining, shifted away from a strategy of promoting industrial peace to one of emphasizing control over labor costs even at the risk of major disruptions in union-management relations, broke with traditional communications and other protocols of bargaining, and demanded major changes in noneconomic terms of the employment contract. Unions responded to threatened deep cuts in employment by accepting wage and work-rule concessions and, where they had the power to do so, negotiating quid pro quos that gained greater employment security and more influence in managerial decision making. In these cases where quid pro quos were negotiated, unions essentially traded short-run cash-saving concessions for noncash benefits that would enhance their ability to represent their members in the future.

Question 3: Are these universal developments? Here the answer is clearly no. These developments have been concentrated in those settings under the severest pressures and where industrial relations change was linked to viable business and representational strategies.

With these issues and questions in mind, we can now turn to a more detailed presentation of the theory and the evidence that have shaped our interpretation of the developments in collective bargaining during the eary 1980s.

The Theoretical Framework

The modifications made to collective bargaining and the middle tier of union industrial relations provide another illustration of the causal sequence presented in our strategic-choice framework. The central propositions of our argument are presented in figure 5.1. Again we stress the importance of interactions between environmental pressures and management's strategic business decisions. However, to explain the timing and pattern of concession bargaining, it also is necessary to recognize the importance of the degree of union coverage. Specifically, the steady erosion of union coverage some firms and industries experienced during the 1960s and 1970s gradually built up pressure for change within collective bargaining. It was not until the deep economic recession of 1981–82, however, when unions faced employment losses that jeopardized the interests of influential senior members and union power weakened so severely that unions could no longer "take wages out of competition."

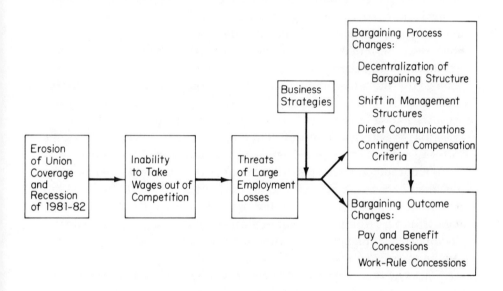

FIGURE 5.1

Forces Producing Changes in Collective Bargaining in the 1980s

These environmental pressures set the stage for significant change in collective bargaining. Business strategy decisions, prompted by the changed economic environment, in turn interacted with environmental pressures to shape the nature and extent of pay and work-rule changes. As outlined in more detail later, the major changes in the process of bargaining that helped management achieve pay and work-rule concessions included a decentralization of the structure of bargaining; greater involvement by line and human resource professionals in the

planning and conduct of negotiations; more extensive and direct communication with rank-and-file workers during bargaining; and a shift
in pay criteria from reliance on wage comparisons and cost-of-living
formulas to more contingent and firm- or plant-specific factors.

The Environmental Pressures on the
Traditional Union Model

As chapter 2 pointed out, the New Deal model of industrial relations
developed in the postwar economic environment of growth and market
expansion, encouraged by government policies and prevailing union
and business values. This model included the use of pattern bargaining
and wage formulas to set wages. Unions' bargaining power was
strengthened by their substantial organization of a number of the nation's core industries. Economic growth and the institutional maturation of the collective bargaining process gave stability to contract
negotiations and led labor and management to prefer a status quo
orientation within bargaining. This stability gave industrial relations
professionals power and influence within managerial hierarchies.

As environmental pressures built up, however, union power gradually
declined in a number of industries during the 1970s. To understand
why that decline initially was not associated with downward adjustments in bargaining settlements requires recognition of the political
factors that influence union wage policies. Stated succinctly, it is the
median union voter (typically with a number of years of seniority),
and not the marginal union member, whose job must be threatened
before unions are likely to significantly lower their wage targets.[7] Thus
it is the threat of large employment declines that cut deep into union
membership, not the hard-to-discern loss of potential future members
or the layoff of small numbers of current members, that leads unions
to lower their wage expectations.

Pressures of intensified competition from either international or
domestic nonunion competitors were the driving force that induced
labor and management eventually to make major modifications in their
traditional bargaining approach. The growth in the union/nonunion
wage differential that had occurred in the 1970s only served to increase
the competitive pressure from the nonunion sector. In addition, in

industries such as airlines, trucking, and communication, deregulation opened the door to new entrants and produced abrupt increases in cost competition. Furthermore, the economic pressure for cost cutting in the union sector was exacerbated by the deep macroeconomic recession that occurred in the early 1980s.

As these competitive pressures mounted, unions confronted large-scale layoffs and plant closings. Between 1980 and 1984, for example, the Bureau of Labor Statistics estimated approximately 2 million jobs were lost in manufacturing; of these, slightly more than half were jobs of union members.[8] Employment among the major auto producers and parts suppliers dropped from a December 1978 peak of 800,800 to 487,700 in January 1983.[9] Industry employment dropped from its previous peak levels (usually attained in 1979) to recession lows (usually reached in 1983): 44 percent in the steel industry, 48 percent in the farm machinery industry, and 50 percent in copper mining.[10] More generally, unions feared that unless they agreed to concessionary modifications in either existing or new contracts, they would face even more substantial declines in employment. As they were less able to take wages out of competition, these unions faced a significant decline in their bargaining power.

Peter Cappelli's analysis of concessionary agreements reached in 1982[11] reveals the important role played by actual or threatened employment loss to large numbers of union members. In the first half of 1982, 210 cases of concession bargaining were reported (concession bargaining is defined as negotiatons that are under "distress," including those where attempts are made to reopen contracts or to seek rollbacks in the terms of contracts). Ninety-six percent of these 210 cases report that employment security was involved in the form of either threats of layoffs or plant closings. Ninety percent of the cases had actually experienced layoffs or temporary closings just prior to negotiations. Further, unions granted concessions only where employment was threatened (there were no rollbacks in the 4 percent of cases where layoffs or plant closings were not threatened.)[12] These results are reinforced by the Conference Board survey data discussed in previous chapters. Regression analysis of wage changes negotiated in 1982 and 1983 found that marginal employment declines did not significantly lower the rate of wage increase. However, those bargaining units that experienced a 40 percent or greater drop in employment in the early 1980s negotiated settlements approximately 3 percent below those negotiated in bargaining units with no employment declines.[13]

115

SLOWING THE RISE IN WAGES AND UNIT LABOR COSTS

In the 1980s concession bargaining produced contractual outcomes that differed markedly from past settlements. Many agreements implemented either pay cuts or freezes. In 1982, 1.5 million workers (44 percent of those covered by new major collective bargaining agreements) received first-year wage cuts or freezes.[14] In 1983, 15 percent of workers covered by major agreements received wage cuts and another 22 percent accepted wage freezes. Daniel Mitchell's summary of the BLS data on wage freezes and pay cuts that occurred in collective bargaining contracts covering 1,000 or more workers showed that between 1980 and 1984, about 50 percent of union members under these contracts experienced a pay freeze or cut for at least one year.[15] Many experienced cuts or freezes of a longer duration.

We already noted that Mitchell's estimates, as well as our own, suggest the aggregate impacts of wage concessions have been to lower the rate of wage increases negotiated under collective bargaining by between 1 and 3 percent compared to what they would have been if the trends of the pre-1980s had continued. These wage concessions contributed to the national slowdown in the rate of compensation increases documented in table 5.1. As the figures in the first row of the table show, the rate of compensation adjustments provided over the life of major collective bargaining agreements also declined substantially in 1982, and throughout 1983 and 1984 they stayed at levels that were low in comparison to previous trends. Part of this decline reflected the diminishing contribution of cost-of-living escalator clauses in union contracts. Not only had the pace of inflation slowed, but in a number of agreements COLA payments were deferred or temporarily eliminated. Whereas COLA payments had accounted for 33.7 percent of effective wage adjustments in major collective bargaining agreements in 1981, in 1983 they accounted for only 15 percent of those wage adjustments.[16]

A slowdown also occurred in the growth of wages and salaries in the nonunion sector, illustrated by the figures in row 3 of the table. But as a comparison of the figures in rows 2 and 3 shows, as of 1983, nonunion employment costs started rising faster than union costs. This began to reverse the substantial widening of the union/nonunion differential that had occurred in the 1970s.

The slowdown in pay growth was particularly acute in the most heavily unionized firms, as their unions often were hit the hardest by competitive pressures and suffered the greatest losses in bargaining

TABLE 5.1

Percentage Changes in Compensation and Prices, 1979–84

	1979	1980	1981	1982	1983	1984
Compensation Adjustments over Life of Contracts Covering 5,000 Workers or More	6.6	7.1	8.3	2.8	3.0	2.8
Employment Costs (wages, salaries, and benefits)						
Union	9.0	10.9	9.6	6.5	4.6	3.4
Nonunion	8.5	8.0	8.5	6.1	5.2	4.5
Annual Percentage Increase in the Consumer Price Index (December to December)	13.3	12.4	8.9	3.9	3.8	4.0

SOURCES: For compensation adjustments, *Current Wage Developments,* BLS, 37 (2), (1985): table 15; for employment costs, *Current Wage Developments,* BLS, various issues; for annual increase in the CPI, *Economic Report of the President* (Washington, D.C.: U.S. Government Printing Office, 1985), table 5–56.

power. For example, regression analysis of data from the 1983 Conference Board survey found that more highly unionized firms negotiated lower wage increases than less unionized firms.[17] This is a clear departure from the patterns of wage outcomes negotiated in the 1970s.[18]

Some of the slowdown in union and nonunion compensation growth that occurred after 1982 was in response to a slowdown in the rate of inflation (measured by the consumer price index [CPI]), a slowdown that was in part precipitated by declines in the price of oil and a weakening in consumer demand caused by the recession. At the same time, the slowdown in compensation growth, through its effects on production costs and product prices, made a significant contribution to the decline in the rate of inflation. However, the exact extent to which the wage slowdown caused the price slowdown or vice-versa is difficult to determine.[19]

WORK-RULE CHANGES

In their efforts to slow the growth in unit labor costs and respond to environmental pressures, labor and management often included changes in work rules as part of concessionary labor agreements. In itself, this is not unusual. The tendency for employers to address work-rule provisions more aggressively during periods of slack demand or intensified competition has been well documented in the collective bargaining literature. Sumner Slichter described the intensified competition between union and nonunion plants that occurred during the various recessions and the Depression of the 1930s.[20] The recession of 1958 and 1959 also produced a round of management efforts to take a "hard line" on work rules and to regain some of the prerogatives that were incrementally lost during the expansionary period of World War II and the postwar era.[21] The productivity bargaining literature of the 1950s and early 1970s represents another installment in the discussion of how work rules are subject to periodic buyouts of existing practices.[22] Finally, the 1972 recession prompted Peter Henle to document the cases of "reverse collective bargaining" that occurred during the downturn.[23] However, although pay and work-rule concessions did appear in collective bargaining in the past, particularly during deep recessions, the recent extent of such concessions is unprecedented in the post–Great Depression period.

According to 1983 Conference Board survey data, 63 percent of the surveyed firms said they had received work-rule concessions in recent bargaining.[24] The general focus of management's efforts was a push for increased flexibility in human resource management. This push was evident in management proposals for such things as broader job classifications, more managerial discretion in the allocation of overtime, more liberal subcontracting rights, and restrictions on voluntary transfers or other movements across jobs.[25]

Notable work-rule changes include the 1982 revisions to the National Master Freight Agreement (NMFA), allowing over-the-road truck drivers with less-than-full loads to make local pickups and eliminating some penalty pay provisions. Other important changes outside the Master Freight Agreement were negotiated by a number of firms within the trucking industry. As discussed in more detail later, airline industry bargaining also led to important work-rule changes, typically involving increases in pilot and flight attendant flying time and a broadening of job classifications among ground crews.

EXPANSION OF THE BARGAINING AGENDA

As labor and management in union firms searched for a response to intensified competitive pressures, they often modified collective bargaining by introducing new subjects into the negotiations. In many cases this entailed making changes at either the workplace or strategic levels of industrial relations practice.

One way this expansion in the bargaining agenda appeared was through the improvements or quid pro quos labor gained in exchange for concessions in pay or work rules. Unions received quid pro quos in 52 of the earlier-mentioned sample of 210 episodes of concessionary bargaining. Sixty percent of these agreements contained quid pro quos for employment guarantees; 35 percent provided future wage and benefit improvements; 10 percent provided additional information on firm performance; and 8 percent provided for some involvement in company decisions.

Employment Security. A number of firms improved job security. Harkening back to the type of productivity bargaining that occurred in the West Coast longshoring industry in the early 1960s, American Airlines introduced lifetime job guarantees to existing workers and lowered the pay of new hires during 1983 negotiations. A guaranteed income stream program was created in the 1982 agreements at Ford and GM to compensate high-seniority auto workers permanently laid off because of plant closings and other reasons. In 1984 a "jobs bank" was created at these companies guaranteeing six years of income support or redeployment to workers displaced by technological change, outsourcing (contracting work out to another plant or firm), or negotiated productivity improvements. In 1982 plant-closing moratoriums were adopted in the automobile and meatpacking industries, while the necessity of prior notice of plant closing was introduced into the electrical products industry. In the trucking industry, a form of employment guarantee in the 1982 and 1985 national agreements was provided by limiting management's freedom to create nonunion subsidiaries.

The dominance of employment security as a quid pro quo for concessions is not surprising, given the number of layoffs that occurred in the eary 1980s. For most of the post–World War II period, employment insecurity took the form of layoffs that were temporary or occasionally of longer duration (when recessions were particularly severe). But for most workers these periods of unemployment were followed by recall. In turn, the union response had been to encourage income maintenance via supplemental unemployment benefits coupled with state unemployment insurance programs. With the extensive amount of restructuring that started in the late 1970s, however, workers with substantial seniority could no longer assume that they would be called back in the face of plant shutdowns and the worldwide consolidation and technological updating of manufacturing facilities. This led workers and their unions to upgrade the priority given employment security on their negotiating agenda.

The development of new work structures geared toward greater flexibility in the deployment of the workforce has also spurred interest in employment security. Traditionally, plants were organized along the conventional lines of occupations generally found in the external labor market, lessening the difficulties associated with layoffs by making alternative employment more easily available. But as firms pushed for fewer classifications and more firm-specific training, workers sought assurances for employment continuity. Without such assurances, workers fear that specialized training will make them ill-equipped for jobs in the external labor market.

Generally speaking, the new employment security arrangements protect workers against job loss due to decisions where management has some *choice*, such as outsourcing, the speed at which new technology is introduced, and other efforts to improve productivity. The new employment guarantees do not deal with displacement caused by a general falloff in demand. Thus these programs deal with internal decisions rather than with externally generated pressures to reduce employment levels.

A related theme is that employment security has come to be seen as much as an objective to be achieved jointly by the parties as a benefit that is embodied in the collective bargaining agreement. The arrangements at Xerox, GM, and Ford, for example, where workers are given a chance to propose changes in work rules and arrangements to keep work inhouse, are based on the assumption that more flexibility and productivity lead to greater employment security. This contrasts with the more traditional assumption that granting employment security is a good idea because it leads to greater productivity by removing fear and resistance to change.

The joint nature of labor and management's heightened concern for employment security can also be seen in the comprehensive development and training programs that have been fashioned in a number of industries. One of the most ambitious is the program created in 1982 between Ford and the UAW with funds that started at approximately $10 million a year (generated by a five-cents-an-hour contribution) and increased considerably in later years as both employment and the company's contribution rate increased. Another noteworthy program has been created by Boeing and the International Association of Machinists (IAM) to prepare workers, both active and on layoff, for new skill areas associated with new technologies such as computer-aided design (CAD) and computer-aided manufacturing (CAM), robotics, and composite materials. In some respects these programs and funds are reminiscent of the surge of special efforts created under the banner of Automation Funds during the 1960s.[26] The current programs, however, go much beyond the earlier ones. Today's programs focus on all workers, helping those who are laid off as well as those who are employed to adapt to new skill requirements. In addition, some of the new programs are prepared to spend monies to help workers find employment outside their initial employer. Companies increasingly have accepted the responsibility of preparing workers to return to the labor market.

Not all efforts to introduce greater employment security with more flexible production methods have succeeded. GM and Ford, along with the UAW, sought to link employment security and redesigned plant work rules, referred to as the pilot employment guarantee, in their 1982 national agreements. But as of 1985, only one site at Ford and none at GM (out of a contemplated eight sites) finalized an agreement to implement this program.

In general, the extent of enhanced employment security has grown significantly in the early 1980s. This expansion has furthered at the middle level of collective bargaining the type of joint collaboration that has become more evident in workplace QWL programs. The contract language creating the Ford-UAW Employee Development and Training Program, as an example, is very similar to the language outlining their Employee Involvement Program. In the next chapter we examine more closely the linkages that often exist across employment security and QWL programs.

THE INFLUENCE OF BUSINESS STRATEGY: THE AIRLINES INDUSTRY

Even though actual or threatened employment loss served as the primary motivation for radical adjustments in collective bargaining, the extent, nature, and consequences of concession bargaining varied widely across firms facing similar pressures. To understand why this variation in response occurred requires consideration of different business strategies adopted by different firms. Peter Cappelli's analysis of the course of recent bargaining in the airlines industry illustrates this point.

Table 5.2 outlines the relationship between business strategies and various aspects of labor relations for the major unionized carriers during the period from deregulation until 1984.[27] In the table the carriers are grouped into rows according to their product-market strategies since deregulation. Carriers in the first group (Avoided Competition) went against the conventional wisdom, avoiding longer trunk routes and concentrating on regional markets. When most trunk carriers abandoned these markets for longer routes, these carriers were typically left with little or no competition. U.S. Air, for example, was the monopoly nonstop carrier on half of its top fifty routes.[28] In short, their business strategies allowed them to avoid many of the competitive pressures associated with deregulation.

Carriers in the second group (Strong) have been hit squarely with route and price competition since deregulation. Unlike many other airlines, however, their financial resources were sufficient to provide the option of restructuring their operations to meet competitive pressures. These carriers were able to offer at least the potential for growth (often contingent on changes in labor relations).

Although carriers in the third group (Vulnerable) were also hard hit by competition, they have chosen to address competitive pressures by drawing back from their traditional markets. Both TWA and Pan Am lost tremendous amounts of money in their domestic markets but were supported at some points by their international routes (which are not deregulated) or by profits from other businesses in their holding companies. These carriers had somewhat fewer options than those in the second group; in particular, their ability to offer growth was much more limited.

Carriers in the final group (Near Bankruptcy) include those hardest hit by competition. These carriers had fewer options than those in the third group, largely because they were weaker financially. Almost without exception, they have pursued short-run business strategies aimed at staving off bankruptcy.

The column headings in the table outline aspects of changing labor relations in air transport that vary across carriers. The first column, No Changes, identifies those carriers whose labor relations have remained more or less unchanged after deregulation. Those carriers whose business strategies provided market niches that did not have severe competitive pressures did not need to change their form of labor relations. The remaining carriers have all faced severe competitive pressures and have seen labor relations change radically.

The second column, Extensive Relief, identifies those carriers that have received substantial labor-cost concessions—wage or work rule—from their unions. What is perhaps most interesting about this pattern is that it does not break down according to the carriers' financial position. For example, carriers in the second group received much more significant concessions than did those in the third group, even though

TABLE 5.2

Changes in Airline Industrial Relations and Business Strategies (1981–83)

		No Changes	Extensive Relief	Early Relief (wages—temporary)	Quids			Relationships	
					Work Rules	Jobs	Equity	Coop	Broken
Avoided Competition	Northwest	x			1	1		x	
	Piedmont	x							
	Ozark	x			2	2		x	
	US Air	x						x	
Strong	American		x		x	x			
	United		x		x	x			
	Delta		x		x	x			
Vulnerable	Pan Am			3				3	
	TWA								
Near Bankruptcy	Braniff		x	x			x	4	
	Continental		x	x					x
	Eastern		x	x			x	5	
	Frontier		x						
	Republic		x	x			x	x	
	Western		x	x			x	x	x

NOTES: 1. Northwest received limited work-rule changes for flight attendants in return for job security.
2. Ozark made the same trade with its flight attendants.
3. Pan Am received wage relief during its financial crisis and had cooperative relations during the crisis.
4. Braniff's labor relations turned cooperative during the short period before its reorganization.
5. Eastern's labor relations, like Pan Am's, initially turned cooperative during its financial crisis and then soured as finances improved.

SOURCE: AIRCon data on contract changes, corporate reports, interviews, and popular press for business strategies.

those in the latter group were in considerably worse financial condition. In other words, apparently it is not simply the threat of bankruptcy that determines the extent of concessions.

The key determinant of whether concessions were secured was whether unions were confronted with substantial unemployment at existing labor-cost levels. Unions at carriers in the fourth group obviously faced that risk as their carriers teetered near bankruptcy. Carriers in the second group were able to formulate business strategies so that unions were confronted with the possibility of substantial unemployment if the status quo was maintained and fewer employment losses if concessions were granted. For example, United was the first carrier to secure major concessions from its pilots. As the result of an arbitration award, United's 737 aircraft were operating with three-man cockpit crews, which United argued was unprofitable. It threatened to sell off its fleet of 737's and abandon their routes, sharply reducing pilot positions, unless the pilots granted relief.[29] Similarly, in 1983 American obtained perhaps the most extensive contract changes in the history of the industry. American Airline's senior vice-president for marketing was quoted as saying that the carrier had decided to implement one of the following business strategy options if concessions were not granted: shrink its airline business within the holding company, abandon the airline business altogether, or start a new (probably nonunion) carrier.[30] American Airline's unions had rejected concession demands in 1981 and 1982 when the carrier was in worse shape financially, a fact that suggests that this new business strategy, not the degree of financial pressure on the firm, was the key. To some extent, Delta put similar pressures on its pilots by making its orders for the new generation of aircraft contingent upon union concessions.

In contrast, through 1984 Pan Am and TWA had not imposed that type of unemployment threat on their unions, although employment had been declining gradually for several years in both firms. Even though both carriers had tremendous losses in their domestic markets, they were not in danger of bankruptcy because of support from their holding companies and from international operations. Nor did they confront their unions with business strategies that might force major changes in labor relations. As noted in the table, Pan Am did receive concessions when it lost its lines of credit in 1981–82 and appeared in some danger of defaulting. Then in early 1985, Pan Am negotiated concessionary agreements with its employees after a strike during which the company threatened to either hire permanent re-

124

placements for striking employees or go out of business.

The next set of headings in the table, Early Relief and Work Rules, describe the major concessions secured by the carriers. Most have received some wage concessions, typically revisions in pay formulas for flight personnel, as well as some work-rule changes (often outside of the contract). The difficulty has been in securing permanent changes. Management typically asks for wage concessions when there is short-run crisis, often cash-flow problems, and unions see little reason to grant permanent changes when the problem may well disappear. This contrasts with such business decisions as subcontracting a given operation, which are more likely to lead to permanent changes because they impose a permanent threat to employment. The work rules that management have been most interested in changing are those concerning the cross-utilization of employees, which is especially important in smaller work units where work demands vary. These changes have been difficult to secure, however, because such arrangements cut across the various craft unions and involve complicated jurisdictional issues.

Firms able to provide employment security—explicitly or implicitly through business growth—have been more successful at securing work-rule concessions. The most successful carriers in this regard have been listed in the strong group in the table. In addition to presenting the threat of potential unemployment, these carriers have been able to offer employment guarantees if work-rule concessions are granted. At United, pilots were offered a no-layoff agreement if they accepted the two-man crew rule on 737's.[31] American Airlines offered virtually all its employees a lifetime employment guarantee if concessions were accepted.[32] Delta has historically had implicit employment guarantees for full-time workers, making it easier for them to secure work-rule changes from their pilots.[33] It should be noted, however, that Delta did not seek or impose major concessions from its largely nonunion workforce in the early 1980s. As a result, by 1986 Delta was positioned as the high-labor-cost carrier among the major airlines competing for East Coast routes.

The remaining carriers have had little success in securing work-rule changes. As TWA's chief executive officer noted, "What's gotten productivity is promises of jobs. . . . I can't offer that without a program for growth."[34] Neither TWA nor Pan Am could offer such a plan, and the other carriers were doing their best just to stay afloat. Indeed, when pressed for productivity changes, Eastern's machinists agreed to change informal work rules but would not alter contractual rules, presumably so that the changes would not be permanent and could be taken back if jobs were lost.[35] At Republic, union employees originally had agreed to make productivity changes amounting to 8 percent of labor costs. They eventually decided, however, to take an 8 percent pay cut instead, presumably because the lack of growth at the carrier would have otherwise led to unemployment. At Western, all employees initially took a 10 percent wage cut (the second pay cut for the pilots). Then in 1984 another 12.5 percent wage cut was implemented along with extensive work-rule changes. This second round of cuts was unique in the industry in that the contracts did not contain provisions to "snap back" wages and work rules to their previous levels at some future time. Again in 1984 the pilots at Western took an even larger pay cut to avoid major layoffs. Flight attendants and ground personnel also agreed to a combination of wage cuts and work-rule changes. The mechanics, on the other hand, took no pay cuts at all, making their concessions entirely in the form of work-rule changes and some layoffs. Their response presumably reflects the superior prospects for mechanics in the external labor market.

Where unions could not get job security, they often sought other quid pro quos in return for concessions. Unions at carriers in the top two groups secured a limited range of quid pro quos because they had job security, their most important concern, and because the concessions were not crucial to the survival of the carriers. The carriers in the Near Bankruptcy row, in contrast, clearly needed union concessions for survival but were not able to offer employment guarantees. In order to help secure union concessions, they were much more likely to grant unions a broadened role in management affairs and workers a greater ownership stake in the company. Equity in the company was a benefit typically granted when carriers needed wage concessions to generate capital. By the end of 1984, employees owned 33 percent of Western, 25 percent of Eastern, 15 percent of Republic, and 13 percent of Pan Am. Moreover, all of these carriers agreed to provide unions seats on their boards of directors and access to competitive business information previously held to be solely the province of management. These are the situations where concession bargaining has not only reduced wages but also produced fundamental changes in the roles of the parties at the strategic level of industrial relations.

The final column, Broken Relationships, identifies those carriers that have sought to break existing collective bargaining arrangements with unions. These situations seem to occur where management's strategic plan demanded reductions in labor costs so drastic they could not be accommodated by traditional collective bargaining arrangements. In these cases, management has not tried to break unions through traditional forms of confrontation but rather has attempted to go around them. Frontier, for example, was successful until 1983, when its finances soured quickly. Its chairman asserted that Frontier could not wait any longer to get union concessions and announced the formation of a nonunion, low-cost subsidiary (Horizon) to fly the trunk routes where price competition was a problem.[36]

Continental serves as the most visible example of this approach. Following an unfriendly takeover by Texas International in 1981, management tried unsuccessfully to win approval of its concession demands. These demands included substantial wage cuts, work-rule changes, and layoffs—a difficult package for unions to accept, particularly given the absence of goodwill and trust following the takeover. In September 1983 the company filed for Chapter 11 bankruptcy and unilaterally and substantially reduced its wages and changed work rules, citing the failure to achieve concessions as the reason. In October Continental pilots went on strike, joining striking mechanics and flight attendants. But with a reorganized route structure and the help of newly hired staff and some employees who chose to cross picket lines, Continental continued to fly. The unions subsequently lost court challenges to Continental's tactics and, by early 1984, Continental had restored 70 percent of its prestrike capacity.[37] (Not until late 1985 was a back-to-work agreement worked out with the pilots' union at Continental).[38]

As these examples illustrate, in the airlines and other industries, changes at the middle tier of industrial relations are affected not only by changes in the environment but also by the diverse strategic business decisions made at higher levels of the industrial relations system. In turn, in some cases the quid pro quos for concessions have produced fundamental changes in the structure of industrial relations within the firm by altering the roles of management and the unions at both the strategic and workplace levels. This provides further support for our thesis that a complex interaction occurs between a more demanding competitive environment and the shaping of key business decisions, an interaction that produces options and diversity in industrial relations outcomes. Thus a complete explanation of the recent changes in industrial relations requires consideration of variables that encompass these interactions.

Bargaining Structure and Process Changes

The changes made to collective bargaining in the early 1980s entailed more than just adjustments in pay levels and work rules. As labor and management struggled to respond to environmental pressures, they made significant changes in the bargaining process as well. Indeed, these changes often served as the mechanisms through which management was able to achieve significant changes in bargaining outcomes. These process changes reversed many of the structures, patterns, and procedures that had taken years to build up within bargaining relationships. For that reason these changes are likely to have longer-lasting effects than many of the pay and work-rule concessions, which may be reversed (less likely for work rules) if and when economic conditions gradually improve and competitive pressures ease. Important bargaining-process changes include a decentralization of bargaining structures; shifts in the role of internal industrial relations staffs and functions; new communication policies; an increased emphasis on contingent compensation criteria; and a changing pattern of strike activity.

DECENTRALIZATION IN BARGAINING STRUCTURES

Economic pressures produced the decentralization of longstanding formal and informal bargaining structures in a number of industries.[39] This decentralization took the form of an erosion of intra-industry (intercompany) pattern bargaining in industries such as automobiles, rubber, and meatpacking. Within the trucking industry, the influence of the National Master Freight Agreement declined as regional and company modifications and deviations from the national agreement emerged. In 1982 the number of companies covered by the Basic Steel Agreement dropped from eight to six. Furthermore, in the 1982 steel negotiations the Wage Policy Committee of the United Steelworkers (USW) established different bargaining goals for such "distressed" industries as basic steel and such "healthy" industries as nonferrous metal or containers. This produced a weakening of the interindustry (intra-union) pattern bargaining that had traditionally characterized USW negotiations. Moreover, in 1985, as they prepared for contract renegotiation, management in the companies that had participated in coordinated bargaining in 1982 announced that they would each bargain separately with the USW. This put an end to the industry's thirty-year tradition of coordinated bargaining.[40] Even industries such as printing, with a tradition of more decentralized bargaining, underwent a similar erosion of pattern bargaining.[41]

In these and other industries a second form of decentralization emerged as a result of a downward shift in the level at which issues were resolved; this involved a movement from national-level to company- or plant-level resolution. Examples of this shift occurred in the rubber, steel, and automobile industries, where plant-level modifications in work rules were frequently introduced as part of the efforts to lower costs and keep business in-house. A number of plant agreements in the auto industry introduced pay systems and transfer rights that differed from prevailing industry practices.[42]

The decentralization underway in the structure of bargaining reversed the trend toward centralized and pattern bargaining that had emerged in the post–World War II period. The earlier centralization of bargaining structures had been helped along by the extensive union coverage in these industries. In effect, intensified competitive pressures in the late 1970s and early 1980s had forced decentralization as part of the process whereby wage and work-rule concessions were introduced in response to heightened competition and an associated erosion of union coverage.

The trucking industry illustrates both the long time periods and struggles that were associated with the creation of centralized bargaining structures and the parties' earlier reluctance to modify those structures in periods of stress. Contracts covering over-the-road drivers had been set before and immediately after World War II in company-level negotiations. In the 1950s, however, president of the Teamsters Union Jimmy Hoffa was able to induce the signing of regional agreements.[43] Hoffa's efforts to centralize negotiations went a step further in 1964 when a National Master Freight Agreement set common increases in wages and fringe benefits and a number of work rules for over-the-road drivers, although regional agreements still supplemented the terms of the national agreement.

In the early 1970s the economic environment for trucking bargaining began to change as the number of independent and unorganized drivers increased significantly in the "full truckload" portion of the industry. The underbidding of unionized carriers by these new entrants, along with extensive price cutting by union carriers in the "less than truckload" portion of the industry, put pressure on labor and management to abandon the national agreement so as to allow companies to separately fashion their response to this new competition. This pressure increased markedly with the passage of the Motor Carrier Act of 1980 and the decision of the Interstate Commerce Commission to allow free entry and rate competition in the industry.

Although these pressures intensified throughout the 1970s, the Teamsters union resisted abandoning the centralized negotiations it had fought so long and hard to introduce. Not until the early 1980s were a number of companies able to introduce wage and other employment terms that differed from those in the national contract. Just as the movement to a centralized bargaining structure was a slow and deliberate process, so was the reverse shift to more decentralized bargaining. It would appear, therefore, that this recent movement toward more decentralized bargaining is a change not likely to be reversed easily or quickly.

Variations in business strategies also affect the extent to which bargaining has been decentralized as a consequence of more intense competition. The trucking industry again serves as a good illustration. The breakup of centralized bargaining in trucking has been much more extensive in "full truckload" carriers than in "less-than-full-load" (LTL) companies. This is because companies in the full-load business have been more vulnerable to nonunion independent operators who can enter the industry by contracting for business that carries a full truckload of goods from the manufacturer directly to the customer. We will review the experiences of one such company later in this chapter. In contrast, the LTL business is more asset-intensive, requiring extensive feeder networks and terminals or break-bulk centers. Additionally, the LTL carriers, drivers, and warehouse workers have traditionally been members of the Teamsters union. The National Master Freight Agreement was initiated largely to control this segment of the industry. Thus it has been hard for new nonunion companies to enter this segment of the industry given the tremendous infrastructures required. In contrast, deregulation provided the opportunity for the entry of nonunion companies into the full-load segment of the industry. Again we see how in this industry the firm's environment and business strategy influence the nature of changes in the structure, process, and results of collective bargaining.

MANAGEMENT STRUCTURE FOR INDUSTRIAL RELATIONS

A second structural development involved shifts in decision-making power within management and changes in the position of industrial relations staffs. As we noted in previous chapters, the shift in management strategies toward nonunion operations and the growth of employee participation processes served to reduce the power and influence of industrial relations professionals; so, too, did the rise of concession bargaining in the 1980s. This shift in power showed up most clearly in the more frequent direct intervention of operation and financial executives in negotiations.[44] In some cases the top industrial relations executives were replaced. In the airline industry, for example, five of twenty-three vice-presidents of industrial relations were dismissed in 1982 alone.

Within many firms, the traditional professional industrial relations staff members resisted changes being urged on them by other professionals in the personnel/human resources management function or by top management to reduce substantially the growth in labor costs. Such resistance meant jeopardizing the labor peace and stability in union-management relations they had been so successful in achieving in previous years.

In short, by the late 1970s many industrial relations managers had become isolated within the management decision-making hierarchy, and the criteria they had used for building and maintaining their power within management were becoming less relevant for coping with emergent competitive pressures.[45] In order to achieve significant changes in bargaining, the behavior of industrial relations professionals had to change; if this was not possible, the individuals making the key bargaining decisions had to change. In General Motors these pressures led to a reorganization of the corporate personnel and industrial relations staffs in 1981, as well as the creation of a new strategic-planning group within the industrial relations staff. In other companies bargaining teams increasingly were led by chief executive officers and consisted more heavily of representatives from operations and finance departments. In one firm we studied, the planning process for upcoming contract negotiations was revised so as to directly involve executive and operating management. In the past, these duties had been under the exclusive control of the industrial relations staff and top executives had been involved in labor relations only when they had to approve the parameters for the negotiating team *prior* to bargaining and approve the contract *after* it had been negotiated. In general, lower-level op-

131

erating and executive managers now are becoming involved more extensively in setting bargaining goals and strategy and, in some cases, participating in the actual negotiation process.

DIRECT COMMUNICATION STRATEGIES

The decentralization of bargaining structures and the response to economic pressures often involved extensive efforts to change the expectations of rank-and-file workers. A strategy frequently used to achieve this change was to increase the flow of information about the firm's economic state and the industry's competitive conditions. This approach contrasted with the traditional pattern of limiting the flow of information from management to union leaders and the rank and file and carefully channeling all communications during negotiations through official spokespersons. The new communications efforts were frequently used to gain acceptance for bargaining outcomes that more closely tied compensation and work practices to the firm's productivity and cash-flow requirements. The need to change expectations while at the same time avoiding a strike challenged management and union officials alike to combine their previous emphasis on stability with a new emphasis on modifying labor costs.

The new strategies were often designed to bypass union officials and appeal directly to individual workers. They put forward the company's message in an effort to influence both the union's bargaining positions and contract ratification votes. Such campaigns often got underway long before bargaining actually took place. In some other cases, the companies' communication strategies focused on changing union leaders' perceptions of economic conditions and constraints. For example, the Cummins Engine Company began its effort to change employee attitudes by sending groups of union officials along with management representatives across the country to attend conferences and investigate cooperative programs in other industries more than a year before bargaining over a new contract began.

American Airlines negotiations for its pathbreaking 1983 agreement, which included a two-tier pay system, provides an example of management's use of communication tactics. American wanted to alter work rules so as to increase the flexibility of personnel deployment. The company felt that the rank and file would have no strong objections to those changes but that union leadership would strongly oppose them. Thus the company did not want the union to explain its arguments to the rank and file but wanted to make those arguments directly to the workers. American began its campaign for new work practices with articles in the company newspaper, home mailings, and video presentations at work. These presentations argued that employment would fall by 50 percent if the carrier's cost structure were not brought down to the level that would make it profitable enough to replace aging aircraft. In return for contract changes, the company offered a series of quid pro quos, including lifetime job security for existing workers.

During contract negotiations, management updated presentations to the rank and file, which included detailed financial arguments and consideration of union proposals. In addition, American established a "hotline" to answer specific questions from workers. The proposed contract eventually was ratified by the membership against the opposition of the local and international union leadership.

In other industries and firms where the expanded communication process during negotiations occurred with the support of union leaders, a commitment to sharing information on an ongoing basis resulted. In the automobile industry, for example, the extensive sharing of information in 1982 negotiations led to the establishment of ongoing "Mutual Growth Forums" where workers and managers discuss business pressures and upcoming decisions. Excerpts from the letter of agreement establishing these forums at Ford illustrate the far-reaching nature of this development and the extent to which it represents a significant departure from the traditional collective bargaining practices:

This forum . . . provides a new framework designed to promote better Management-Union relations through better communications, systematic fact finding, and advance discussion of certain business developments that are of material interest and significance to the Union, the employees, and the Company. . . .

The parties recognize that information to be made available frequently is of a sensitive nature and may have important competitive implications. Accordingly, they agree that information and data shared at these meetings will be accorded appropriate confidential treatment and will not be disclosed to outside firms, agencies or persons without the consent of the party providing it.[46]

The letter of agreement then goes on to outline the range of topics plant-level and corporate-level forums are expected to discuss, including such things as the general operating performance of the plant and the company, the quality of products, administrative matters, and pilot projects or experiments in human resource development. Thus, in this particular case, what started out as an effort to change expectations of rank-and-file workers in order to secure concessions has resulted in lasting changes in the structure and process of communications throughout the organization.

CONTINGENT COMPENSATION CRITERIA AND PRACTICES

In the face of more intense competition and increasingly volatile and uncertain product markets, in the early 1980s management pushed for a modification of pay-setting criteria. Management preferred to substitute localized and contingent pay procedures that varied with the performance of the firm or the local labor market for the traditional patterns and formulas. For example, Conference Board surveys conducted in 1978 and 1983 showed a sharp decrease between these two years in the ranking of industry patterns as a pay criterion and a rise in the importance of expected profits and company productivity or labor-cost trends.[47] The movement toward more localized and contingent pay criteria did not necessarily lead to the abandonment of contractual cost-of-living escalators. There was some reduction in the extent of COLA coverage, as discussed earlier, but COLA's were continued in a majority of major collective bargaining agreements. Yet increasingly modifications were introduced into the "across the board" pay formulas that had traditionally been used as supplements to cost-of-living adjustments.

In the automobile, airlines, and meatpacking industries, there was a shift away from the use of a COLA and other formula mechanisms toward profit sharing and other "contingent" compensation mechanisms that more directly tie pay to company performance. For example, a variable earnings plan was introduced at Braniff (before bankruptcy), Eastern, and Western Airlines in 1983. This shift in pay criteria reversed traditional negotiating practices that, in the process of taking wages out of competition, had placed heavy emphasis on external wage comparisons and formula escalators rather than on the firm's profit levels or cues from the local labor market.

STRIKES

Three features stand out in strike activity in the early 1980s compared to prior periods. First, strike frequency declined to its lowest levels since World War II. In 1981 there were 2,577 work stoppages involving six or more workers. As Robert Flanagan notes, "One has to go back to the late 1930s, when the extent of union organization was much smaller than it is now, to find years in which work stoppages were this low."[48] Second, while strikes produced a positive return to union members in the 1970s,[49] in the 1980s strikes appeared to be defensive weapons used only as a last resort, in some cases by unions fighting for their continued existence. Third, those strikes that did occur were more hostile, violent, and emotional than earlier strikes.

In some cases the modifications in pay and work rules came only after bitter strikes that, in turn, occasionally ended with the elimination of union representation. Wilson Meatpacking and Continental Airlines underwent bitter strikes and used bankruptcy protection to impose substantially lower pay and less costly work rules after their unions refused to agree to those terms in negotiations. Other meatpacking and some trucking firms also used reorganizations in ownership to gain lower labor costs. Some of these firms closed unionized operations and then reopened on a nonunion basis, hiring the same workers back on significantly less favorable terms.[50]

How victory in a strike enabled management to radically alter work rules and work organization is illustrated by one manufacturing plant included in our field research. In this firm, workers went on strike after refusing management's demands for major changes in work practices. After a long strike, during which supervisors were able to keep the plant in operation, workers returned to work on management's terms. A team system of work organization replaced a highly detailed job classification system and ended a tradition whereby shop stewards continually negotiated work-rule practices with individual supervisors. A pay-for-knowledge system was instituted and all workers received higher hourly pay. Workers, however, were required to learn and move across a variety of jobs. The traditional codification (and continuous amendment) of formal rules was replaced by the flexibility inherent in the team structure and by increased direct informal communication between workers and their supervisors.

The early 1980s, generally, were characterized by an increased willingness on management's part to hire replacements in an attempt to break strikes. In firms such as Phelps Dodge, management succeeded in those efforts and eventually the previous union was dislodged in a decertification vote held among the ranks of the now-permanent replacement workforce.[51] Events at Phelps Dodge are summarized in more detail in table 5.3.

Not all acrimonious strikes, however, ended with the demise of union representation. Greyhound hired replacements for its striking drivers after they refused to agree to contract concessions. But after Greyhound

TABLE 5.3
A Chronology of Events at Phelps Dodge Copper Facilities

1967–1980

In 1967 the International Union of Mine, Mill and Smelter Workers merged with the United Steelworkers Union (USW). Along with other unions in the copper industry, the USW then pressed in contract bargaining for coordinated bargaining in an effort to standardize wages and other contract terms across plants and companies in the copper industry. These efforts met with some, although not complete, success.

Phelps Dodge opened a smelter in New Mexico in the early 1970s and was successful in keeping it unorganized.

At Phelps Dodge's unionized copper facilities in Arizona and its refining operations in El Paso, Texas, strikes occurred during contract negotiations in 1971, 1974, 1977, and 1980.

1982

Facing sharp declines in the price of and demand for copper, Phelps Dodge temporarily closed its Arizona and New Mexico mining facilities and instituted a number of cost-reduction policies, including executive pay cuts and salaried employee layoffs.

April 1983

A contract settlement was reached at Kennecott Copper Corporation and was approved by the unions' coordinated bargaining committees as the "pattern" settlement they hoped to negotiate elsewhere in the copper industry.

July 1, 1983

A strike started at Phelps Dodge's Arizona and El Paso, Texas, operations after the company refused to agree to follow the Kennecot pattern in new contracts.

August 1983

Phelps Dodge began hiring permanent replacements for striking employees.

August 1984

A thirteen-union coalition, led by the USW, launched a "corporate campaign" against Phelps Dodge and its executives. At stockholder meetings, including those of Manufacturers Hanover Trust (a major creditor of Phelps Dodge), the coalition pressed its campaign.

October 1984

An election was held to decertify all unions at Phelps Dodge's Arizona and El Paso operations. The employees voted to decertify and the vote was subsequently challenged in the NLRB and the courts by the unions (unsuccessfully).

and its unionized drivers eventually agreed to a new labor agreement (which did include wage concessions), the unionized drivers returned to their jobs.[52]

Companies and work sites have varied substantially in the degree to which they modified traditional bargaining practices and in the interactions that occurred across the various modifications. Yet much can be learned by looking closely at the experiences of one firm. Negotiations at Schneider Transport provide a graphic illustration of the sort of changes in the bargaining process that often were required in order for firms to achieve significant concessions or changes in pay levels, pay design, and work rules. We present this case to illustrate how important, and indeed necessary were changes in the process and structure of bargaining to the achievement of significant changes in the outcomes of bargaining.

Concession Bargaining at Schneider Transport

Schneider Transport has been in the trucking industry for over thirty years. Its most rapid growth occurred in the 1960s and 1970s, and in 1985 it employed approximately 1,600 drivers and generated nearly $200 million in sales. Schneider Transport is a fully-owned subsidiary of Schneider National, which had nationwide trucking and related volume of $500 million.

From its beginning Schneider Transport (Schneider) was a very paternalistic employer. It attempted to establish close relations with employees and to treat them well. As the company grew it acquired a number of Teamster contracts and eventually was covered under the National Master Freight Agreement (NMFA). After it was included in the NMFA, a new position, the Director of Industrial Relations, was added to Schneider Transport's management structure to work closely with Schneider's line management.

The firm's first real labor-relations challenges occurred during the 1976 negotiations. The industry association developed a new method of compensation for drivers and included it in the agreement negotiated with the Teamsters that covered Schneider's drivers. The agreement involved changing from a pay system based on payment for miles driven and hours worked loading and unloading to a new system that rewarded drivers based on a percentage of the shipment revenue. Management argued that the miles-and-hours-type pay was easily abused, since there was no good way to verify the time spent working at the hundreds of load and unload sites. In addition, a concept called "comparison pay" was included in the agreement to protect drivers if their pay under the new system fell below what they would have received under the old. As it turned out, the negotiations process reached agreement on this new pay concept and method very late in bargaining. In fact, neither the Teamsters nor Schneider had time to prepare the drivers for this new system. Instead it was announced to them after the negotiations had been completed. Thus, the drivers were not aware that a new system was going to be brought to them for ratification. As a result, the company experienced a brief walkout that ended when the company gave assurances that it would definitely pay the comparison pay wherever warranted.

Labor relations at Schneider were mixed between 1976 and 1979. A high level of grievances occurred because of the drivers' distrust of both the company and the union under the new pay system. At the same time, the company was in a very rapid growth period. Schneider doubled in size from a sales volume of $50 million to $100 million during this period. The growth was a result of general economic prosperity and Schneider's efforts to become the largest full-truckload carrier in the nation. The company could see that deregulation was approaching and would present a major opportunity. Management felt, however, that the labor issues needed to be resolved in a way that resulted in a more competitive contract as well as a driver force that was in touch with the evolving new marketplace.

The climate of low trust and high conflict continued within the firm through the years leading to the 1979 negotiations. The company was very clear that even more changes were required to be competitive in the new trucking industry. In fact, more changes in the level and method of pay were accomplished in the 1979 negotiations. In response a group of disgruntled drivers organized a rival faction within the local union. This in turn resulted in a wildcat strike after the 1979 contract was negotiated with the Teamsters. The contract was ratified, several leaders of the strike were discharged, and the company and its drivers went back to work.

During the mid- to late 1970s the company could see that the mood of the Congress and the steadfast insistence of shippers were going to convince the ICC to deregulate the trucking industry. The airline industry deregulation bill passed in 1978. Further, Schneider's goal was to develop into a full-service nationwide carrier poised to grow to meet the needs of its largest customers. They could see that it would take time to improve relationships with the Teamsters and the Schneider Transport drivers and to negotiate, over time, a contract that was competitive with nonunion carriers. To accomplish their growth goals the corporation began setting up independent contractor operations in the West, Southwest, and Southeast. Under this independent contracting arrangement, nonunion subsidiaries were established in which the drivers, being independent contractors, owned their own tractors and were affiliated with the company on a long-term lease basis. A large number of independent contractor firms had always existed in the industry. As deregulation occurred, however, there was an influx of independent contractors. This put price and cost pressure on Teamster companies. Schneider estimated that its labor costs were approximately 30 percent above the costs required to run an independent contractor firm.

In view of this cost differential and the increase in the number of its competitors who used these subcontractors as deregulation evolved, Schneider National, the holding company for Schneider Transport, chose to develop its nationwide growth with independent contractor operations. By 1982 Schneider National had several of these operations in place and had reached a nationwide sales volume of approximately $300 million.

ORGANIZATIONAL INNOVATIONS

With the new organizational structure and the planned growth came a new management structure. The president of Schneider National decided to develop a more professional management group and in 1979 hired (1) an experienced executive to serve as the president of Schneider Transport; (2) an experienced professional as the vice-president of Human Resources Management; and (3) an Organizational Development (OD) specialist. The hiring of all three of these professionals signaled a new approach to managing employees in the firm.

The key ingredients of the new human resource management strategy as it applied to Schneider included:

1. The development of new communications systems and processes between the company and the drivers, and between the company and the union;
2. The development of a more employee-centered high-commitment work system for managing the workforce;
3. The development of greater driver and union awareness of the competitive conditions facing the company and its workforce and the relationship between those competitive conditions and job security; and
4. The reduction in labor costs of the company through a combination of a reduction in pay for nonproductive time, the implementation of an entirely new pay design that rewarded productive behavior and fostered employee involvement in running the business, and the movement out from underneath the NMFA.

The first step in implementing this new strategy centered on the development of a major training program developed and implemented by human resources, the fuel department, and operations. Over a period of eighteen months, starting in 1979, approximately 1,100 of the 1,500 drivers were brought into headquarters over a three-day period in groups of fifteen to twenty. The business training that took place was new for the drivers. Fuel efficiency was the focus because each $\frac{1}{10}$-mile-per-gallon improvement was worth $750,000 of profit enhancement. The training goals went beyond this, however.

The training program was the first major step to get the drivers and managers to see that a major behavior and performance change on their part was going to be necessary to compete in the deregulated trucking industry. On the third day of the program the new president of Schneider Transport met with the drivers and operations supervisors to discuss in detail the industry, the plan for Schneider, and the new stance on human resources. All subjects were open for discussion, including the independent contractor operations initiated in the west and south. Cost comparisons and rate structures in the industry were discussed, with a focus on the importance of wage, fringe, and fuel costs. All the material was also sent directly to drivers' homes in letters from the president and key operations management.

Several other new programs were initiated in the 1979 to 1982 time frame. One was called Operations Handshake where, once per quarter, drivers and managers collaborated to take important business information to the field. Motor homes were rented and placed at various truckstops across the country. Small groups of drivers would meet with the manager-driver presenting teams and discuss subjects that ranged from industry competitiveness to equipment design to specific information from customers.

Another innovation introduced was the Performance Recognition Program (PRP). This program required drivers and supervisors to sit down face to face on at least a quarterly basis. Supervisors shared business results with drivers, talked about how the company was doing, and discussed their personal lives. To facilitate the business discussion the company created a driver performance report that provided individual performance data against standards that had been established in a number of key areas, which were primarily cost-related (like fuel usage) or in some cases service factors (like the timeliness of pick-up and delivery). Supervisors and drivers were to agree on meeting specific performance objectives, and progress was reviewed against these objectives.

140

Additionally, several drivers had the opportunity to engage in non-driving activities, such as the recruiting of other drivers and safety improvement activities. When drivers participated in these nondriving duties they received about $400 a week, which was substantially less than the average wage of $700. However, there were always far more candidates for those kinds of opportunities than the company was able to provide. Some drivers had the chance to become supervisors. When supervisory positions became available, the company conducted its own Management Assessment Program (MAP) to identify potential candidates. Drivers and other nonexempt staff would find out about MAP sessions through a job-posting system. Twelve drivers had become supervisors during the 1979 to 1982 period. When a driver became a supervisor he took about a $10,000 initial pay cut. The intrinsic rewards of being a supervisor and the life-style seemed to make up for the initial decrease in pay. Eventually, the supervisor could surpass his earnings as a driver if he performed well and/or was promoted to positions of increased responsibility.

In the fall of 1980 the chief operating officer of the company formed a new group for planning the 1982 negotiations called the "Industrial Relations and Human Resource Planning Group." The group's members included four managers of the company's operating divisions, the director of Industrial Relations, and the vice-president of Human Resource Management. Their central task was to think about "where we had to be at the point where the contract expired and to determine what needed to be achieved in these contract negotiations." The group defined its task in terms of four major concerns. First, they were concerned with the amount and type of business communication and learning that drivers need to have prior to the beginning of formal negotiations. Second, they were concerned about the type of communication and knowledge that various managers and supervisors needed. Third, they focused on developing an analytical base for assessing all of the relevant costs associated with their operations and with the operations of their competitors. Fourth, they were asked to develop a new, more collaborative approach to the Teamsters' locals and national bargainers.

Out of the planning process emerged a negotiation strategy that focused on two objectives: the ability to negotiate a separate contract outside of the NMFA between the company and the Teamsters; and the achievement of a new pay structure and system that allowed the company to compete with the more cost-effective carriers that were forming in the new deregulated full-load trucking industry environment. The new design sought to achieve a significant increase in productivity as well as lower costs per mile.

The company then formally requested separate negotiation authority from the international union. The president of the company met with the top leaders of the international union to present the case for separate negotiations, and laid out the competitive situation directly with data on the differential labor costs, trends in revenue and erosion of the business, and other pertinent information. The international representatives agreed to allow separate negotiations, which were conducted with the team that included the president of the company, the director of industrial relations, and selected operations managers.

The negotiations resulted in an agreement that incorporated many of the changes in the pay system that the company proposed. It eliminated much of the "nonproductive" pay of the past. It involved a significant pay reduction (15 percent) for each mile driven, but the driver was given the opportunity to drive more miles in a year. Depending on how the drivers adjusted to the new system, the pay reduction per mile could be largely offset by driving more miles. The new design allowed the company to achieve a significant increase in productivity as well as lower costs per mile.

RATIFICATION STRATEGY

The company developed a very comprehensive and new approach to ratifying the contract. It should be noted that this was the first time that the Teamster drivers in this company had the opportunity to ratify their own agreement, since in the past they were only one very small part of the voting group under the NMFA. The company decided, therefore, that it needed a very active communications program to carry through the ratification process. This was important not only because there were so many changes in the pay system under the new agreement but also because, as a company representative stated, the Teamsters "by and large had had little experience dealing with their members on contract proposals involving major changes from past practice and pay reductions."

The heavy emphasis on direct communications with individual workers prior to the negotiations process helped to lay the groundwork for changing expectations, for gaining trust and credibility with the drivers, and for getting the drivers to focus on the competitive realities facing the company. The emphasis on developing a stronger line management and supervisory structure was also consistent with the desire to develop closer lines of communications, closer working relationships, and better trust within the firm from the rank-and-file drivers up through the entire management structure. It was part of an effort to "get line management to understand its new role and take responsibility for its relationships with individual workers."

Drivers at Schneider first rejected the proposed contract by a vote of 30 percent for and 70 percent against ratification. Management then initiated another set of communication meetings with small driver groups. The president, key operating management, and even the founder of the corporation spoke at these meetings in an effort to convince drivers that if the proposed contract was rejected, Schneider Transport management would close down a substantial part of the business. This direct and personal communication apparently made a substantial impact; in a second vote, drivers accepted the proposed contract by a margin of 55 percent for, 45 percent against.

LESSONS OF SCHNEIDER TRANSPORT

This case illustrates how the chain of events outlined in figure 5.1 modified the process and the results of negotiations in the early 1980s. This company reoriented its business strategy and then introduced changes in the way it managed and bargained with its employees. This reorientation of human resource management at Schneider brought changes in the process and outcomes of collective bargaining.

Notable bargaining process changes include the pullout from coverage by the Master Freight Agreement and the negotiation of a separate company agreement; more direct communication with drivers regarding business conditions and alternatives; and the direct participation of operating management in the contract negotiation process, a participation that replaced the previous dominance of the industry association's industrial relations staff. The key changes provided in the new contract at Schneider are a pay and work system that rewards productive behavior and encourages direct involvement of the driver in the operation of the business. In the extent to which changes in bargaining outcomes were accompanied by significant changes in the bargaining process and in the association that prevailed between changes in the firm's corporate strategy and human resource management, the collective bargaining that took place at Schneider is representative of the type of bargaining that occurred in the 1980s in many other industries.

Summary

This chapter shows how environmental pressures motivated labor and management to modify traditional collective bargaining practices. By the early 1980s unionized firms were hard-pressed to respond to heightened competition and an economic environment that put a premium on cost control, flexibility, and adaptability. The patterns, structures, and processes of collective bargaining that evolved out of the New Deal industrial relations system were no longer compatible with prevailing economic realities. The entry of unorganized competitors (international and domestic) and unions' inability to counteract that entry with successful organizing strategies produced a major weakening of unions' bargaining power. No longer able to take wages out of competition, union firms were forced to abandon the pattern bargaining and the standard wage formulas that had provided steady pay gains over the postwar period.

Pay concessions and work-rule modifications were accompanied by alterations in the bargaining process, including a decentralization within bargaining and realignments within managerial hierarchies that lowered the status and influence of traditional industrial relations professionals. As they struggled to cope with environmental pressures, in some cases labor and management expanded the bargaining agenda so as to include such things as novel employment security programs. In some other cases, unions' loss of bargaining power was so extreme as to make them unable to resist either management's unilateral imposition of contract concessions or their eventual removal through bankruptcy or the hiring of permanent replacements during strikes.

Changes in the middle (collective bargaining) level of union industrial relations systems thereby became intertwined with changes occurring at lower and higher levels of these sytems. This showed up in the complicated package of work-rule and work-organization changes that often accompanied pay and other contractual modifications. Business strategies and the strategic involvement of labor also played a crucial role in the course and design of contractual changes. For example, unions were more willing to agree to greater flexibility in work rules and to experiment with worker-participation programs where their bargaining structure enabled them to influence managerial decisions in a way that assured them of a role in the firm's future. And business strategies influenced the nature of labor relations options and altered union and worker preferences for available options.

As for the future, we believe that major changes introduced into collective bargaining are likely to continue where the parties continue to be exposed to extreme competitive pressures. In such situations it is difficult to envision a return to the wage-setting practices that characterized the New Deal industrial relations system.

In a few cases, in their efforts to respond to economic pressures labor and management already have introduced the rudiments of what eventually might amount to a new industrial relations system. This new system appears to link more localized and contingent compensation, more flexible and team-oriented work organization, enhanced job security, and broader worker and union involvement in production and strategic decision making.

To fully understand the potential form and likely success of this alternative industrial relations system, it is necessary to look more closely at the changes underway in unionized settings at the workplace and strategic levels.

CHAPTER

6

Changing Workplace
Industrial Relations in
Unionized Settings

CHAPTER 4 documented the
pressures on unionized industrial relations systems as a result of the
innovations and lower costs found in many newer nonunion workplace
systems. Chapter 5 examined the efforts of companies and unions to
respond to these and other environmental pressures through changes
at the level of contract negotiations. Our analysis of these recent
changes in collective bargaining, especially concession bargaining,
shows that they often have a close relationship with changes underway
at the workplace level. In this chapter we shall illustrate the interrelated
nature of the various levels of an industrial relations system by examining the changes introduced jointly by labor and management as
part of their efforts to respond to accumulating pressures at the unionized workplace.

Two central questions regarding the innovations being introduced
in unionized workplaces need to be addressed: Are the changes being
experimented with and introduced in selected settings significant

enough to help close the competitive gap that exists with the most innovative nonunion settings? Are the changes diffusing to a wide enough proportion of union settings and being institutionalized in ways that will lead to further adaptation and innovation and eventually to what might be called a "new industrial relations system"?

The workplace changes being introduced jointly have two basic objectives: (1) to increase the participation and involvement of individuals and informal work groups so as to overcome adversarial relations and increase employee motivation, commitment, and problem-solving potential; and (2) to alter the organization of work so as to simplify work rules, lower costs, and increase flexibility in the management of human resources. As our discussion of the actual implementation of various change processes will show, some innovative work designs set out to accomplish both of these objectives simultaneously.

Participation processes operate under a variety of popular labels, such as quality of working life (QWL), quality circles (QCs), employee involvement (EI), labor-management participation teams (LMPT), and operating teams. While there are subtle differences among these processes, for the purposes of our analysis it will be sufficient to use the broad label of QWL to refer to them. Both the QWL and the work-redesign efforts have occurred separately from or, increasingly, in combination with technological changes. Moreover, these efforts have occurred in existing plants with existing workforces, in new union plants that carry over workers from old plants that have closed, and in new union plants that operate with new unionized workforces. Thus our examples will draw from each of these different settings and combinations of innovations. The contemporary responses to workplace innovations of labor and management representatives cannot be understood readily unless we first appreciate the controversial and, in many ways, the problematic historical paths that QWL and other workplace innovations have traveled over the course of their development and evolution.

Historical Context of Workplace Changes

Table 6.1 summarizes the three broad types of participation processes uncovered in our research, the various components in each type, and the cases discussed later in this chapter used to illustrate each type.

Type 1 represents a narrow QWL program that focuses primarily on workplace issues; those in type 2 go beyond QWL issues to address work-organization issues and thereby get linked to collective bargaining issues; those in type 3 go on to yet a broader agenda and are linked to strategic issues. The cases that follow document how in some worksites, an initial workplace QWL program moved in an evolutionary course from type 1, to type 2, and then to type 3 issues and domains. In these worksites the QWL processes started with a limited focus on workplace issues, but then broadened (often during the early 1980s) to more fully address competitive pressures and the employment-security interests of workers and their unions. The cases also show how the broadening of these efforts was a necessary product of the connections that exist across the three levels of industrial relations systems.

Previous chapters noted that efforts to introduce new systems of worker participation and/or work organization often met with resistance from union leaders and labor relations managers. This resistance arose because the earliest proponents of QWL programs challenged the basic assumptions of the traditional system of job-control unionism and workplace organization that prevailed within collective bargaining in the post–New Deal period.[1]

THE PROBLEMATIC HISTORY OF QWL

QWL processes are based on the simple proposition that increased employee involvement in task-related decisions and greater collaboration between workers and managers can help both groups. Why then should so many union leaders and industrial relations professionals within management be so skeptical or resistant to introducing these concepts? One reason is that QWL programs have a focus that is very different from collective bargaining processes. While the traditional workplace industrial relations system that developed under collective bargaining stressed the management of contractual relations and due process, the QWL proponents focused on the psychological needs and motivations of individual employees. Thus, whereas QWL theorists and organizational development consultants stressed the values of individual participation, cooperation, problem solving, and the building of trust through informal participatory processes, collective bargaining focused on the management of inherent conflicts, due process in resolving conflicts over individual or group rights, and uniformity in the application of work rules and practices.

To a large degree these differences in focus reflected differences in

TABLE 6.1
Types of Workplace Innovations

QWL Program Components	TYPE 1 Limited QWL Focus	TYPE 2 Extensive Links to Collective Bargaining Changes	TYPE 3 Extensive Links to Strategic Issues
Components Focused on the Workplace	Quality Circles Enhanced Worker-Supervisor Communications Worker Attitude Surveys	Quality Circles Enhanced Worker-Supervisor Communications Worker Attitude Surveys	Quality Circles Enhanced Worker-Supervisor Communications Worker Attitude Surveys
Components Linking to Collective Issues		Teams Work Restructuring Pay-for-Knowledge Workers and Union Receive Business Information	Teams Work Restructuring Pay-for-Knowledge Workers and Union Receive Business Information
Components Linking to Strategic Issues			Employment Security Gain Sharing Union Representation on Managerial Planning Committees Union Involvement in Employment Adjustment and Training
Cases Discussed	Auto industry early and mid-1970s Steel plants AT&T worksites	Auto industry late 1970s (especially in operating team plants) Xerox Rochester Complex	Fiero Auto Plant Selected Steel Companies in 1986 Packard Electric Warren Complex

underlying assumptions regarding the nature of the employment relationship. These differing underlying assumptions were particularly important in their contribution to the problems that arose when labor and management in unionized settings tried to integrate collective

149

bargaining and QWL processes. Many union leaders feared that QWL processes would undermine the role of the local union and the sanctity of the collective bargaining contract. These fears were fueled by the fact that most of the earliest applications of QWL principles were in nonunion settings and were designed, in part, as a union-avoidance strategy. Indeed, the active and extensive use of QWL and other work-place innovations by American managers and behavioral science consultants throughout the 1960s and 1970s as part of the broader union-avoidance strategies served as the most significant obstacle to the acceptance and diffusion of similar innovations in unionized settings in the 1970s. Most American union leaders saw the QWL movement as a hostile force, devoid of any sensitivity to or understanding of the history of U.S. industrial relations and unwilling to accept the need for unions as independent and legitimate representatives of worker interests.

This resistance to QWL processes slowed their diffusion. When experimental programs did get underway in unionized firms during the 1970s, they remained limited to particular pockets of activity and to a relatively small number of locations and workers. We believe that one important reason for this is that most line managers did not see QWL as making a significant contribution to improving organizational performance. Nor did they yet see a significant shift in the values of top corporate executives that would support long-term investment and commitment to QWL processes for the sake of improving individual worker satisfaction and motivation. QWL was still a behavioral science program, perceived as yet another fad of behavioral science theorists and organizational development consultants, but not something that would enhance the bottom-line results for which plant and division managers are rewarded. It was not until the late 1970s and early 1980s that these programs caught the attention of many line managers, when pressures to increase productivity, improve product quality, and lower costs intensified as a result of the deteriorating American economy and the growing popularity of Japanese managerial techniques. These pressures induced line managers to pay more attention to workplace issues and encouraged broader experimentation with QWL programs that held out the promise of more cooperative and flexible labor-management relations.

An example of this slow diffusion of QWL programs during the early and mid-1970s, followed by a rapid escalation of interest in QWL-type processes, is found in the auto industry.[2] The American auto industry's experimentation with worker-participation programs began in the late

1960s. The early programs arose in response to increased absenteeism and an increase in shop-floor problems (the increase in grievance rates and local contractual demands discussed in chapters 2 and 4). They focused on improving communication and relationships between workers and supervisors. An expansion of QWL-type programs was spurred further by the well-publicized strike at General Motor's Lordstown (Ohio) assembly plant in 1972, which led to wide-ranging discussions in and out of the industry concerning the workplace environment and worker motivation.

In 1973 a letter of understanding was added to the GM-UAW national agreement. It recognized:

... the desirability of mutual effort to improve the quality of work life for the employees. In consultation with union representatives, certain projects have been undertaken by management in the field of organizational development, involving the participation of represented employees. These and other projects and experiments which may be undertaken in the future are designed to improve the quality of work life thereby advantaging the worker by making work a more satisfying experience, advantaging the Corporation by leading to a reduction in employee absenteeism and turnover, and advantaging the consumer through improvement in the quality of the products manufactured.[3]

A joint national committee was created to review and encourage the QWL projects envisioned by this letter. A variety of experimental projects followed. Among these was a program to enhance upward communication via a survey of worker attitudes at the GM-Lakewood (Georgia) assembly plant, which showed signs of early success. At a van assembly plant in Detroit, assembly-line operations in one work area were replaced by a team (stall) work organization. Later, the QWL program at the GM-Tarrytown (New York) assembly plant was heralded for its success at substantially reducing absentee and grievance rates and improving worker attitudes.[4]

The pace and extent of these experimental programs varied widely within companies and across the auto industry. At Ford, program development stalled after a few unsuccessful pilot projects and was not revived until the end of the decade. Meanwhile, at Chrysler and American Motors, very few participation projects were initiated during the 1970s. At GM, where the widest diversity of programs emerged under the leadership of Irving Bluestone of the UAW and Stephen Fuller, Vice-President of Personnel at GM, there were failures as well as successes. For example, the team organization at the van assembly plant just mentioned failed to reach performance expectations and soon ended. The new cooperative relationship at the Lakewood assembly plant lasted only for a few years and then evaporated when plant management changed. In some other plants, such as Tarrytown, the worker-participation programs continued to be successful throughout the 1970s.

Table 6.2 illustrates the slow diffusion of QWL processes across one division of General Motors between 1973 and 1979. The upsurge in the number of plants initiating a QWL program can be seen toward the end of the decade—an upsurge spurred by the sharp economic downturn experienced by the domestic auto industry that started in late 1979. For example, in 1977, four years after top corporate and union officials agreed to promote QWL, nineteen of the twenty-two plants in this division had not initiated a QWL program for hourly employees. Even in 1979, sixteen of the plants still had no QWL program. By 1980, following a dramatic downturn in sales and employment in this division and in other parts of the industry, all but nine of the plants had introduced QWL to some fraction of their hourly workforces. Even then, however, only four out of twenty-two, or less than 20 percent, of the plants in this division had diffused the QWL process to a majority of their hourly workers. These data illustrate that active experimentation with a QWL process often comes only after significant external pressure and that diffusion of these programs often is a very slow process.

TABLE 6.2

*Numbers of GM Body Plants with Varying
Percentages of Hourly Workers Involved
in QWL Programs (N = 22)*

Year	0	1–10%	11–49%	50% +
1977	19	0	1	2
1978	17	2	1	2
1979	16	2	2	2
1980	9	7	2	4

A 1985 survey from a national sample of workers sheds further light on the extent of diffusion of QWL processes. Thirty-six percent of the survey respondents reported that some form of QWL or employee involvement process had been implemented at their place of employment. About two-thirds of those employed in organizations with a QWL process (or approximately 23 percent of the total workforce) indicated that they *personally* had participated in such a process. Moreover, large firms were significantly more likely to have an employee involvement process than were small firms. Fifty-nine percent of the firms with one thousand or more employees were reported to have an employee involvement program. It is also interesting to note that union members were equally likely to be involved in a participation program as nonunion workers.[5] While these data provide only a general profile, they are consistent with the more intensive, company-specific data summarized previously: Despite the extensive discussion concerning the value of worker participation, still only a minority of the American workforce has gained experience with this process, and it is generally limited to those larger organizations with reputations for innovative personnel practices in other areas of management. And even among those firms that have implemented a process, a significant percentage of employees remained uninvolved.

The Effects of QWL Processes

The main motivation for the expansion of QWL processes in the late 1970s and early 1980s was the hope that they would improve organizational effectiveness and cost competitiveness. Consequently, the long-run viability of these efforts depended on their ability to deliver concrete and measurable results. It therefore is important to examine whether there is any evidence to support the proposition that QWL processes improve organizational effectiveness. Despite voluminous press accounts of the "success" of various QWL programs, few studies actually have documented the quantitative impacts of these programs on industrial relations or organizational performance. Before summarizing the evidence on the effects of QWL programs we have collected in various quantitative and case-study analyses, it is important to recognize why it is so difficult to derive precise estimates of the "independent" effects that QWL efforts exert on organizational performance.

For one thing, our theoretical framework posits that important interactions occur across the various levels of an industrial relations system. This suggests the need to follow workplace industrial relations experiments through at least one complete contract negotiations cycle, from the start of an experiment through the next negotiation of a collective bargaining agreement, in order to accurately assess their staying power. With this longer time frame it is possible to assess success at integrating principles and processes across these two levels of industrial relations activity. Moreover, it is important to examine the staying power of workplace changes over a longer period of time, particularly through changes in the business cycle or in business conditions, as key union or management leaders change, and especially as union leaders stand for reelection and as new business strategies are adopted. While it is not always possible to study every experiment or example of change over this extended series of events, it is essential to gauge the effects that events occurring at higher levels of the industrial relations system exert on the diffusion and institutionalization of workplace changes.

QWL efforts may also serve as an initial starting point for further organizational changes that have larger economic payoffs to the firm and its employees. That is, standing alone, QWL programs may not appear to have significant economic effects. But by opening up new communications and problem-solving channels and by increasing trust, QWL processes may lead managers, union leaders, and workers to adopt more significant work-organization, technological, investment, or other policy changes that have greater returns. For this reason we need to be cautious about assigning precise quantitative estimates to the independent effects of QWL interventions. Some of these long-term stimulative effects of QWL programs are revealed in our case studies reported later.

Given these caveats, what are our estimates of the effects of QWL programs on organizational performance? Quantitative estimates of the effects of narrowly focused QWL interventions are provided by data from fifty plants in two divisions of General Motors.[6] Using the data sets introduced in chapter 4, we estimated the direct effects of QWL activity in these plants on measures of labor efficiency and product quality. We also estimated the indirect effects that QWL activity exerted on these outcomes by way of improvements in the performance of grievance procedures (conflict management) and other measures of individual employee attitudes and behavior.

The QWL activities underway in these plants at the time of our research were narrowly focused type 1 programs; they did not include major revisions in either work rules or work organization. Their primary focus was on improving the communication between workers and supervisors, addressing housekeeping issues such as workers' requests for better lighting or ventilation, and on solving workplace production problems. The most important activity by which these objectives were to be accomplished was through quality circles that met voluntarily for approximately one hour per week on paid time.

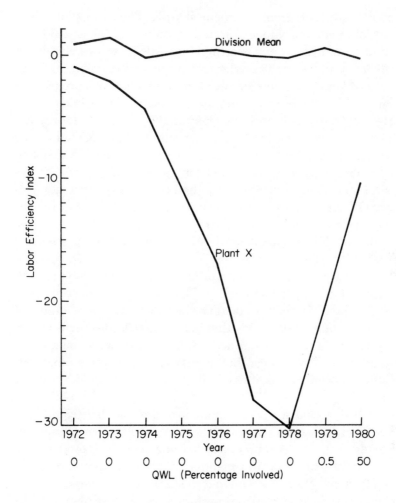

FIGURE 6.1

Plant Direct Labor Efficiency Versus Division Mean

While the specific results of the two studies vary slightly, the overall results are quite consistent. First, in each sample a number of individual plants achieved significant improvements in product quality and labor efficiency after introducing QWL efforts. That is, a number of successful examples of QWL could be identified, some of which displayed stable improvements over several years and across the swings in the business cycle over the course of the 1970s.

Figure 6.1 shows the improvement in the efficiency with which labor was utilized in one GM plant when the hourly workforce's involvement

155

in the plant's QWL program was rising sharply. The figure plots plant X's direct labor efficiency index (an index comparing the actual labor hours used to industrial engineering standards), the average direct labor efficiency index for the other plants in this division, and the percentage of hourly workers involved in plant X's QWL program in each year. The direct labor efficiency index of plant X increased relative to the rest of the plants in its division after 1978 when QWL program participation also was on the rise in the plant. Plant X's efficiency improvement after 1978 reversed the sharp relative decline that had occurred over the previous six years (at its low point, plant X was using labor 30 percent less efficiently than the division average). Advocates of QWL programs commonly use evidence such as this to generate support and help justify program diffusion to other settings, whether or not the causal attribution is warranted from a scientific standpoint.

Overall, however, both studies found QWL programs to have a small but positive effect on product quality. That is, holding constant variables measuring differences in quality due to variations in volume of output, amount of overtime, and other industrial relations performance measures, those plants with more active QWL programs had marginally better product quality ratings than plants with less active programs. In one study this effect was statistically significant while in the other it was not.[7]

Neither study found either an economic or a statistically significant effect for QWL programs on labor efficiency, and neither found consistent evidence that QWL processes led to a *sustained* lower rate of grievances or absenteeism in a manner that would suggest a strong indirect effect of QWL on economic performance through the improvements in industrial relations performance in these plants. To be sure, some short-run improvements in industrial relations performance were occurring in some plants with higher levels of QWL activity; however, we did not find that these improvements generalized across the plants to the point where an average and stable effect could be observed.

Our finding of QWL program's small effect on quality but not on labor efficiency is consistent with the view expressed earlier that improved trust and individual commitment is likely to have a bigger effect on those dimensions of organizational performance that are more directly under employees' control. In this case, quality improvement can be traced more directly to problems that employees and their supervisors can solve through increased communication, training, and motivation. On the other hand, labor efficiency and costs are subject to the influence of a wider variety of factors, such as staffing levels, scheduling problems, the organization of work, and the accumulation of work rules.

These are merely initial results for the effects of type 1 QWL programs. Remember, these data cover experiences prior to 1981 only, and the number of QWL programs in many auto plants increased dramatically after the industry's sales downturn, which began in late 1979.

Many managers and union officials in the auto industry offer considerably stronger testimonials to the contributions of QWL efforts than these results suggest.[8] This is not surprising, since their experience tells them that, as our case studies will demonstrate, a type 1 QWL program is only a small but perhaps a necessary step in their larger efforts to change industrial relations practices and outcomes to improve economic performance and employment opportunities. In the minds of most practitioners, it is difficult to isolate QWL programs' independent contributions (or lack thereof). Our case studies document the complicated dynamic interaction that QWL activities have as the parties broaden their efforts by addressing issues involving work organization, collective bargaining, and strategic decision making. This explains why it is so hard for both practitioners and researchers to isolate QWL effects.

But we should not let this difficulty keep us from recognizing one implication of these quantitative results: Specifically, in the auto plants analyzed, QWL efforts that focused merely on improving trust and problem solving without making other organizational changes were not able to achieve major sustainable improvements in labor costs and produced only small improvements in product quality. If this result is generalizable to broader settings (and our case-study evidence suggests it is), then QWL programs alone are unlikely to be sufficient to close the competitive gap between union and nonunion systems. While they may be a good starting point, they are not a good ending point.

TYPE 2 WORKPLACE INNOVATIONS—THE CASE OF THE
AUTOMOBILE INDUSTRY

Whether they met with success or failure, most of the early worker-participation programs were kept separate from collective bargaining. Both labor and management viewed the programs as vehicles for im-

proving worker-supervisor relations and addressing housekeeping issues regarding worker comfort.[9] But in the early 1980s, when labor
and management looked to cooperative programs to provide part of
the answer to economic pressures, this separation between cooperative
programs and other workplace and industrial relations activities proved
artificial. Developments in the auto industry are worth tracing in detail
because they illustrate our conclusion that worker-involvement programs inevitably interact closely with events underway at the two other
levels of industrial relations and that the most successful worker-
participation programs involve work reorganization and a broadening
of unions' participation in decision making.

In the mid-1970s GM opened a number of new plants in the South
that started up without UAW representation.[10] In a number of these
plants, work organization and pay procedures differed markedly from
GM's practices in its unionized facilities. In this way GM was following
the course of other previously heavily unionized firms discussed in
chapter 3—it introduced into its greenfield sites the comprehensive
personnel practices being developed by nonunion firms.

Most of GM's nonunion southern plants used an "operating team"
system that put hourly workers into ten- to fifteen-person work teams.
A broadening of job tasks in the teams was encouraged through a pay-
for-knowledge system that provided higher pay in a stepwise fashion
when workers proved competency in a larger number of tasks. Management also experimented with intensive orientation and training
programs and other methods to increase communication within the
plants.

The UAW, perceiving these unorganized plants to be a threat to its
unity and bargaining power, launched a series of organizing campaigns.
During these campaigns, some workers and union officials came to
perceive operating teams as a device to keep the union out the plants.
This produced a complicated relationship between team use and the
union status of these plants. In some plants, such as GM's assembly
plant in Oklahoma City, after it was organized the local union negotiated successfully to remove the team system. At other plants, such
as the Delco-Remy plant in Albany, Georgia, the local union agreed
to the continued operation of the team system, but only after acquiring
representation rights.

By the early 1980s the UAW (or in the case of GM's Packard Electric
division, the IUE) had gained the right to represent all hourly workers
in GM's southern plants. A series of clauses added to its national

contracts with GM assisted the UAW in its organizing efforts. As part of the 1976 national agreement, GM agreed to remain neutral in election campaigns. (Much controversy developed over whether GM did in fact maintain strict neutrality in the organizing campaigns that followed.) In the 1979 national GM-UAW contract an accretion clause was added and later amended. As noted in chapter 3, UAW leaders threatened to disrupt operations elsewhere inside GM, through local strikes or through withdrawal of support for ongoing QWL programs, if the corporation continued to oppose union representation in its new plants. The key to the UAW's success was that as a national union, it possessed enough bargaining power to intervene at the strategic level of the industrial relations system to stop the threat of nonunion southern plants.

The sharp economic decline in the auto industry in the late 1970s precipitated the development of a second generation and wider range of worker-participation programs. The scale of the industry's economic decline was massive. By July 1982 the number of production workers employed in the industry had dropped 36 percent from its peak level in December 1978. Furthermore, shifts in the demand for autos, heightened international competition, and the resulting imperative for rapid technological change suggested that employment levels were unlikely to return to anywhere near their earlier peaks.[11] In addition, the enormous success of the Japanese auto production system raised doubts about the soundness of American labor relations practices and helped to induce a new wave of experimentation.

The economic troubles of the American auto industry after 1979 have led to significant changes in the conduct of labor-management relations.[12] These changes have included the initiation of quality circles at the shop-floor level and enhanced communication between workers and management through other less formal channels. To preserve jobs, a number of plants have modified local agreements and work-rule practices. In the process, the role of union officers has changed dramatically. Union officials in many plants now communicate frequently with management outside of normal collective bargaining channels and receive information regarding business plans, new technologies, and supplier relations—information on subjects earlier deemed to be exclusive managerial prerogatives.

At Ford, worker-participation programs generally had been inactive throughout the 1970s, but their rapid growth during the early 1980s was stimulated by the economic pressures just discussed and by the appointments of new labor and management representatives: Donald Ephlin as the vice-president of the Ford-UAW department and Peter Pestillo as Ford's vice-president of industrial relations. A further push for participation programs came in the national agreements at GM and Ford, signed in 1982, which created new training programs, guaranteed income-stream benefits, pilot employment-guarantee projects, plant-closing moratoriums, and outsourcing limitations. These agreements also included significant pay concessions (the removal of the annual improvement factor and deferral of COLA payments) and reduced the number of paid holidays by nine per year.[13] The net impact of all these changes in collective bargaining at the plant level was to put greater pressure on managers and union leaders to improve quality, productivity, and labor relations.

This elaboration of worker-participation programs in the early 1980s confronted two central issues. First, economic pressure clearly was a major force that spurred these programs and raised the issue of how they were to relate to other cost-cutting measures. Second, labor and management faced a decision regarding whether or not participation programs were to expand to the point that they entailed a more systematic transformation of industrial relations.

Movement in the direction of a fundamental transformation was spurred in part by the spread of the operating-team system to a larger number of plants. In the early 1980s GM began to introduce the system into all its new plants and into a number of others that were redesigned to produce a new product or infused with a major investment in new technology.[14] The operating-team system entails a fundamental reorganization of shop-floor labor relations because it integrates changes in work organization with increases in worker decision making. The operating team provides both a reduction in job classifications and a broadening of jobs. The latter occurs in part by virtue of the fact that workers in the teams perform their own inspection and some repair work. In some of the team plants, workers have also taken on some material handling, housekeeping, and minor machine maintenance tasks. Worker input occurs when the work teams influence the allocation and, in some cases, the design of their tasks. Regular team meetings also provide a forum for workers to discuss production problems and the financial performance of their work area. The extent of information provided to workers in the team meetings and the degree to which supervisors end up dominating team decisions varies substantially across teams and plants. Yet the mix of work restructuring and worker involvement occurs in all teams.

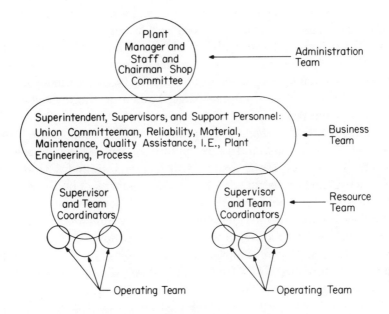

FIGURE 6.2

Pontiac Fiero Team Concept

In some plants using the team system the local union receives extensive financial and operating information. This also occurred in plants where QWL programs that initially focused on quality circles expanded to include increased communication between plant management and the local union. However, this process has been pushed the farthest in a number of team plants. For example, the parties at the GM plant in Pontiac, Michigan, (which produces the Fiero sports car) redesigned the plant's entire reporting structure into a team format. A brief look at the new structure illustrates the radical changes this approach implies for the traditional principles of "job-control" unionism and "management manages and the union grieves."

The organizational structure of the Fiero plant is outlined in figure 6.2. At the lowest level are the operating teams. The top administrative team includes the plant manager and the chairman of the bargaining committee for the local UAW union. As the UAW chairman stated, "This makes him a member of the plant manager's staff and a participant in *all* staff meetings." So far, the UAW shop chairman has had access to all of the plant's financial and economic performance data and participated on the plant's five-year planning committee, which

161

reported to GM's executive board. The business and resource teams at Fiero also integrate hourly workers and union officials into the resolution of production and quality problems and give them access to a wide range of financial and performance data. One key to the cooperative relationship that exists at Fiero is the fact that the local union participated in the planning meetings that set up the revised organizational structure.

Not all of GM's team plants have such a cooperative labor-management relationship. In some plants the local union opposed the introduction of the team system and has maintained a traditional arm's-length relationship with plant management. The team plants also differ in their actual work organization. For example, the Fiero plant does not use the pay-for-knowledge system and has roughly forty classifications for production workers (which, however, is still many less than the hundred or so of classifications typically found in assembly plants). Meanwhile, GM's Cadillac-Livonia (Michigan) plant has a single job classification for production workers and uses a six-step pay-for-knowledge system. However, GM's team system illustrates how worker-participation programs can be linked to major changes in work organization and in the local union's participation in plant operations.

We would like to present some hard data concerning the impact of type 2 innovations on workplace outcomes. Unfortunately, such data are not yet available. After the operating-team concept meets the test of time, especially the duration of at least one cycle of contract negotiations, it should be possible to conduct the type of analysis that we have done for type 1 QWL innovations. Based on the improvements in efficiency and quality that such installations have generated in nonunion plants (see chapter 4), we would expect the results to be positive.

THE DYNAMICS OF QWL PROCESSES: SPECIFIC CASES

A number of other case studies our research team has conducted over the last six years provide further evidence regarding the effects QWL efforts have exerted on organizational performance. Many of the cases summarized here are drawn from our more detailed study of the effects of worker-participation processes on unions and the collective bargaining process.[15] Here our aim is to illustrate how the data reinforce several of the key conclusions just suggested. In summary, these cases document the slowness of QWL programs' diffusion process in existing large organizations; the pressures management and union officials experience to go beyond a narrow QWL process into type 2 workplace innovations by using QWL procedural and problem-solving aspects to modify work organization; and the development in a few workplaces of a third generation of changes (type 3) that link workplace innovations to broader changes in collective bargaining and longer-term strategic decision making.

Xerox and the Amalgamated Clothing and Textile Workers. The relation of Xerox Corporation and Local 14B of the Amalgamated Clothing and Textile Workers Union (ACTWU) in the firm's major manufacturing facilities in Rochester, New York, illustrates many of our conclusions. This union represents all of the production and maintenance employees of Xerox and has done so since the 1930s. Moreover, the relationship between the union and the company has been highly cooperative over the years; only one short strike has occurred in the past two decades.

While Xerox enjoyed a strong profit and growth record throughout the 1950s and 1960s, during the 1970s the company's share of its major market (office copiers) fell from over 90 to slightly under 50 percent as a result of intensified Japanese and domestic (nonunion) competition. These mounting pressures, along with the effects of the general recession of 1981–83, led Xerox to make a number of changes in business strategy, including an effort to diversify into a broader range of office equipment (computers, word processors, office systems) and, most important, for our purposes, to focus more directly on reducing manufacturing costs through staff reductions, productivity improvements, cost controls, and technological changes.

In 1980 (before the major shift in business strategy but after a decade of shrinking market share), Xerox and the union jointly agreed to experiment with a narrowly focused QWL process that, in its design, closely approximated a quality circle program. A steering committee was established composed of equal numbers of union and company representatives. Union and company facilitators of problem-solving groups were chosen and trained, and volunteers were given forty hours of training in problem solving, statistical methods, and group dynamics.

Since the original impetus for the QWL process came from the chairman of the corporation, there was strong commitment at the top of the firm. Corporate organizational development and industrial relations staff officials were also highly supportive and worked together in implementing the process. Interviews with management and union representatives and QWL facilitators clearly documented that many middle managers and first-line supervisors initially resisted the process. Like their top-management counterparts, top union representatives, although somewhat skeptical at the outset, became forceful advocates and supporters of the QWL process early in its implementation and remained strong supporters throughout its evolution. Rank-and-file workers displayed mixed views of the process, depending on whether or not they chose to participate in a QWL team, their specific experiences with the process, and, most important, their interpretation of events that occurred at higher levels of the bargaining relationship. This can best be seen by briefly reviewing the evolution of the QWL process as it unfolded over a four-year period. During this time substantial layoffs took place as the company shifted business strategies; a new collective bargaining agreement was negotiated that contained significant fringe-benefit concessions, including a highly controversial change in absenteeism policy and an employment guarantee for existing workers; and finally, the QWL process was broadened to encompass changes in the organization of specific work units.

An early challenge to the continuity of the QWL process came about two years into the experiment when management concluded that it needed to subcontract out the production and assembly of wiring harnesses, a highly labor-intensive part of the production process. By this time approximately 25 percent of the four thousand employees in the bargaining unit had been trained in QWL procedures and had participated on a QWL team at one time or another. Not all who had been trained continued as team participants, however, since the layoffs taking place in the plants at this time were disrupting many established teams and causing trained QWL employees to be bumped into jobs where no teams existed.

When the subcontracting decision was announced, the key union leaders (and strong QWL supporters), along with several key industrial relations and line managers, protested that the decision was not only inconsistent with the spirit of the QWL process but could threaten its continuity. After some discussion, a decision was made to give the problem to a task force of workers, supervisors, and technical staff in the wiring harness area to see if they could identify changes that would reduce the costs of producing these parts in-house by approximately $3.2 million, the estimate of the savings available if the work were contracted to outside vendors.

After several months of deliberation and data analysis, the task force produced a series of recommendations for changing work organization, including such things as the way jobs are assigned, the way work is scheduled, the provisions governing transfer into and out of the work area, the use of part-timers to buffer volume surges, and the scope of responsibilities of production and maintenance jobs. These recommendations obviously violated one of the key principles built into the original language governing the QWL process, namely that no QWL team or group could act to modify the terms and conditions of the collective bargaining agreement. Moreover, some of the suggested changes were equally threatening to management since they went well beyond the authority of the teams, such as recommendations to change accounting charges for overhead, alter the plant's physical layout, and drastically reduce the number of supervisors.

After considerable discussion the company and union decided to implement those recommendations that had no major contractual implications or that the parties could agree to as midcontract modifications. The remaining items and the larger policy issues were deferred until the negotiation of the next bargaining agreement.

As these negotiations began, both parties recognized that the QWL process had reached a critical point. Because of the large number of layoffs and significant resistance by some middle managers and supervisors, rank-and-file support for the QWL process had reached a plateau and was beginning to wane. Those employees who had taken the risks of getting involved in and supporting the QWL process at an early stage were beginning to question whether employees would share in the increased productivity, effort, and savings they believed would result from the process (although no quantitative data on cost savings were collected, plant managers did become supporters of the QWL process since they saw their plant's economic results improve). Furthermore, many employees feared that any productivity improvements would only lead to reductions in employment and an erosion in job security. They did not believe that declines in employment due to reductions in manning levels would be offset by the increases in employment that would follow from improvements in cost competitiveness.

Going into bargaining, it was clear to the union leaders that some form of employment and/or income security arrangement would need to be negotiated if the QWL process was not to atrophy further. Management, on the other hand, saw these negotiations as critical to its larger strategy of reducing manufacturing costs and specifically saw the wiring harness task force experiment as having potential for fundamental workplace reform in other areas.

Negotiations resulted in a guarantee of no layoffs for the existing workforce in these facilities for the three-year term of the new agreement. In return, the company was given the right to implement the remaining wiring harness task force recommendations *and* to use that same task force approach in other work units identified as potential candidates for subcontracting. The new contract also contained some important changes designed to control health-care costs and absenteeism and other changes that did not affect the evolution of the QWL process.

One and one-half years after the ratification of this agreement, interviews with union and management officials as well as survey data collected from rank-and-file workers indicated that the wiring harness recommendations were implemented and four other task force teams had been commissioned. These teams also made suggestions that required modifications of specific contract provisions and broad managerial policies that normally would have fallen outside the authority of team members—and only one of the teams was not able to generate sufficient recommendations to reduce costs to the level of outside vendors. In addition, the diffusion of the QWL process slowed considerably after the results of the new agreement began to be felt by the rank and file. Volunteers for QWL training became harder to find, eventually the company made QWL training mandatory for hourly employees. After three and one-half years, QWL had diffused (measured by the number of bargaining-unit employees participating in problem-solving teams) to only about 30 percent of the hourly workforce, and for many of these employees QWL participation involved only once-a-week attendance in a quality circle that discussed a limited agenda of issues.

At the same time, a variety of other participation and work-restructuring activities were started by employee groups determined to tailor the process to their needs. Strong rank-and-file opposition developed toward the absenteeism and health-care policy changes introduced into the contract. Some employees believed the company was being inconsistent in asking for high trust and commitment from QWL team participants and yet demonstrating a lack of trust by instituting a tough new absenteeism policy and forcing employees to share health-care costs.

Despite these setbacks, the QWL process continues. Discussion of task force team recommendations and proposals for additional teams have occurred and made incremental changes in the organization of work that are highly acclaimed by both line managers and union representatives. While both management and union representatives recognize the fragility of the QWL process and the rank-and-file commitment to it, they remain dedicated and optimistic about its future prospects. Union and some management officials recognized that the next step in institutionalizing this experiment is likely to require some form of sharing the cost savings or productivity/profitability gains achieved partly as a result of the QWL process. As a consequence, during contract negotiations in 1986 the parties agreed to design a pilot gain-sharing program. This is likely to be a key topic on the future agenda of collective bargaining in other instances where the parties wish to make workplace innovations a permanent fixture of their relationship.

Xerox's slow progress in QWL processes may come as a surprise to some readers since it could be expected that the changes instituted at the middle level of the system (for example, no layoffs) would provide the linkage and support for further changes at the lowest level (for example, greater diffusion of the process to the workforce). While it is our belief that QWL-type processes will not diffuse widely and become institutionalized without accompanying and reinforcing changes at higher levels of the system, these companion changes do not guarantee a transformation in workplace relations. The plateauing of Quality Circle activity that occurred at Xerox may be temporary, it may reflect the "selection effect" (the firm has for the moment run out of volunteer workers predisposed to participation), it may reflect inadequate linkages (for example, the absence of gain sharing), or it may be a natural state—implying an organizational future much more varied in process and structure. These are matters for future research.

What we can say is that the Xerox/ACTWU case illustrates how what began as a first-generation, narrowly focused type 1 QWL process evolved over time to a type 2 innovation as it became an integral part of the firm's efforts to reduce costs and increase productivity through work reorganization and the union's efforts to promote employment security and to save jobs. Moreover, what started out (as do most QWL processes) with specific contractual language indicating that the process was a supplement to collective bargaining and would not change any contractual provisions became interwoven with contractual issues as the parties began exploring alternative means of organizing work, cutting costs, and saving jobs. In turn, the diffusion of QWL teams and their acceptance by rank-and-file workers were adversely affected by the larger strategic management decision to shift to a cost-control/ staff-reduction strategy and by the changes in the collective bargaining contract provisions governing absenteeism and health insurance. Finally, it is clear that QWL processes would have experienced severe setbacks if the parties had not addressed worker concerns for job security in the 1983 negotiations and again during the negotiations in 1986.

In short, this case illustrates the slowness of the diffusion process; the interwoven nature of QWL, collective bargaining, and strategic decision making; and the pressures exerted by employers facing severe cost competition to expand the QWL process to address through work reorganization bigger productivity-improvement opportunities. Finally, this case also illustrates the important influence of a bargaining relationship that historically was characterized by a high level of trust between the union and the company and a QWL process that was supported by the joint commitment of the union and the company. Without this historical base and shared commitment, it is unlikely that the parties would have been successful in negotiating agreements that institutionalized the QWL process into their ongoing relationship.

Packard Electric and the Electrical Workers. This case involves Local 717 of the International Union of Electrical Workers (IUE) and the Packard Electric Company, a subsidiary of General Motors based in Warren, Ohio. Here a worker-participation program led to a substantial increase in union and worker involvement in business decision making, experiments involving new forms of work organization, and the negotiation of a lifetime job-security guarantee.

The series of events that led to the emergence of increased worker and union involvement began in 1973 when Packard Electric management announced that no more hiring or capital investment would take place in the cluster of plants in Warren, which employed 13,500 hourly IUE-represented workers. As a supplier of wire harnesses and other electrical products to General Motors, the Warren complex had undergone substantial growth over the previous decade. Yet management argued that cost pressures required the generation of cheaper sources of supply. New Packard Electric plants were subsequently opened in Clinton and Brookhaven, Mississippi, and Juarez, Mexico, all of which initially operated without union representation.[16] The Brookhaven plant (opened in 1978) used a team form of work organization, pay-for-knowledge, and a participatory management style. The new southern plants were fairly small in size (Clinton employed

1,200 workers while Brookhaven employed 450 by 1980). However, their employment impacts on the Warren complex were made larger because these plants made extensive use of a number of "dedicated supplier" plants. Packard Electric supplied parts and materials to these vendor plants, which employed labor at low wages to assemble and then return the finished parts to Packard.[17]

During the mid-1970s, workers at the Warren complex watched employment decline through attrition. At the same time, management held to their pledge not to put any further capital investments in Warren. In 1978 a new local union president and new chairman of the bargaining committee were elected on a platform supporting closer cooperation with management in an attempt to save jobs. A joint union-management committee known as the "Jobs Committee" was then established to "develop an ongoing union-management approach that will maintain job security and identify opportunities for hiring in the Warren operations."

Between 1978 and 1980 the Jobs Committee encouraged a variety of employee involvement and joint problem-solving activities. This included the creation of a number of labor and management task forces to address specific production problems. The main accomplishment of the committee was an agreement providing for the construction of five new "branch" plants in the Warren area that would have new work-organization and design features. Local union officials participated actively in decisions regarding the design of these new branch plants and the nature of work organization in them. Several of the production lines in the new plants now operate as semi-autonomous work groups, while others rely more heavily on more informal employee involvement and statistical process-control groups to achieve their productivity objectives. Overall, the branch plants have many fewer job classifications than the main Warren plants.

While the creation of these branch plants saved some jobs in the Warren facilities, workers' fears of job loss were not eliminated. In fact, these fears were exacerbated by the auto sales slump that began in early 1980 and by the large number of layoffs that followed among the Warren workforce. At the same time, the local IUE union and many workers were aware of the expansion occurring in the late 1970s in Packard's plants in Mexico as well as in Spain, Portugal, Ireland, and West Germany. With the wider availability of alternative suppliers, in 1981 Packard Electric management announced that 3,900 jobs in the Warren complex were "noncompetitive" and would be eliminated. After discussions with the union, however, Packard management made a commitment to accomplish this employment reduction through attrition and not permanently lay off employees. Yet, even with these assurances, the IUE leadership was concerned about the long-run decline in employment at Warren.

Management and union leaders then began intensive discussions regarding various changes in pay and work rules that could be introduced in order to reduce the competitive gap between costs at Warren and those of alternate suppliers. A plan was finally ratified by the membership in the fall of 1984—but the search for a viable program that all parties would accept involved a number of developments along the way. A first proposal that would have created a new entry rate of $4.50 per hour in wages and $1.50 in fringe benefits was turned down overwhelmingly by the membership in August 1983. Subsequently the leader of the opposition to this proposal was elected chairman of the union's bargaining committee. A newly constituted Jobs Committee then submitted a revised package, which was ratified, to the membership in December 1984.[18] Under the wage terms of this agreement, new hires will be paid 55 percent of the rate received by permanent employees; 10 percent of this wage differential will be removed each year through extra pay increases until parity is achieved. The new agreement encouraged greater union input into business decision making and also includes a novel job-security program, guaranteeing that any employees hired before 1982 will never be permanently laid off due to either a shift in work to other locations or technological change. In these protections, the Warren local agreement is similar to the job bank provided other GM employees in the UAW national agreement negotiated in the fall of 1984. The IUE Warren agreement, however, is unique in that it provides these guarantees for the workers for their lifetime and eliminates the possibility of temporary layoffs of longer than six months due to declines in the volume of available work. Permanent layoffs are allowed if for cost reasons production of a part now produced by Packard Electric is shifted to a firm not allied with General Motors.

Packard Electric hourly employees covered by the no-permanent-layoff guarantee can be temporarily laid off for up to six months and will receive their regular supplementary and state unemployment assistance during that period. After six months, these employees must be recalled to work. To ease the problems this would present to management during future business downturns, two other important provisions were included in the agreement: Management will be permitted to hire new employees on a part-time basis and expects to make more extensive use of both part-time hourly and salaried workers in the future. Furthermore, the local union agreed to allow recalled permanent employees to be used flexibly if such recalls occur during business downturns. The union expressed its willingness to temporarily assign these workers to nontraditional jobs, which would be monitored by the local union as part of its enhanced role in plant operation decisions.

Labor and management at Packard have taken a number of steps to expand and shift the role of the Jobs Committee. The broad intent of the new agreement is to make the Warren complex more competitive with outside suppliers. New plant-level jobs committees will have the responsibility and authority to suggest and help implement new forms of work organization and training that will further that objective. In part this will be accomplished through expansion of the worker-participation programs and work-organization changes (fewer job classifications and semi-autonomous work teams) already underway in various parts of the Warren complex. These plant-level jobs committees are part of other steps underway at Warren to shift managerial decision making downward so that plant operations are more decentralized.

The broader business strategy that motivates labor's and management's efforts is the intent to gradually shift work at Warren away from assembly operations and to tasks requiring higher skills, namely to more parts production and product development. In that way the focus of the 1984 contractual agreement at Warren was very different from the 1983 rejected plan, which sought to maintain job security by keeping assembly work at Warren through the payment of substantially lower wages.

The biggest change underway may well be the extent to which local union officials receive information regarding and participate in business decisions. The parties have created informally an administrative structure that is very similar to the structure at GM's Fiero plant, and local union leadership in Warren attends many of management's staff meetings. This broader involvement provides a way for the local union to link the various programs underway at the plant and shop-floor levels and forces a connection between worker-participation activities and actions that increase workers' job security.

LESS SUCCESSFUL EXAMPLES OF QWL PROCESSES

The Xerox and Packard cases represent successful examples of joint union-management QWL processes. These firms have been able to maintain the continuity and momentum of the process over time by linking QWL activities to the problems being confronted by the parties at higher levels of their relationships. However, not all joint QWL efforts are successful in weathering the challenges encountered over the course of a bargaining cycle or through changes in higher-level business and union strategies. The experiences of the United Steelworkers and some of the major steel producers with labor-management participation teams in the early 1980s illustrate the difficulties in sustaining cooperative efforts at the workplace when they are not reinforced by higher-level collective bargaining and strategic decisions.

The contrast with the more successful efforts is most clearly illustrated by the history of LMPTs in U.S. Steel. Although this company traditionally led the industry in negotiations with the USW and therefore was a key party to the 1980 and 1982 contracts, which contained language authorizing experimentation with LMPTs on a plant-by-plant basis, significant activity was begun in only two of its plants. No company-wide steering or oversight committee process was put in place to guide these efforts. The effort at one plant was relatively short-lived. A series of collective bargaining conflicts over work-rule changes imposed by the company in 1983 plus local union leaders' distrust of management commitment to reinvestment in the steel industry led the local union in one plant to withdraw from the LMPT process. In the other plant the process continued in one work area; however, the closing of the plant's foundry has reduced activity to only four problem-solving teams. Thus, despite the existence of contract language that calls for the formulation of the LMPTs and despite the support of the international union, only limited activity in one plant took hold in the largest steel company in the country.

Instead of encouraging LMPTs, U.S. Steel management chose a more direct strategy of technological change and workforce reductions to improve its productivity and cost position. Corporate strategists never viewed LMPTs as critical to the achievement of the company's key business objectives. Instead, it better served the company's strategy to keep the union at arm's length and to maintain the adversarial relationship that has been characteristic of relations between "Big Steel" and the USW.

For a somewhat different reason a highly successful workplace-level cooperative effort in another part of the industry has faced difficulties because of an unsupportive strategic business plan. The LMPT process in the Aliquippa (Pennsylvania) plant of the Jones and Laughlin Company was the first LMPT to start after signing of the 1980 contract and quickly became the showcase example within the steel industry. At its peak, the parties had approximately forty problem-solving teams in place. The process survived considerable workforce reductions and the concessionary round of industry-level contract negotiations that took place in 1982. The parties were also successful in introducing significant flexibility in work organization among craft workers by reducing the number of craft classifications from twenty-six to three. Unfortunately, however, in 1985 Jones and Laughlin announced the closing of a major part of the Aliquippa facility as part of its overall restructuring and consolidation. After the LTV company parent acquired the production facilities of Republic Steel, it had excess steel-making capacity; and despite the progress made in the Aliquippa works, that plant was still the most logical candidate for closure. As of this writing employment is down to 800 workers. Yet the LMPT process has survived even this drastic restructuring. Four problem-solving teams are in operation and plans are underway to add several more. Thus, while the process did survive, it could not counteract the larger strategic considerations that led to the partial shutdown and loss of jobs.

These experiences in the steel industry illustrate two key points that should be kept in mind in evaluating the potential of workplace-level participation and work-organization reforms. First, without a commitment from management and supporting policy changes at the level of business strategy and collective bargaining, labor-management cooperation in the workplace is unlikely to diffuse widely across a firm and is likely to be vulnerable to conflicts arising at these higher levels of the labor-management relationship. This explains why relatively little cooperative activity got started at U.S. Steel and why those QWL processes that did get underway were held hostage to collective bargaining and strategic-level differences between the company and the union. Second, the partial closing of Jones and Laughlin's Aliquippa plant demonstrates that even highly successful workplace efforts cannot be sustained over the long run unless they are embedded within a viable business plan for the facility.

By 1986 the worker participation programs in a number of steel companies had been rejuvenated and broadened. The expansion of these participation programs often was linked to the negotiation of wage concessions in return for profit sharing, employee stock ownership, and union involvement in business decisions. At Wheeling-Pittsburgh Steel Corporation, for example, a Joint Strategic Decisions Board oversees operating performance, product quality, capital investment, new technology, and facility utilization. In a number of companies, such as LTV, Bethlehem, and National Steel, some traditional work rules are being replaced by semi-autonomous work teams, and in other ways workers and union officers are participating in operating decisions. Thus in steel, as in autos, early experimentation with narrow forms of participation provided the experience and the trust necessary for the union and several of the companies to move on to much broader models of participation and restructuring of roles. This took place not only at the workplace but also at the levels of collective bargaining and strategic decision making.

PARTIAL SUCCESS: AT&T AND THE COMMUNICATIONS WORKERS

Other researchers have also provided evidence of QWL programs that had limited success. For example, just prior to AT&T's divestiture the U.S. Department of Labor sponsored the preparation of case studies at ten QWL programs that AT&T jointly administered with the Communication Workers of America (CWA).[19] As of October 1983 these parties had approximately 1,200 problem-solving groups in operation at various AT&T worksites around the country. Of the ten cases studied, the researchers found that "two or three of them appeared to be quite successful, two or three were in trouble; some received a great deal of support from the management and the union, others faced serious resistance; four had been in operation for over two years and three for less than seven months."[20]

More specifically, survey results showed that compared to nonparticipating workers, QWL participants reported higher marks for job satisfaction and for evaluations of supervisory relations and union performance as well as feelings of greater participation in decision making. In short, as in our own attitude surveys, attitudinal relations at these workplaces seemed, on average, to improve for those participating in QWL processes. But there was little evidence of significant improvements in organizational efficiency or in QWL participants' evaluations of relationships with the company as a whole or with higher management. In sum, the authors concluded that the effects of QWL programs in the Bell System during their first three years were positive but limited. Most teams had succeeded in solving some local problems but had not yet moved on to organization-wide problems nor diffused or become institutionalized to the point of no longer being viewed as a "special program."

In line with our claim that reinforcing changes at the strategic level are necessary before workplace changes have a chance to be institutionalized, it is interesting to note that the cooperative efforts between AT&T and the CWA at the top of the system apparently have plateaued. Despite the creation of joint committees for QWL, job classifications, and technology, and despite a trip to investigate developments in Scandinavia, the parties have not, at least up to now, been able to produce a joint vision statement or substantive outcomes. No doubt the intense competitive pressures on both labor and management stimulated by deregulation and divestiture contributed to this plateauing. The parties have not yet found a way of maintaining cooperation while confronting pressures that adversely impact the union and the employment security of its members.

Thus at this stage in the history of joint union-management workplace innovations, there are examples both of success and failure, with a large number of narrow processes continuing and achieving the "positive but limited" results described in the AT&T/CWA study. Our research suggests that the workplace innovations that have the most significant impacts on the firm's organizational performance and employee attitudes are the ones that have broadened beyond their original QWL charter to modify the way work is organized and to tackle issues that lie at the heart of competitive problems and the employment security interests of the workers.[21] But to do this successfully the parties must confront directly the relationships between workplace participation and reform and issues that arise at the contract negotiations and strategic levels.

Conclusions

The success of QWL programs and other workplace reform efforts over time depends on the ability of the organization to reinforce and sustain high levels of trust. As we have argued throughout, and particularly in regard to changes introduced at the workplace, the maintenance of trust will be influenced heavily by the extent to which the strategies and events unfolding at higher levels of the industrial relations system are consistent with and linked to the development of greater trust at the workplace. Thus QWL efforts are more likely to succeed if reinforced by interactions at higher levels of the industrial relations system.

Recall the workplace industrial relations system model introduced in chapter 4. There we argued, and provided empirical evidence to demonstrate, that high-conflict/low-trust relationships can lead to low levels of organization performance. To the extent that QWL efforts can increase the level of trust, improve the management of conflict, promote more effective problem solving, and assist in the introduction of more flexible forms of work organization, these efforts can improve organizational performance. The magnitude of these improvements, however, will vary across organizational settings and depend on a range of factors, such as the firm's technological or market constraints. Our case-study evidence suggests that where QWL programs expand in scope so as to include major changes in work rules and work organization, they can produce sizable improvements in organizational performance and the quality of working life.

Our case studies and previous research show that it is difficult and politically risky for both union and management officials to introduce and manage union-management change efforts.[22] Consequently, for these efforts to be sustained and diffused, all parties—management, workers, and union leaders—must achieve tangible improvements in the goals that each values. To achieve these rewards, the expansion of worker-participation programs and the introduction of new forms of work organization often have been accompanied by changes in contract terms negotiated in collective bargaining. At Xerox and Packard Electric, worker and union involvement were encouraged by measures adopted as part of a package of modifications made to a local collective bargaining agreement. In both firms this package included new job-security programs and pay outcomes that differed from previous patterns. In these and other firms the expansion of shop-floor worker participation also was spurred by or associated with increased worker and union involvement in strategic issues. This involvement in strategic issues was critical because it both assured the union that worker participation was not a step toward the demise of union representation and because it helped convince workers and the union that enhanced employment security would follow. But expansion of the process to the strategic level of decision making does not occur easily or automatically. Indeed, we have observed this expansion only in cases where unions are strong and relatively secure to begin with. As we will discuss more fully in the next chapter, management tends to closely guard control over issues that have traditionally been viewed as its prerogatives. This leads to a rather ironic conclusion, considering the origins of QWL activities. If linkage to strategic decision making is essential for workplace participation to be successful in the long run, a strong union presence and active support for the process are also essential.

Nonunion firms or those with weak unions are unlikely to develop or sustain this full form of worker participation.

To fully understand labor's and management's response to the many challenges they confronted in the early 1980s, it is thus essential to analyze more closely the many changes underway at the strategic level of unionized industrial relations systems and the extent to which successful models of union participation in strategic decision making are emerging.

7

Union Engagement of Strategic Business Decisions

UNDER the strategy of business unionism preferred by the AFL unions in the early years of this century and then endorsed and institutionalized by the National Labor Relations Act in 1935, American unions have depended on collective bargaining to negotiate contracts that regulate the impacts of managerial decisions. Union involvement does not extend to the strategic business decisions that affect the enterprise and employment conditions. Yet in the face of the many changes underway in U.S. industrial relations, there is a growing movement away from this pattern, as unions increasingly seek to influence strategic business decisions rather than wait to negotiate only the impacts of those decisions.

The overriding reason for this shift is that management initiatives above and below the level of traditional contract negotiations have produced a mismatch between existing union strategies for organizing and representing workers and employers' human resource strategies. In this chapter we focus on those cases where unions have embarked on efforts to overcome this mismatch by utilizing their existing bargaining leverage to pressure employers to modify their business strategies and in other ways become more involved in strategic management issues. A number of unions have been led into such new efforts in part as an outgrowth of the expansion occurring in the bargaining agenda and/or in workplace-level participation processes in a number of firms. In some cases changes in collective bargaining and worker participation have produced increased worker and union involvement in business decisions concerning such matters as new investments, workforce adjustment strategies, new technology, and new forms of work organization. Not all of these new efforts, however, have been successful. As this chapter shows, labor and management find it hard to integrate joint resolution of strategic business issues with collective bargaining and workplace issues and procedures.

To understand why this search for a new pattern at the strategic level is so difficult, it is necessary to review the extent to which involvement at this level represents a significant break with the New Deal industrial relations system.

A Strategic-Choice Model of Union Participation in Management

Recall that one of the basic principles of the New Deal collective bargaining model was that "management manages and workers and their unions grieve or negotiate the impacts of management decisions through collective bargaining." The reluctance of labor leaders to engage management in joint consultations or to seek shared decision-making power reflects the longstanding business unionism traditions of the labor movement, the practical fear of being coopted into supporting unpleasant choices, and the political risks associated with getting too closely identified with management and losing touch with rank-and-file interests.[1] Thus a union's decision to seek a role in management decision making requires a break from these deeply held views concerning what is an appropriate strategy.

Just as management's beliefs serve as a mental filter through which its strategic choices are screened, seeking a role in management represents an equally fundamental shift on the part of union leaders' values and strategic thinking. Following the model of strategic choice, union leaders are not likely to reach for these new approaches unless they are experiencing a deep crisis or severe pressures to try something new. Moreover, like other social innovations, any shift in union strategies can be expected to go through a trial-and-error period in which small numbers of leaders try new approaches, others resist them, and still others evaluate the results of the experiments. Only if the new approaches produce enough tangible benefits and begin to gain the endorsement and support of others do they begin to diffuse to settings where the pressures that led to the initial experimentation are not present. At this stage of the innovation process the new strategies have a chance of being institutionalized into ongoing practices, but the eventual outcome is far from clear.

The trial-and-error process is characterized by a great deal of internal union political debate and conflict; some union leaders argue that getting involved with management breaks with revered traditions and threatens to erode the independence that historically gave unions the bargaining power needed to achieve their hard-won collective bargaining gains. Thus, just as in earlier eras of significant transition in the American labor movement,[2] we can expect this period to be one of active debate and political turmoil. Whether or not seeking a significant role in strategic management issues emerges out of this period as a generally accepted practice of American unions depends not only on the objective environmental conditions that make the approach reasonable but also on which labor leaders win these internal political debates.

In the case of a shift toward union participation in management, an additional key structural consideration must be added to the innovation model: the power of unions to achieve an expanded role in management decision making in the face of American management's historical resistance to sharing power with unions. Given management's instinctive opposition to sharing power, especially over issues considered to be its prerogatives, there is little chance of any involvement unless a union has sufficient power to force management to deal with it at the strategic level. As was noted in chapter 3, unions that represent only a small percentage of a firm's workers or that deal with large firms through decentralized bargaining structures generally cannot engage top executives in strategic discussions. Thus in most of the examples that follow unions represent a high percentage of the blue-collar workers and deal with management on collective bargaining matters at centralized levels.

NEW ATTITUDES TOWARD INVOLVEMENT IN STRATEGIC ISSUES

Despite the traditional reluctance of union leaders to participate in management and the deep managerial resistance to it, the growing importance of the top tier of managerial decision making has led to a significant shift in philosophy among some union leaders and a growing willingness to experiment with new strategies. These leaders appear to be convinced that significant changes in traditional union strategies will be required to stem the decline in union jobs and to enable the labor movement to recapture its former innovative position in industrial relations. Some excerpts from the comments of union leaders who participated in an interim report on our research illustrate these views[3]:

I would be interested in seeing some experimentation in representation on boards. I think you have some other examples (besides Chrysler), such as the plywood factories in the West. I think we might proceed here in ways somewhat similar to the ways the labor movement came into QWL. In 1972, the early stage, there was no pell-mell change. Initially it was the UAW who started the experiments. That was a good ten years ago so it certainly has been a slow development. I don't know of any companies that are inviting us into the board rooms, but given the opportunity, I think we'd want to experiment so we can evaluate it.
—John Carmichael, Business Agent, Newspaper Guild

I, as a union leader, could not give workers an answer in Youngstown, a city completely devastated by steel-plant shutdowns. The shutdowns affected ten thousand steelworkers who are looking for answers. We have a right to participate in such grave social decisions. Everybody around us was raising the issue of whether we are moving across traditional union lines to get involved. We have no choice but to do so. . . . We have a right to be involved, and that is what our members expect us to do. . . . Most unions fail to realize that basically their members do want to participate in all such decisions that affect them. The whole concept of a democratic society now stops at the industrial gate. Once you open that up, you would be surprised to see that workers want to be involved in the decision-making process on everything that affects them in their workplace. We have to extend the whole concept of the right to participate at the strategy level so that we can be part of corporate decisions.
—Sam Camens, National Staff, United Steelworkers

As to how we represent our members, there are no barriers as to what is off limits. Whatever is legal we should try to do. . . . We must get into new areas as quid pro quos for economic restraint. I think we have to do more and more of getting into decision making. General Motors did not invite us into QWL either. And as for the right to speak at the Ford Board [meetings], well, they didn't offer that to me either; I took it.
—Don Ephlin, Vice-President, United Auto Workers

We as labor organizations need to think about how we leverage our financial power. The financial institutions in this country are the ones that most directly affect the big economic decisions and we need a voice there. . . . When we talk about corporate strategy, we have to realize that we have it within our power to influence whether and how these institutions help finance industry's activities. Our pension funds, our investments, and our treasuries provide tools to get their attention.
—Doris Lackey, National Union Staff, Bricklayers

Organized labor should take advantage of the boardroom openings as soon as possible. . . . Besides the boardroom, though, we need to get involved in decision making at the plant or division or other relevant operating levels of a company as well.
—Michael Bennett, Local Union President, United Auto Workers

An attempt has to be made to expand union involvement in order to deal with a process that has been underway since World War II of building megacompanies through acquisitions and expansion. It is this process, to a great extent, that has changed the urge of unions to control companies. The corporate structure is not now responsive to collective bargaining, especially decentralized collective bargaining, if it ever was. The corporate decision-making process has changed, as well as our ability to influence it.
—Richard Prosten, Industrial Union Department, AFL-CIO

While we do not have adequate data to determine how representative are the views expressed by these labor leaders, it is clear that traditional attitudes are changing. As the quote by Richard Prosten suggests, the major impetus for this change is the growing awareness that important decisions that lie beyond the scope of collective bargaining are made at the level of corporate strategy formulation. Union leaders have begun to conclude that to represent their members effectively in this context, they must develop strategies to engage management at this level. The changes in beliefs have produced a variety of experimental approaches toward gaining a role for unions in management decision making. We now turn to a review of several examples of these efforts.

Industry-level Strategic Interactions

In highly competitive industries composed of multiple employers and a single or a small number of unions, historically a number of industry-level labor-management committees have been formed to discuss problems of mutual interest. These committees represent early efforts by unions to discuss broad issues of mutual concern to labor and management outside of the formal structure and process of collective bargaining. Although these committees have rarely led to extensive union or worker involvement in strategic business issues, they are a good place to start in our review of specific cases. An illustrative example of such a committee was started in the retail food industry in 1974 as part of the federal government's wage and price control program.

THE RETAIL FOOD INDUSTRY COMMITTEE

The initial stimulus to form the Joint Labor-Management Committee of the retail food industry (JLMC) came from the federal government in the early 1970s.[4] A retail industry committee was formed as a subcommittee of the Pay Board as part of the federal government's efforts to control wage and price inflation. An agreement to continue the committee as a privately funded and constituted entity was spurred by federal regulators' discussion of the possibility of greatly reducing the extent of federal regulation of the retail industry. The original policy statement of the new committee listed the following four objectives:

(1) The Committee shall serve as a forum for initiating and maintaining wage and benefit data collection programs and for the exchange of information to strengthen the ability of the industry (labor and management) to reach constructive decisions in collective bargaining. . . .

(2) . . . the Committee . . . will have to be sensitive to interference with normal collective bargaining and respect the autonomy of the individual organizations. The Committee cannot and should not be a mandatory settlement organization. However, with reliable data that is kept current and utilizing its role in encouraging open communication and exchange of information on a national basis, the Committee may be able to assist the industry in contract discussions that might otherwise lead to major confrontations. . . .

(3) The Committee shall be a national forum for discussions of a variety of longer range industry problems that often surface in local negotiations and which may benefit from national attention to secure mutually beneficial results.

(4) . . . the fundamental work of the Committee would be to see the Committee as an ongoing forum to broaden the base of com-

munication between labor and management at all levels and on all subjects of mutual concern to labor and management.[5]

Analysis of the minutes of committee meetings and interviews with several key committee staff and members suggests that the JLMC has generally stayed true to these objectives in its first ten years. The style of interaction has been more integrative than distributive although at times labor or management representatives have threatened to walk off the committee because of specific conflicts in collective bargaining. For example, in 1984 a key union representative indicated his union would "rethink" its membership on the committee because of what he viewed as extremely bad faith behavior in collective bargaining by one member company.

Despite these isolated examples of tactical sparring, committee participants have generally sought to engage in mutual problem solving. Indeed, the desire to maintain a cooperative climate sometimes has inhibited frank discussion of issues where the parties' interests were clearly divergent. A summary of notes made by one of the authors after attending one of the committee meetings of chief executives of the member companies and union presidents illustrates this point:

I sensed there was a lot of holding back on the part of the managers who attended. On many of the issues discussed (multi-employer pension funds, health care cost containment, contract language problems, two-tiered wage structures, etc.), they didn't seem to open up or follow through with hard questions. When I mentioned this point to a member of the committee's staff he noted that sometimes the committee members are "too nice." Management appears to be reluctant to really open up and discuss what is on their minds for fear of threatening the union leaders and producing a more hostile environment. The committee staff member also feels that some of the reluctance of the CEO's to open up results from concerns expressed to them by their industrial relations managers. These industrial relations managers constantly caution the CEO's not to say anything in the high-level meetings which will come back to jeopardize them in negotiations that are ongoing or that will occur at a later date.

This reluctance to discuss the basic issues of concern to either party seems to be a characteristic of many labor-management committees. That is, as long as the committee can avoid highly divisive issues and still maintain significant motivation to continue by focusing attention on more integrative issues, the committee can survive. Survival is threatened, however, under three conditions. The first is that the committee simply fails to make concrete and tangible progress on issues of joint concern. The second is when a highly divisive issue is raised and splits the group apart. The third is when an issue arises such as the problem raised by the union leader who threatened to quit the committee. Such situations usually reflect the internal political pressures generated on a union (or management) leader by conflicts occurring at the collective bargaining level. It is politically difficult for an elected leader to continue to meet in a cooperative joint process at the industry level while labor and management are engaged in intense conflict on other issues at the bargaining table. This is a phenomenon that has been documented as contributing to the demise of many in-plant, community, and national labor-management committees.[6]

What have been the JLMC's major accomplishments over its first decade? Interviews with representatives of the committee and examination of documents recording committee deliberations suggest a number of achievements. Probably the most important accomplishment, and the one most frequently cited by those interviewed, has been the committee's opening up of lines of communication between top union leaders and the chief executive officers of the major companies with whom the unions have contracts. In a decentralized industry with a highly decentralized bargaining structure, this is an extremely important function and a significant achievement. As one member of the committee stated, "I have a much better understanding of the political problems the top union representatives have in getting their local unions to go along with their views." A staff member of the committee put it this way: "Corporate executives now understand that union leaders simply cannot issue edicts to their local union leaders and expect that they will fall in line."

Similarly, corporate committee members were quick to give examples of specific problems that they were able to bring to the attention of top union leaders during the informal discussions that always occur at such gatherings. Thus the committee has been quite successful in fostering informal communication and mutual education.

The committee also has been able to support or conduct several major long-term research projects on industry problems. Major studies completed by the committee include (1) a study of the effects of new technology in stores and warehouses; (2) a study of the occupational safety and health standards governing warehouses, which produced consensus within the industry and agreement with the federal government to eliminate a host of outmoded standards and to add several new ones governing new technologies and work methods; (3) a major study of health hazards from exposure to meat wrappers that led to the introduction of new, safer materials and work methods; (4) a study

185

of health-care cost-containment strategies for health and welfare funds; (4) a study of multiemployer pension funds and unfunded liability problems; and (5) several major studies of the contract language problems employers perceive to be inhibiting their competitiveness as well as counterpart studies of language and wage-bargaining problems of concern to the major unions. While the advisory nature and centralized structure of the committee often limits translation of these findings into concrete action, considerable information has been generated and disseminated.

Over the years the committee chairman and staff members have also assisted directly and indirectly in mediating collective bargaining disputes. Although the priority given to this activity has changed over the years, the function is performed as requested.

One of the chief executive officers indicated that serving on the committee also performed an extremely important symbolic function for him. It signaled to his managers and employees the importance he attaches to effective employee relations. It also shows his industrial relations staff that he sees relations with employees and their union representatives as being important enough to "not leave it solely to the professionals."

Finally, some of the committee's dialogue and research laid the groundwork for important strategic bargains between individual companies and unions. For example, out of one series of studies and discussions came an agreement in principle between one of the major unions and the firms participating on the committee to establish several new, lower wage classifications that would allow firms to compete in new markets for beauty aids, floral shops, pharmacies, delicatessens, and other newer services. In return the companies agreed to extend union recognition to these new units.

While these achievements are notable and useful, it is also clear that the committee has not been successful in altering or responding to the underlying structural changes taking place in the retail food industry. These changes have produced a steady erosion of market share for the unionized firms, an even larger erosion of the share of the industry organized by unions, and pressures for concession bargains and two-tiered wage agreements in those markets hardest hit by new nonunion competition. Thus, despite all the positive developments just outlined, the basic forces affecting company performance, union membership, and collective bargaining have not been significantly altered by the joint committee.

The major limitation of the committee's operation is its inability to link the broad discussion of problems to specific activities occurring in collective bargaining or on the shop floor. In large part this weakness derives from the fact that joint committees that could either carry through on the issues discussed at the national level or derive more local solutions to problems have not been created. This does not imply that the industry-level committee has been a waste of time. The joint national committee has provided a valuable new channel for labor and management leaders to communicate with one another and contributed to the resolution of several important problems; but at the same time it must be recognized that the committee is a mechanism through which the union has gained only limited influence over the direction of the industry or involvement in the strategic business issues facing participating firms.

PARTICIPATION IN NEW TECHNOLOGY DEVELOPMENT

The Tailored Clothing Technology Corporation [(TC)^2] program has been underway for the past several years in the men's clothing industry. This project represents a dramatic example of a union, in this case the Amalgamated Clothing and Textile Workers Union (ACTWU), getting involved at a very early and basic stage in the research-and-development effort to mechanize the production of garments in order to help stem the flow of imported goods. By contrast, most unions in the United States limit their involvement with new technology to its consequences, that is, *after* management has made the strategic decision to introduce it. A few unions do get involved with the initial decision, if management is willing to discuss a projected development that it has in mind. In this instance, however, the union is involved in developing machinery not yet available on the market.

The ACTWU and the International Ladies Garment Workers Union (ILGWU) have been involved in strategic matters throughout the history of the garment and textile industries. These industries are characterized by many small employers with considerable ease of entry (and also substantial involuntarily exit). Unions, therefore, have historically served as a stabilizing force for the organized portions of these industries. For example, during the early 1900s unions provided technical assistance in running the many small shops on a modern basis.[7] By doing so the unions were able to transform what otherwise would have been a proliferation of sweatshops into enterprises capable of supporting a living wage and acceptable working conditions.

At the macro level of the industry, the unions have always wrestled

187

with trade-offs between, for example, wage policies, imports, emerging nonunion competition, and viability of the organized sector. Thus, for certain sectors in a transition period, such as the remnants of the unionized garment and textile operations in New England, wages have been allowed to fall below those of the newer nonunion shops in the South. All of this can be seen as a form of private industrial policy.

By the same token, these unions have been eager to prevent runaway shops and have negotiated strong limitations governing the movement of operations without union approval. These unions have also worked vigorously to control imports and have been key participants in the fashioning of tariff programs, such as the multifiber agreement. The ACTWU has also made effective use of corporate campaigns against companies that have resisted unionization, such as Farah and J. P. Stevens.[8] These two instances serve as dramatic examples of how the ACTWU has operated at the highest levels of corporate decision making in an effort to strengthen its base of membership in the industry.

Thus $(TC)^2$ must be seen as the latest example in a succession of strategic initiatives by the major unions in the garment industry. The genesis of the project started with a study conducted by John Dunlop in the mid-1970s that examined the outlook for men's tailored clothing.[9] The report concluded that there would be a continued rapid growth of imports, to account for at least 50 percent in all product areas by the late 1980s. The first step in the implementation of a program to preserve a job base (and to take advantage of the baby-boom cohort entering into the prime period of clothing purchases) was to initiate a comprehensive training program in order to "make the clothing industry more productive and competitive." This program, which operated during the late 1970s, combined funds from the U.S. Department of Labor with industry contributions. However, this program was phased out by the Reagan administration.

The stage was, therefore, set for development of a more basic program. Starting with a contribution of $50,000 from the ACTWU and each of the major companies plus funds from the Economic Development Administration of the Commerce Department, a project was begun in October of 1980 to develop a prototype machine that could mechanize the operation of fashioning a sleeve. With a board of directors consisting of representatives from the union and companies as well as neutrals, funding for the project has reached several million dollars per year. Equipment capable of automatically sewing the sleeves of a man's suit was designed and developed by the Draper Laboratories of Cambridge, Massachusetts, and is expected to be ready for initial testing in 1986.

It is too early to gauge the ultimate success of this project. Nevertheless, it contains a number of important features that are worth watching as the project moves from the technology design phase to its implementation in specific firms. As it does so, the ability of the union and of industry employers to carry their cooperative efforts to lower levels of their relationship will determine whether or not this experiment results in tangible gains for the industry, textile workers, and the union.

Whether or not union participation in the design of new technology is translated into greater acceptance (less management resistance) in specific firms remains to be seen. Also, this new technology has the potential to displace at least 20 percent of the workers in the industry. The union feels that in the long run more jobs will be saved by enabling production to remain in the United States than will be lost as a result of the labor-saving technology. This implies that the parties will need to evolve their cooperative efforts to a further stage, namely, to design and conduct training and adjustment programs for workers displaced by the technology. Finally, union involvement in the earliest stages of technological development may set the stage for the union becoming involved with a wide array of companies and industries that supply new technology to the clothing industry. Just as the union pioneered industrial engineering techniques when the industry needed standardization, the union will very likely now begin playing a strategic role with equipment suppliers to this industry. This case represents perhaps the most advanced form of union participation in technology strategy found in American industry. Only time will tell, however, whether the union will be successful in translating this role into tangible employment and income-security benefits for its members.

Cases of Formal Board Representation

The most visible way unions have increased their involvement in strategic business issues recently within specific firms is through the placement of one or more union representatives on a company's board of directors. Chrysler, Pan Am, Eastern Airlines, Western Airlines, Wheeling-Pittsburgh Steel Corporation, Weirton Steel, Rath Meatpacking, and several trucking firms all have done so. In all of these cases the union was granted formal representation on the board of directors as part of a negotiated package that included wage and work-rule concessions. The cases differ markedly, however, in their subsequent financial performance and in the extent to which formal representation on the board of directors was linked to other forms of union and worker involvement. The experiences of Rath Meatpacking Company and Western Airlines illustrate this wide divergence.

RATH MEATPACKING

A threat of bankruptcy at Rath Meatpacking in 1978 led the local union to negotiate an employee buy-out of the corporation by means of an employee stock ownership plan (ESOP) in which workers gained 60 percent of the stock and ten of sixteen seats on the board of directors. While the international union leadership advised against this plan, the local union and rank-and-file workers viewed it as the only alternative to company bankruptcy and the loss of their jobs.

The subsequent interaction between management and union officials at Rath vacillated between highly integrative and highly adversarial behavior; in fact, researchers Tove Hammer and Robert Stern used the metaphor of a Yo-Yo to describe the interaction pattern.[10] Specifically, the initial cooperative pattern first gave way, after two years of board membership, to a more adversarial pattern. Political pressures began building up within the union as economic losses continued, no significant changes in plant operations or management were observed, and workers began questioning what had happened to the $5 million in wage and benefit deferrals they had given up. As these pressures escalated, the union began demanding that its representatives on the board vote as a unified block and promote the union's list of proposals at board meetings. A return to a more cooperative relationship occurred when the chief executive officer was replaced and several union officials moved into key managerial positions. Adversarial relations returned, however, as financial losses continued to mount, management demanded further wage concessions, and a wildcat strike occurred over a work-rule dispute. The company ultimately filed for protection under Chapter 11 of the Bankruptcy Code, the labor contract was set aside by the Bankruptcy Court, and the company was radically reorganized.

The primary reason this experiment failed is because the company was unable to identify and pursue a viable business strategy. The pay and work-rule concessions workers granted helped to give Rath some breathing space to search for an economically viable strategy, but these concessions could not substitute for such a strategy. In the end, the firm needed more than just concessions from its workforce.

At Rath the parties also confronted another problem typical of firms that put union representatives on the board of directors as part of a concession package negotiated during a financial crisis: placement of union representatives on the board alone did not lead to an abrupt change in worker trust in management, nor did it produce a major alteration in worker-manager relations. Workers change their deep-seated attitudes toward management slowly, and only if other forums for worker and union involvement in decision making that supplement formal board representation are introduced. Workers often rightfully view a seat on the board of directors as a cosmetic change. To be successful, formal union representation on a company board must be supported by other changes at the workplace, in collective bargaining, and in day-to-day management decision making. But Rath was either unwilling to make or incapable of making these supporting changes. So in the end union formal representation on the board served as an important quid pro quo for the negotiation of concessionary changes but did not fundamentally alter either labor-management relations or the firm's economic performance.

WESTERN AIRLINES[11]

The experience with formal board representation for the unions at Western Airlines is particularly instructive for our purposes because it illustrates (1) the differential degrees of interest or acceptance by union leaders of the new union roles at the strategic level and (2) the general lack of interest of rank-and-file workers in board representation per se. Employee board representation at Western Airlines, like that at Rath, was the result of a series of crisis negotiations beginning in the fall of 1983. After extensive top management turnover and in-creasingly severe financial losses, a series of painful negotiations be-tween Western and its five unions yielded a wage and work-rule concession package that included employee board representation as well as profit sharing and stock ownership (where employees were granted 32 percent of the company's common stock outstanding, at a value of 50 cents for each dollar conceded).

The package, called the Partnership Plan, was renegotiated in the fall of 1984. These negotiations, part of Western's "Competitive Action Plan," or CAP, refined the management quid pro quos in exchange for further wage and work-rule concessions. At this point, the employee stock plan was revised to become a full-fledged Employee Stock Ownership Plan (ESOP), giving employees (rather than a trustee) full voting rights for their shares in the company.

At the same time, the employee board representation provision was expanded as well. While the original Partnership Plan had allowed for two union representatives on the board, the CAP increased that number to four. The original two employee board representatives were in fact never chosen, since Western's four major unions never agreed on which two would get the board seats.

The first point just mentioned—union leaders' different perceptions of their new roles—is illustrated in a number of ways. For instance, three of the unions placed union representatives on the board of directors, while a fourth, the Teamsters, chose an "outsider" to minimize potential conflict of interest. Further, one of the union leaders years ago took the initiative to get a shop-floor employee involvement program installed, while leaders of the other five unions are not at all interested in this kind of worker participation.

The second point that is illustrated by the Western case is the generally low level of worker interest in union board representation. In a survey of employee attitudes, conducted late in 1985, employees on average much preferred profit sharing to board representation, stock ownership, or employee involvement. The average response, on a scale of "Strongly Agree" through "Strongly Disagree," to the statement "Now that we have CAP, I have a greater chance to participate in the management of Western Airlines" was "disagree." The response to a similar question about board representation in particular fell between "agree" and "disagree," but closer to the latter.

Despite the fact that for many Western workers the developments at the strategic level have been very remote, that they are only interested in the cash value of these changes, and that the unions remain unenthusiastic or ambivalent about this form of high-level participation, any overall evaluation of this experiment must be cautious. The major unknown at this time is whether the changes put in place at the strategic level will eventually be paralleled by equivalent changes at the workplace level. Major efforts are underway, particularly for ground personnel, to develop worker involvement. But as of early 1986, it is unclear how this effort to "deepen" the structural changes at the top will work out in practice. In some interesting ways, the state of this relationship lies somewhere between the traditional and the yet-to-be-realized new system, similar to the Xerox and ACTWU story reviewed in the last chapter. However, the direction of evolution is quite different, since Western is pursuing a "top-down" sequence and Xerox a "bottom-up" sequence.

Strategic Involvement Through Stock Ownership

During the period between 1983 to 1985 sixteen conversions to employee stock ownership and board representation for workers occurred in the over-the-road trucking industry. The Teamsters Union has developed a number of working principles as they have responded to the prospect of bankruptcy—an event that has affected approximately 20 percent of the capacity in this industry since deregulation took effect in 1980.[12] Review of these principles will illustrate how one union has sorted through the need to represent its members at the strategic level without compromising its ability to continue to serve as an independent bargaining agent for workers in reorganized firms as well as in healthier firms.

The first response of the Teamsters was to agree with the industry representatives that some type of general relief was in order. Accordingly, in late 1983 national union and industry representatives negotiated a two-tier wage contract. The membership, however, rejected the agreement by a margin of nine to one. The Teamsters then adopted a case-by-case approach to dealing with economic pressure. The common principle guiding each case, however, was that the union would adopt what we might call a "limited engagement strategy"—one in which management is left free to manage the firm subject to indirect union representation on the board and the union remains in a position where it can continue to bargain as usual with firms that are not experiencing severe financial distress. Moreover, the Teamsters' strategy does not involve any significant new roles for workers or union leaders at the workplace level of industrial relations. The union uses the following guidelines to manage this case-by-case approach.

First, before national union leaders will consider a major concession, a company must demonstrate genuine economic duress. Second, a financial plan is required to show how the requested concessions will be deployed. The union prefers to have the savings used for new equipment and other capital improvements rather than lowering prices. But in general, the Teamsters' philosophy is to leave to management the job of running the business. Thus the union does not seek to participate in day-to-day management decisions nor to dictate how concessions should be used.

Third, the Teamsters are firm about the extent of control that they require as a quid pro quo for concessions. On the one hand, they want the workers and their representatives to play an important ownership role and consequently they set a minimum of 40 percent of the outstanding stock. On the other hand, in keeping with the philosophy to let management run the business, the Teamsters put a ceiling of 49 percent on the workers' ownership of the firm. Generally the stock is voted as a trust.

The union has adopted the guideline that board members are not to be Teamsters Union members or officers. However, they are nominated by the union and are expected to represent the workers' and the union's interests in corporate decision making. That is, these board members must endorse the principle of collective bargaining and oppose strategic moves (such as the opening of a nonunion subsidiary) that would undermine or hurt the union.

The Teamsters also insist that the stock be purchased from the concessions via a payroll deduction plan and that no workers commit savings to the stock ownership plan. Participation is voluntary, so in this sense the ESOP is different from a concession agreement in which everyone takes the same cut in wages and benefits. Yet, in practice, most firms (and their creditors) require 80 to 90 percent employee participation in the ESOP and the wage-reduction plan before implementing it.

This example illustrates several key points about union involvement in strategic business decisions. Again, in this instance no involvement at the strategic level would have taken place without the development of dire economic circumstances. As Norman Weintraub, Director of Research for the Teamsters, stated: "Companies that are not in trouble do not want to share ownership."[13] The union has attempted to maintain the national wage scale for as much of the industry as possible and to respond in a pragmatic way to minimize potential job loss where firms are at or approaching bankruptcy. In several instances the ESOP approach has only bought time and the firms have eventually gone out of business. While it could be argued that the Teamsters should work out concession-ownership packages for firms before severe financial pressures develop, as a practical matter, this would be difficult to do because once concessions were given to firms that are not at *in extremis,* it would be impossible for the union to avoid the pressures for similar concessions from other employers. Thus the Teamsters have become involved at the strategic level as a pragmatic response to the task of simultaneously maximizing pay and benefits for as many workers as possible while responding to severe job-loss challenges at the edges of the industry. Whether this limited engagement strategy proves to be sufficient or whether it leads to a more comprehensive change in the roles and practices of union and management at the collective bargaining and workplace levels is another question worth watching in the years ahead.

Corporate Campaigns

In recent years several unions have embarked on public relations campaigns designed to put pressure on corporations to change their policies of resisting union organizing or bargaining efforts. These campaigns represent another channel through which unions are attempting to become involved in strategic business issues. Most of these "corporate campaigns," as they have been labeled, have been accompanied by strategies designed to put pressure on a target firm indirectly by pressuring individuals or other firms that do business with or have interlocking directorate ties with the firm. Unlike the other forms of strategic interactions, corporate campaigns tend to have specific and visible objectives. The intent is to continue the pressure on the firm only as long as it takes to change the company's policies and achieve the specific organizing or bargaining objectives of concern. To illustrate this approach we briefly review the campaign against Litton Industries, coordinated by the Industrial Union Department (IUD) of the AFL-CIO.[14]

LITTON INDUSTRIES

In the early 1980s several national unions approached the IUD to discuss the problems they were experiencing in organizing and negotiating contracts with plants owned by Litton Industries, a large and

195

highly diversified U.S. corporation. The IUD eventually decided to coordinate a public relations campaign against Litton in an effort to achieve a change in its labor relations policies. Because Litton is a major defense contractor, the IUD chose a strategy designed to publicize Litton as a major labor-law violator to federal government officials. Thus the IUD asked the House Education and Labor Subcommittee to hold hearings to consider debarring Litton from future government contracts in light of its alleged labor-law record. Examination of the record led the General Counsel of the National Labor Relations Board to decide to consolidate eleven future cases involving Litton plants or divisions in order to consider whether a corporate pattern of violations was occurring. Research was also initiated by the IUD to determine the record of unionization and decertification of bargaining units of facilities acquired by Litton. Finally, Litton stock was purchased and plans were made to speak out at the annual meeting of Litton stockholders in 1983.

Prior to the meeting, an agreement was negotiated between the company and the IUD to set up a joint union-management study committee with a neutral chairman to: "(1) study the allegations of the union against the company; (2) determine how industrial relations between the company and its unions can be improved; and (3) recommend how productivity can be improved."[15] Thus what was initiated as a highly distributive set of pressure tactics was transformed into an integrative, problem-solving study process.

The committee issued its final report approximately a year later. There were two major outcomes of the process. First, several specific disputes between the company and the unions representing employees in specific plants were resolved. An initial contract dispute that had been at impasse was signed and a large backlog of grievances that reflected the aftermath of a bitter strike was resolved. The committee was unsuccessful in mediating a third dispute in which it got involved. Second, the union representatives were able to open up a new channel of direct communications with the chairman and chief executive officer of Litton. Prior to the campaign all union contacts with the company were handled through the company's labor relations and legal staff, and all contacts were maintained on a decentralized, plant-by-plant basis. One union representative on the committee commented that this new channel of communications was the most significant achievement of the effort. On the other hand, no substantive changes were achieved in the corporation's business strategies, managerial values, or industrial relations policies. For example, the company stated to the committee that it intended to continue to reallocate its resources out of the mature industries (which generally happen to be organized plants) and to transform the firm in ways that will allow it to become "an advanced electronic defense, high-tech, and resource exploration and geophysical services company and that those businesses which do not fit in will be divested."[16] Litton also did not indicate any change in the values that would guide its approach to union organizing in the future. According to the committee chairman's report, the firm's basic philosophy will be continued: "Litton states categorically that it operates on a decentralized basis, with its divisions preferring to operate without unions. The company notes that this preference for a non-union atmosphere is legal and this right to express its opinion is allowed by law."

Thus, while a number of specific problems were resolved and improved and more direct communications with the chief executive officer were achieved, no long-run influence was achieved over the strategies, values, or the basic industrial relations policies that have made it difficult for unions to organize and represent workers of this firm. The union's inability to penetrate strategic business issues more extensively derives from the weakness of its bargaining position at Litton. Litton clearly was not willing to grant the union or workers greater access to strategic issues unless forced to do so. The unions and the IUD had utilized a combination of internal and external pressure to induce Litton to engage in the dialogue that did occur and to introduce the changes just outlined. But this pressure was not sufficient to induce the firm to revise further its relationships with the unions and workers.

Strategic Involvement from the Bottom Up

Union involvement in strategic business decisions need not start with union participation on high-level committees such as boards of directors or joint industry-level committees. In fact, in recent years increased union and worker involvement has often developed "from the bottom up," through shop-floor or plant-level activities. These activities often have been an outgrowth of the worker-participation programs discussed in chapter 6. The Fiero and Packard Electric work sites illustrate how union involvement in strategic business issues can develop in this way.

197

GM FIERO AND THE UAW

A hierarchy of committees oversees plant operations at GM's Fiero plant. Notably, the UAW has representatives on all these committees. At the top of the committee structure is the "administrative team," which includes the plant manager, senior plant staff, and the chairman of the local union's bargaining committee. This team addresses the plant's long-run planning issues. For example, the administrative team receives information regarding current and forecast sales of the plant's product (the Fiero sports car). Based on these forecasts, the team discusses employment forecasts and considers adjustment strategies to bring the available workforce in line with projected personnel needs. If sales are running low and projected to stay low, the team will discuss the need for and form of future layoffs. Similarly, the administrative team receives advance information regarding model changes and discusses the adjustments in technology, plant layout, and personnel (size and work tasks) needed to accommodate them. The team also engages in long-run planning. In 1985, for example, the administrative team at Fiero prepared the plant's five-year business plan for GM's executive committee.

Through participation on this administrative team and the associated access to the financial and other data, the union chairman of the bargaining committee participates in or, at the least, is notified of strategic business decisions to a much greater extent than usual. At the same time, there are limits to the union chairman's participation in business decisions. The administrative team structure does not allow the bargaining chairman to participate in corporate decisions concerning plants other than Fiero. Furthermore, although the bargaining chairman participated in the preparation and presentation of the plant's five-year business plan, the UAW has no formal representation on the corporate executive committee or the corporate board of directors and thus has no direct channel to affect corporate decisions regarding the plant's five-year plan.

There are, however, some channels through which the UAW is involved in corporate strategic decisions that extend beyond the scope of the Fiero and other plant-level committees. The 1982 national agreement between GM and the UAW provided the head of the UAW's GM department with the opportunity to address the board of directors of the corporation twice a year (a similar clause was included in the 1982 Ford-UAW agreement). This representative also communicates regularly, on an informal basis, with GM corporate officers. Interviews suggest that the amount and depth of this informal communication increased substantially in recent years. As will be discussed, the union's participation in the planning process for GM's Saturn project provides another channel for national-level union involvement in strategic business issues.

It is also important to note that through their participation on the other committees, local union officials and workers get involved in business issues that traditionally lie beyond the scope of collective bargaining. For example, the shop-floor "operating teams" within the Fiero plant have more extensive responsibility for production quality and relations with suppliers than in the past. In their efforts to solve production problems, workers at Fiero can (and frequently do) directly contact suppliers and sometimes visit them. Production workers at Fiero also receive advance warning from the plant's industrial engineers regarding upcoming changes in technologies and are given the opportunity to make suggestions regarding how best to carry out those changes. In some cases this has led to major modifications in plans regarding the layout and utilization of new equipment.

Increased participation by workers in shop-floor decisions is not unique to Fiero. Workers in many auto plants (at GM and Ford) have been given increased responsibility for production quality as part of the industry's efforts to respond to heightened cost competition. This has produced situations similar to that at Fiero, where workers can now directly contact suppliers, receive advance information regarding equipment changes, and make recommendations regarding those changes.

Yet there are limits to the extent of worker involvement in strategic business decisions that derive from these shop-floor activities. It is one thing for workers to make suggestions regarding the layout or use of new machinery; it is another thing for workers to have a direct say in the actual design of that technology or in other critical financial or production issues. Where Fiero is different from most other experiments in increased worker participation is the extent to which the organizational structure of the plant provides channels for union representatives to participate in the broader business decisions that shape shop-floor issues.

PACKARD ELECTRIC AND THE IUE

Chapter 6 presented the terms of the agreement signed in December 1984 between Packard Electric and the IUE that, among other things, provided for employment security and lower pay for new employees. Of interest at this point is the union and worker involvement in strategic business issues that preceded as well as was stimulated by this agreement. On the one hand, in the negotiations that led to the agreement local union officers were given access to financial information and forecasts that the union was never privy to in traditional collective bargaining. Clearly, the primary reason management gave the union access to this information was to try to convince it of the precarious situation at Warren and the need for change.

Union access to financial information did not, however, stop with the negotiation of the 1984 agreement. The discussions between labor and management that began in the late 1970s and those that led up to the 1984 agreement have created a mode of operation whereby local union officials now continually participate in high-level discussions regarding the operation and future of the Warren complex. Furthermore, the 1984 agreement created a number of plant and shop-floor committees that work to implement the agreement. One of the key features of the 1984 agreement was the job-security clause, providing that no "permanent" employee at Packard will be laid off for more than six months and allowing the hiring of temporary and part-time workers. Questions now arise regarding how the parties will adjust workforce utilization and deployment to meet the terms of the 1984 agreement. For example, workers who are recalled after six months of layoff can be assigned to "unconventional job tasks." There are also questions about when temporary workers can be hired and how their work and pay conditions will compare to those of "permanent" employees.

For our purposes, it is important to note that participation in the resolution of these issues involves workers and the union in business decisions that previously were under management's control. Yet, as at Fiero, there are limits to the extent of worker and union involvement in strategic issues at Packard Electric (although field interviews suggest that these limits are changing gradually). Furthermore, the extent of union and worker participation in strategic business issues at Packard will continue to change as the parties adjust to the new economic conditions, as the various new channels of union and worker participation mature, and as labor and management make their own strategic decisions regarding how best to pursue their interests.

THE SATURN PROJECT

An even more extensive form of involvement in strategic business issues is proposed in GM's Saturn project, a complex of new plants designed to produce a new generation of small cars in the late 1980s. Saturn is expected to start production in 1989 in Spring Hill, Tennessee. The proposed design of the plant's work organization and employment conditions is set out in an agreement reached between the UAW and GM in July 1985. On the shop floor at Saturn there will be "operating team" units of ten to fifteen workers that will be in a common job classification and have responsibility for a number of quality-control (inspection), material handling, and inventory-control tasks. The operating team units are modeled after and expand on the system that has been in use on the shop floor at Fiero and a handful of other GM plants in recent years.[17]

Where Saturn's proposed design goes beyond earlier participative structures is in the extent to which the UAW and workers will participate in higher-level planning committees. The Saturn labor agreement outlines a manufacturing advisory committee that will oversee the operation of the complex and include elected union representatives. There also will be a "strategic advisory committee" that will engage in long-term planning and include an elected UAW official.[18] The degree to which this committee structure provides meaningful and sustained union and worker involvement in business issues remains to be seen. Already, however, there has been considerable union involvement. Over the last few years a number of union representatives have been meeting with company officials to plan the work organization to be used at Saturn. This planning committee has received extensive information regarding Saturn's financial constraints and the technology that might be used. This planning process itself represents a novel case in which the UAW has been brought into planning discussions and given access to key strategic information.

General Patterns

The cases summarized in this chapter reveal a number of general patterns. First, since attempts to influence strategic business decisions require a fundamental change in the strategies of unions and employers, the parties initiate this course only when faced with severe environmental pressures. Basically, one or both parties must recognize that traditional collective bargaining is not adequately meeting their needs.

Labor's decision to become more directly involved in strategic business decisions typically must overcome initial resistance to change from within the ranks of one or both of the parties. Increased involvement rarely proceeds very far without a commitment from the key decision makers or powerholders to proceed through an experimental process. For example, design features of the Saturn project have come under severe criticism from some UAW leaders, who see the new agreement as giving up some of the hard-fought collective bargaining gains of the past.[19] At Western Airlines no single union response has emerged among the unions involved. Instead each local union has taken a somewhat different approach depending on its leadership views, the outlook of its rank and file, and the practices of the national unions with which some of these locals are affiliated.

Because efforts to engage management in strategic discussions represent a dramatic expansion of the scope of union influence as well as an extension of union influence to new channels above the normal reach of collective bargaining, unions need to bring considerable leverage or bargaining power to bear in order to get employers to participate in these processes. Thus it is important to note that in each of these cases the unions had a source of bargaining leverage. In the cases of Packard Electric and Fiero (and other experiments underway within the major auto companies), this leverage derived from the fact that the industry was completely organized by the UAW and IUE and the unions retained enough national bargaining power to halt any possible effort by the auto companies to pursue a nonunion option.[20]

At Western Airlines, although the company's financial troubles weakened the union's ability to resist pay concessions, those troubles also weakened the company's capability of surviving a long strike. Economic adversity, in this case as in so many others, made labor and management more dependent on each other. Litton reveals the importance of bargaining leverage by illustrating the limits of union gains in penetrating strategic issues (beyond getting management's attention) where bargaining power is lacking.

Labor and management involvement in strategic business decisions also causes them to face complex issues, the resolution of which requires the collection and analysis of a great deal of factual and analytical data. Union leaders have quickly discovered that they are participating in forums where interests are more multilateral than bilateral. For example, at Western Airlines the banking and investment community became active participants in the labor-negotiating process because they had the power to reject potential settlements on grounds that they were financially unworkable. At Packard Electric, union officers traveled to GM's plants in Mexico to learn firsthand of the competitive pressures those plants posed for the Warren complex.

Union leaders have thereby discovered that effective influence requires that they change their tactical behavior to a more integrative style. Yet their ability to adapt to this new style of interaction has been constrained by the political pressures they feel from their internal critics and from the role conflicts they experience in attempting to balance their responsibilities for representing their specific constituencies against their participation in the larger problem-solving process. A number of union leaders participating on the retail food industry joint committee have faced these role conflicts. Thus, an important determinant of the success of these new efforts at union influence is the parties' ability to manage the mixed-motive nature of these interactions.

Ultimately each party evaluates strategic involvement in terms of the degree to which it furthers the substantive goals that are central to its individual interests. While the rhetoric surrounding these processes often focuses on general social or economic welfare issues and the desirability of moving toward more cooperative relationships, the process has not been made a permanent part of the parties' relationship unless it achieves tangible results. For example, workers at Packard Electric maintained their support for increased union involvement in strategic issues because they saw employment increase in the new branch plants and stabilize overall at the Warren complex. Support for the participative organizational structure from workers at Fiero also derived in part from the steady employment they experienced at a time when many other auto plants were threatened by closing or large layoffs. In contrast, workers at Rath Meatpacking became disillusioned with their stock ownership and their union's role on the board of directors because they saw a continuing decline in the firm's finances and employment.

Summary and Conclusions: The Need for Linkage

Even in the face of these patterns it is difficult to make predictions regarding the future course or implications of increased union and worker involvement in strategic business decisions. The introduction of such participation is so new that labor and management have yet to confront the tough economic and political problems that often led to the demise of earlier high-level labor-management joint initiatives and committees. Furthermore, the limited duration of union involvement in strategic issues makes it impossible to know how workers would react to sustained involvement, and whether these early efforts are likely to blossom—to evolve toward even deeper union and worker engagement of strategic business issues. Although cases like Saturn are still largely on the drawing boards, their growing number indicates that American labor and management are clearly moving through an important period of experimentation with new strategies in organizational governance—strategies that, if diffused and institutionalized, will represent a fundamental departure from the New Deal model of collective bargaining and industrial relations.

Yet, even if these experiments were to develop at a healthy pace, the American labor movement would still face severe problems in spreading this new approach to bargaining relationships where it lacks the power to gain or sustain a meaningful role in strategic managerial decision making. Sustained diffusion and institutionalization may therefore require the active support of public policy. We shall return to this point in chapter 9 when we discuss the choices public policy makers will face in deciding whether or not to support the diffusion and institutionalization of these experiments through changes in national labor policies.

It may be useful at this point to summarize the central conclusions we draw from our analysis of the changes unions and companies are undertaking to close the gap in performance and recapture the innovative position from their nonunion competitors.

1. Standing alone, workplace-level QWL processes, changes in the process and outcomes of collective bargaining, or worker participation or representation in strategic management decision making are not sufficient to close the gap in economic performance and to regain the innovative position in industrial relations. Changes at each of these levels can make positive contributions individually and are necessary if unions and employers are to transform unionized relationships in ways that make them more responsive to their current environments. However, only when the innovations at all three levels are linked together in an integrated fashion do unions and employers appear able to introduce the complete range of changes and sustain their commitment to innovations that both close the competitive gap and recapture the innovative position in industrial relations.

2. Unfortunately, this type of integrated effort is limited to selected, highly unionized bargaining relationships where the union is secure and the employer sees no pragmatic alternative to accepting, working with, and enhancing the role of union. This integrated set of innovations is not diffusing to a broad range of partially organized bargaining relationships and is not likely to be found in completely unorganized firms.

3. Even if this integrated set of changes were to diffuse across the complete range of settings where unions already are organized, it would slow the decline in unionization but would not on its own reverse the downward trend of the past two decades. For unions to reverse the trend, they will need to develop strategies that can better respond to the interests, needs, and expectations of workers in occupations and employment relationships that currently are not organized.

This last statement implies that we need to examine the prospects for organizing nonunion workers. To achieve a turnaround in membership, unions will need to adopt organizing strategies that achieve a better match between the institutional structures of representation and individual worker expectations and interests. We now turn to an examination of these expectations and interests.

American Workers and Industrial Relations Institutions

SO FAR we have analyzed the transformations underway in the strategies of employers and labor unions and the institutional structures and processes of industrial relations. However, our analysis of the forces that will influence the choices that will shape the future of industrial relations would not be complete without consideration of a basic building block for all industrial relations institutions: the goals, expectations, and needs workers bring to their employment relationships. Ultimately, the form and effectiveness of the institutions and processes for managing and representing workers must be well matched to the perceived needs and revealed preferences of the individuals and groups they are designed to serve. In this chapter we review various sets of data that provide a portrait of workers' values, expectations, and stated preferences for alternative participation and representation structures and processes. One overriding question is raised throughout the analysis: What does our research suggest about the ability of the traditional New Deal collective bargaining model or the nonunion human resource management model to meet the needs and expectations of today's workforce? Before we sample the voluminous evidence from surveys and opinion polls on workers' views of their jobs, their employers, and unions, we ask a more basic question: Why do workers' views matter?

Why Workers' Views Matter

In some respects the answer to the question of why workers' views matter seems so obvious as to only require minimal attention. Certainly, any institution that is designed to structure and regulate the employment relationship can be viable only if it is supported by the workers it governs and serves. Two assumptions, however, are involved that require some discussion: (1) that workers are good judges of what is in their own interests and (2) that management cannot be entrusted solely on its own to fathom and to design responses to workers' needs.

The first point has been the subject of a longstanding philosophical debate between those who believe that all employee perceptions of their "needs" are derived from their social context and those who believe that individuals have the ability to identify their own needs and interests.[1]

Our own view is that workers do have a rather well-defined set of economic interests and psychological needs or expectations for their work and careers. However, not all interests or needs can be achieved at any given time or in any specific employment relationship. Nor, as will be discussed more fully later, are the priorities workers attach to different sets of needs uniform across all groups or over time. In this sense worker needs are shaped partly by their environment and partly by their historical experience. For example, workers will, over time, downgrade the priorities they assign to those expectations or needs they lack the power to achieve in a particular employment situation. Thus workers who might otherwise give a high priority to participation in decision making may lower their interest in this aspect of their jobs once they learn that few opportunities for participation are open to them. Similarly, they may upgrade the priorities attached to expectations for participation if they gain favorable experience with it. In this sense, worker needs are influenced by their particular demography and employment context. The important point for our analysis, however, is that all workers have a preference for improving their standards of living, their control over their environment, and their self-esteem through their work. Management policies and representational structures and processes, therefore, play important roles in both helping workers to assign priorities to different goals and providing means and resources for pursuing those goals. Workers, in turn, will evaluate management and union representational processes on whether or not the processes help them meet their work-related goals and expectations.

The second point is based on an important premise of the New Deal labor policy that was noted in chapter 2: that there is a partial but enduring conflict of interests between the goals of employees and their employers. In chapter 6, however, we noted that the newer human-resource management theories and practices reject or ignore the need to provide independent structures and procedures for articulating and accommodating these diverse interests. Instead, informal participation processes and enhanced planning and communications are expected to serve as substitutes for the adversarial procedures of bargaining, contractual rules, and grievance arbitration. Moreover, elements of this new model have spread to a large number of workplaces and, when combined with a determined management effort to avoid unionization, have proven to be a stable system for managing employee relations.

This model's success presents a formidable challenge to both the New Deal collective bargaining model and the normative premises on which it is based. Therefore, we need to ask an equally fundamental question: Are there any sound theoretical or empirical grounds for believing that worker and management interests have become more compatible? It should be clear from our analysis so far that we see no theoretical reason to modify or abandon the basic premise that employment relationships are characterized by both conflicting and common goals. While this premise is no less valid in today's employment settings than it was when institutional economists first articulated it more than half a century ago, the question remains: What do American workers believe? To answer this we turn to the empirical evidence available from attitude surveys and opinion polls.

Contemporary Worker Expectations and Values

Among the many studies of the changing nature and values of the American workforce, the summary statement of Rosabeth Moss Kanter that follows appears to capture most accurately and objectively both the emerging trends and the long-run continuities.[2]

Long-Term Trends in Work Values

Two themes can be said to characterize the ambiance of work in America in 1977—some parts of which represent continuous threads and ongoing trends since World War II, but others of which are new developments or stronger tendencies. One theme can be called cultural or expressive: the concern for work as a source of self-respect and nonmaterial reward—challenge, growth, personal fulfillment, interesting and meaningful work, the opportunity to advance and to accumulate, and the chance to lead a safe, healthy life. The other can be called political: the concern for individual rights and power, for a further extension of principles of equity and justice into the workplace and into the industrial order, for equality and participation both in their general symbolic manifestations and in the form of concrete legal rights. Neither theme denies the extent to which concerns about income and basic material security still dominate the lives of many Americans and propel them into long hours and second jobs. . . .

A more educated work force—as ours has become—is simultaneously a more critical, questioning, and demanding work force, and a potentially more frustrated one if expectations are not met.

SOURCE: Rosabeth Moss Kanter, "Work in America," *Daedalus* 107 (1978):53–54.

Kanter identifies two consistent trends in worker values: (1) the growing expectation that work will provide self-respect, nonmaterial reward, and sustained opportunities for personal growth, and (2) the growing awareness and willingness of employees to assert demands for fulfillment of individual rights, justice, and equality on their jobs. However, these growing and emerging expectations do not displace but rather broaden the basic and historic expectations that workers bring to all employment relationships, namely, the need for material rewards—income, safety, and health and employment security. In a

209

nutshell, the issue facing contemporary industrial relations institutions and practice is how to respond to these varied needs without closing off pursuit of one set at the expense of the other.

While a great deal of empirical evidence supports Kanter's broad conclusions, we will briefly review selected findings that help assess the ability of the traditional collective bargaining and the newer human-resource models of participation and representation to meet the traditional as well as the emerging needs of workers.

WORKER VIEWS OF THEIR JOBS

Table 8.1 provides a summary of survey data on worker values from a large number of organizations. These data expand on Kanter's conclusion by showing that while all workers continue to place a high value on the material rewards of pay and benefits, as one moves up the occupational hierarchy concerns for career advancement, challenging work, and authority and effective supervision take on higher priorities. These rankings of worker values and priorities are drawn from multiple surveys conducted over the 1970s and 1980s by the Opinion Research Corporation (ORC).[3] The central message of these data is that structures and processes for participation and representation need to differ across different occupational groups. No single model or standard set of employment relationship policies and practices will be adequate to meet the expectations of different groups.

TABLE 8.1
Top Five Work Values

Rank	Managers	Professionals	Clerical	Hourly
1	Pay and Benefits	Advancement	Pay and Benefits	Pay and Benefits
2	Advancement	Pay and Benefits	Advancement	Security
3	Authority	Challenge	Supervision	Respect
4	Accomplishment	New Skills	Respect	Supervision
5	Challenge	Supervision	Security	Advancement

SOURCE: William A. Schiemann, ed. *Managing Human Resources/1983 and Beyond* (Princeton, N.J.: Opinion Research Corporation, 1983).

The data collected as part of our research on employee participation summarized in table 8.2 further reinforce these generalizations. When asked the extent to which they wanted to have a say over a variety of workplace, collective bargaining, and managerial or strategic issues, the majority of both blue- and white-collar respondents indicated they wanted "some" or "a lot" of say over both the traditional bargaining issues of pay and grievance handling, and the workplace issues affecting how their job was to be done. Specifically, across all five cases included in the survey, more than 80 percent of the workers agreed that they should have a say over how their work was done. Nearly as many (between 78 and 96 percent) agreed they should have a say over the quality of the products or services they produce. It is instructive to note, however, that a somewhat smaller percentage of workers indicated an interest in gaining a say over those issues that fall within workers' discretion in the most flexible and autonomous work-organization designs, namely decisions about how much work is to be done and who is to be assigned to what tasks. Between approximately 46 and 70 percent of the workers indicated an interest in gaining a say over these issues, with the highest degree of interest among white-collar professionals. Even less interest is expressed in gaining control of the personnel decisions concerning hiring, promotion, and discipline or discharge that are sometimes decentralized to autonomous work groups. Thus on these issues there is a higher variance of opinions across different work settings and occupational groups.[4]

While the traditional bargaining issues of pay and grievance handling continue to be endorsed as priority concerns for worker influence, concerns for gaining influence over specific job-related issues are still paramount. This suggests that contemporary workers may not tolerate union representational strategies that focus narrowly on traditional bargaining issues and ignore their desires for greater direct say on their jobs. Nor are they likely to support participation processes that stress workplace- and task-related involvement at the expense of, or as a substitute for, adequate pay, benefits, and individual due process. Our case studies of the evolution of workplace innovations discussed in chapter 6 further reinforced this conclusion by noting that employee commitment and support for QWL initiatives were more likely to be maintained over time in those settings where employee involvement was effectively linked to the union's strategies for enhancing employment and income security.[5]

Another important feature of the survey data reported in table 8.2 demonstrates the challenge that unions face in garnering rank-and-file support for expanding their role at the strategic level of managerial decision making. As the responses to the questions under the heading of Strategic/Management Issues suggest, workers express a relatively low level of interest in gaining a say over broad areas of managerial decision making such as investment, plant location, and managerial

TABLE 8.2
Interest in Participation by Areas of Concern

| Workplace Issues | Blue-Collar Workers | | | | White-Collar Professionals |
	Case 1	Case 2	Case 3	Case 4	Case 5
The way the work is done—methods and procedures	83[a]	83	91	87	95
The level of quality of work	83	78	88	87	96
How fast the work should be done—the work rate	72	70	81	76	85
How much work people should do in a day	55	43	64	61	70
Who should do what job in your group or section	46	57	51	83	61
Collective Bargaining/Personnel Issues					
When the work day begins and ends	50	33	63	65	76
Pay scales or wages	67	78	82	73	92
Who should be fired if they do a bad job or don't come to work	39	38	39	35	42
Who should be hired into your work group	35	23	32	37	45
Handling complaints or grievances	67	70	72	59	79
Who gets promoted	39	27	42	41	48
Strategic/Management Issues					
The use of new technology on your job	69	70	68	77	79
Management salaries	27	22	13	41	22
Hiring or promotions to upper management	27	8	25	31	44
The selection of your supervisor	42	18	39	52	58
Plant expansions, closings, or new locations	45	22	51	70	40
The way the company invests its profits or spends its money	46	52	41	43	32

NOTE: [a]Figures indicate the percentage of respondents agreeing they want "some say" or "a lot of say."

SOURCE: Unpublished data summarized in Thomas A. Kochan, Harry C. Katz, and Nancy R. Mower, *Worker Participation and American Unions: Threat or Opportunity?* (Kalamazoo, Mich.: Upjohn Institute, 1984).

salaries. This is consistent with data from many other surveys.[6]

Yet under certain conditions contemporary workers are likely to see these issues as priority concerns. First, the one traditional managerial decision area that a strong majority of these workers want to gain greater influence over is the use of new technology. Between two-thirds and three-fourths of survey respondents indicate they want some or a lot of say over this issue. They express as much interest in this issue as in the traditional bargaining issues of pay and grievance handling, perhaps because they see it as directly relevant to their economic security and career opportunities. A second place where strategic issues seem to be of greater interest is in case 4. Here the workers had experienced approximately seven years of union and management cooperative efforts to save jobs and expand employment opportunities by redesigning work systems and joint planning concerning the location, design, and terms of employment of new plant and investments. Thus, as with new technology, workers in this case see a direct link between representation on strategic management issues and their immediate and long-run employment prospects.

These results suggest that American workers will continue to approach the question of involvement in strategic issues in their traditionally pragmatic fashion. Interest will be strong only if their involvement in strategic decisions can be shown to be instrumental to the attainment of specific job and career expectations. As we shall review later, this is a theme that has traditionally dominated worker views of union representation and now appears to describe the approach workers will take to an expansion of union representation or direct participation to new areas.

WORKER VIEWS OF EMPLOYERS

Given this contemporary profile of worker expectations and views, we now need to assess the extent to which workers see current management and/or labor union performance as adequate to meet these needs. Throughout the preceding chapters we have noted that significant innovations in workplace-level participation have been introduced in the newest human resource management systems, first in mainly nonunion settings and more recently in selected unionized workplaces. In chapter 4 it was reported that by 1985, employee participation processes had diffused across approximately 23 percent of the workforce. However, one central question still needs to be asked: Have these and other innovations diffused to a large enough sample

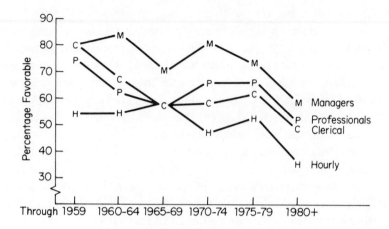

FIGURE 8.1

Ratings of Company as a Place to Work

NOTE: The question asked was: How would you rate this company as a place to work compared with other companies you know or have heard about? The figure shows the percent responding "one of the best" or "above average."

SOURCE: William A. Schiemann, ed., *Managing Human Resources/1983 and Beyond* (Princeton, N.J.: Opinion Research Corporation, 1983).

and been effective in meeting the full range of needs and expectations of the contemporary workforce? In other words, have management policies evolved to the point where they meet workers' needs and expectations well enough to eliminate the need for either traditional union or other forms of employee representation?

Unfortunately, while there are numerous surveys that track trends in job satisfaction among workers over time, no national time series tracks the confidence or trust that employees have in their employers or in the managers who implement human resource policies. However, data from many organizations that speak directly to the confidence workers place in management practices are found in the surveys conducted by the ORC over the past several decades. Figure 8.1 summarizes the trends in ORC survey data on the broad question: How would you rate this company as a place to work compared with other companies you know of or have heard about? The responses show a decline over the past decade across all occupational groups, from hourly workers to clericals, professionals, and managers. In the 1980s between 40 and 60 percent of employees included in ORC surveys rated their organizations "above average" or "among the best" places to work. In the early 1970s between 50 and 80 percent of those surveyed gave their organization this rating. Further data reported by ORC surveys show similar declines in satisfaction with specific employer policies dealing with (1) opportunities for training, (2) ability to achieve one's career goals within the company, (3) fairness in the application of company rules and procedures, (4) managerial responsiveness to employee problems, (5) willingness of management to decentralize decision making, (6) ability of management to stay in touch with employee needs and views, and (7) the ability or competence of top management. On all of these specific items, the percentage of favorable responses declined over the past decade to the point where the average response for all occupational groups on each of these questions was below 50 percent.

While the ORC data are valuable because they provide comparisons over time, their generalizability is suspect because they are drawn from a particular client base rather than from a representative national sample. A 1985 National Survey of Employee Attitudes, however, produced a comparable finding of high job satisfaction but less confidence in employer policies. For example, 84 percent of the respondents indicated they were satisfied with their jobs, 70 percent were satisfied with their organization as a place to work, and, similar to the ORC surveys, only 59 rated their organization as above average or one of the best places to work.[7] Fifty-seven percent expressed satisfaction with their organization's top management.[8] Thus the pattern reported in the ORC data is quite consistent with current data from a representative cross section of the U.S. workforce. This implies that while job satisfaction is quite high among contemporary American workers, about one-half of the workforce remains skeptical of top management's ability or willingness to address the full range of worker interests or expectations.

WORKER VIEWS/EXPECTATIONS OF UNIONS

Similar questions need to be asked concerning the contemporary views of workers toward American unions. Given the nature of the innovations in management policy, do employees still see a need or a unique role for unions, or do they believe that unions performed valuable roles in the past but have outlived their usefulness and are unnecessary for the future? To answer this question we need to distinguish between the general images or perceptions that American workers have toward unions and the roles they play at the workplace and in society from the specific preferences workers express for union representation in their current places of employment.

Dual Images of Unions. Most Americans tend to have two general views of unions. On the one hand, opinion polls dating from the 1940s to the present continually have shown that unions and their leaders are held in low esteem. The majority of the population rank their confidence in union leaders considerably below the confidence they place in government and business leaders. Moreover, unions tend to suffer from a "Big Labor" stereotype. That is, as shown in the 1977 Quality of Employment Survey, most people agree with statements that unions exert strong control over politicians and the electoral process and force their members to go along with unpopular leadership decisions.[9] Thus unions have the image of being large, powerful institutions.

At the same time, the 1977 survey showed that an equally strong majority of the American public views unions as important and effective vehicles for improving the status and representing the job-related needs of employees at the workplace. That is, more than 80 percent of the respondents agreed that unions are effective in improving their members' wages, protecting job security, and protecting workers against unfair employer practices. These favorable views toward unions have carried over into the 1980s. Recent Harris polls, some done for the AFL-CIO Evolution of Work Committee and some for *Business Week*, continue to show the same dual pattern of views toward unions.[10] Moreover, a majority of the public agrees that unions are still necessary to ensure that employees are treated fairly by employers. For example, in the 1984 AFL-CIO–sponsored Harris poll, a similar percentage (69 percent) of the public rejected the notion that unions are relevant only to blue-collar workers. Similarily, 64 percent of the participants in ORC surveys disagreed with the statement that unions are no longer necessary to protect the interests and well-being of the average workers. Thus, while most of the American public has a poor image of unions in general, an equally strong majority agrees that the functions unions traditionally have performed for their members and for the larger society continue to be relevant and needed today.

Specific Views. The general endorsement of the need for unions per se does not translate into a search for union representation by a majority of employees in their specific work settings. Indeed, the evidence from the surveys just reviewed as well as from numerous other studies shows that to induce workers to express a preference for unionizing, takes a combination of (1) deep dissatisfaction with current job and employment conditions, (2) a view that unionization can be helpful or instrumental in improving those job conditions, and (3) a willingness to overcome the general negative image or stereotype of unions. For example, analysis of both the 1977 Quality of Employment survey and the 1984 Harris poll conducted for the AFL-CIO showed that workers who were dissatisfied with their pay, job security, on-the-job recognition, and promotional opportunities were approximately 40 percentage points more likely to express a preference for unionizing than workers who were satisfied with these aspects of their jobs.[11] In the 1984 survey, a perception that unions would be helpful or instrumental in improving one's job conditions increased the probability of voting for unionization another 21 percentage points, while a negative image of unions reduced the willingness to organize by about 24 percentage points.[12]

These results suggest quite clearly that given current circumstances, traditional union-organizing efforts are unlikely to yield substantial new members. Apparently all three of the conditions just mentioned—deep job dissatisfaction, a view that unions are likely to be effective in improving conditions on their particular job, and lack of a negative stereotype or image—are necessary to achieve a 0.5 or greater probability that workers will express a preference for unionizing. Stated in a more practical way, a majority of workers in a specific bargaining unit must possess these views in order for a union to win a representation election. Yet currently most American workers do not hold these views. In fact, in both 1977 and 1984 only 33 percent, or about one-third, of the nonmanagerial labor force expressed a willingness to vote to unionize if offered the opportunity to do so. This is not surprising since in response to other questions in the 1984 survey, more than 80 percent of the nonunion sample expressed general satisfaction with their jobs and, as shown in table 8.3, less than a majority of nonunion workers believe that they would materially improve their wages, working conditions, and degree of participation and recognition by unionizing.

Still, however, one-third of the nonunion workforce does see unionization as a vehicle for improving specific job conditions and would prefer to have a union represent them, if given the opportunity. Further analysis of both the 1977 and the 1984 data confirm that those workers who are most interested in unionization are minorities, women, and low-wage workers. This should not be surprising since econometric evidence clearly shows that the dominant effect of unions has been to improve the wages, benefits, and general working conditions of lower-wage, lower-skill workers who lack individual labor-market power and mobility.[13] Thus the problem for unions is not that there is a lack of

217

TABLE 8.3

Perceived Effects of Unionization on Nonunion Workers' Jobs

| | *If my job were unionized, conditions would:* | | | |
	Get Better (Percentage)	Get Worse (Percentage)	Remain About the Same (Percentage)	Not Sure (Percentage)
Pay	42.2	8.2	46.0	3.6
Job Security	23.7	15.4	58.2	2.8
Recognition	15.1	14.8	66.7	3.4
Fringe Benefits	41.7	7.4	42.0	3.8
Opportunity to Participate	21.4	18.4	57.3	2.9
Health and Safety	22.5	2.3	71.1	4.1
Treatment by Supervisor	15.9	13.8	66.5	3.8
Discrimination against Women	16.7	3.7	74.7	4.9
Discrimination against Minorities	14.7	4.1	76.4	4.8
Chances for Advancement	17.4	11.7	66.6	4.3

SOURCE: 1984 Harris poll conducted for the AFL-CIO Evolution of Work Committee.

individuals interested in membership. Rather, the problem is how to translate that individual interest into majority support within a specific work unit in order for representation to be provided.

Union Performance on the Job. The survey data just reported document how the American public in general and nonunion workers specifically view unions. How do current union members evaluate the performance of their organizations? To get a complete picture, we need to look both at overall evaluations of union performance and at perceptions of performance on specific workplace, collective bargaining, and strategic-level activities. Two overall indicators show that union members in general assign positive evaluations to their union representation. In both the 1977 and the 1984 survey, 75 percent of union members responded that they were satisfied or very satisfied with their unions. In another survey conducted in 1982 as part of the National Longitudinal Survey of adult males, an even stronger endorsement of unionization was found. When current union members were asked how they would vote if a union representation election were held on their current job, 87 percent indicated they would vote to continue union representation.[14]

The data from five of our case studies of union participation in QWL programs summarized in table 8.4 present a more detailed breakdown of union member evaluations of union performance across workplace, collective bargaining, and strategic managerial issues.

TABLE 8.4

Union Performance Ratings on Selected Workplace, Collective Bargaining and Strategic Issues (Percentage Rating Good or Very Good)

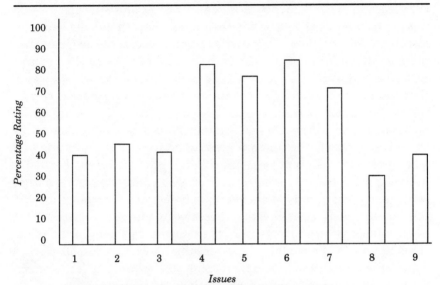

Issues

NOTE: 1. Getting workers a say on how to do their jobs (40 percent)
2. Making the job more interesting (46 percent)
3. Improving productivity (40 percent)
4. Getting good wages (84 percent)
5. Getting good fringe benefits (76 percent)
6. Protecting workers from unfair treatment (83 percent)
7. Handling grievances (69 percent)
8. Getting workers a say in the business (27 percent)
9. Representing worker interests in management decision making (41 percent)

SOURCE: Thomas A. Kochan, Harry Katz, and Nancy Mower, *Worker Participation and American Unions: Threat or Opportunity* (Kalamazoo, Mich.: W. E. Upjohn Institute, 1984) table 4-5, pp. 120–21.

Across all cases, members rated the performance of their union highest on traditional collective bargaining issues. Unions are given consistently lower performance ratings on workplace and on strategic issues. For example, these unions received a good or very good performance rating from 84 percent of the respondents on the issue of getting good wages, 76 percent on getting good fringe benefits, 83 percent on protecting members against unfair treatment, and 69 percent on handling grievances. In contrast, unions received good or very good ratings from 40 percent on gaining workers a say on how to do their jobs, 46 percent on making their jobs more interesting, and 40 percent in improving productivity. Ratings were even lower on strategic issues: 27 percent rated the union good or very good on gaining a say in how the business was run and 40 percent gave them this rating on representing worker interests in management decision making. However, the variation in performance ratings on strategic and workplace issues was quite large depending on whether or not the respondents had been directly involved in a worker-participation process, the scope of that participation effort, and the nature of the union's role in the process. Specifically, further analysis of these data and the cases from which they are drawn showed that the union members who were active in the participation programs underway in two cases evaluated union performance on workplace and strategic issues as more effective. In these two cases (1) the union played an active role in initiating and administering these processes and (2) the processes went beyond a narrow QWL focus to address key concerns about employment security, work organization, and issues traditionally reserved for management.[15] It is not surprising, therefore, that these two unions also received higher overall effectiveness ratings from their members than did the other three unions in the sample. These results imply that just as worker expectations for their jobs and their employers have expanded in recent years, so have union-member expectations for their unions.

While both the traditional collective bargaining model and the newer models of workplace-level participation fill some of the needs of some people, significant gaps remain between the expectations many employees bring to their employment relationship and the performance of existing participation and representation processes and structures. Standing alone, neither model meets both the traditional and the expanded set of expectations. Thus we can expect continued demand for traditional collective bargaining, direct employee participation at the workplace within union and nonunion employment settings, and a desire for greater participation or representation on strategic management issues in situations where workers perceive a tangible link between strategic management decisions and their goals and interests.

Worker Views of Alternative Models

Given the fact that neither the traditional industrial relations system nor the newer human resource management system is an adequate model for a majority of the workforce now or in the forseeable future, a search is underway for alternative models. Two questions need to be asked: What additional means of participation and representation are needed? How can the best features of each system be allowed to grow and diffuse without constraining the other?

The 1985 report of the Evolution of Work Committee of the AFL-CIO began to address the first question as part of its overall effort to explore new opportunities for organizing and representing workers and recouping the membership losses experienced over the past two decades. The following extract cites two of the committee's conclusions and recommendations that are directly related to this question.

The committee stresses the need to (1) develop more effective means for allowing organized workers to resolve problems as individuals on their jobs and (2) provide more individual membership options for those workers who are unable to establish (or uninterested in establishing) a formal collective bargaining relationship with their employer. The basis for these recommendations can be seen in the Harris poll conducted for the committee and in the committee's analyses of the growing number of workers who have temporary or short-term attachments to a single employer. For example, approximately 20 percent of the employed labor force work in part-time jobs. In addition, a small but growing number hold temporary jobs, are consultants or independent contractors, or work for temporary-help agencies and thus are not attached to a single employer.[16] This is clearly an increasingly important segment of the labor force. Moreover, the lack of deep and stable attachment to any given employment relationship poses difficulty for both the traditional union-organizing model and the innovative or high-commitment human resource management model. Thus one objective of the AFL-CIO Evolution of Work Committee was to identify alternative strategies and processes for representing these and nonunion workers in general. The question the committee asked was: Is there interest among unorganized workers in some alternative form of representation?

Selected Recommendations of the AFL-CIO
Evolution of Work Committee

1.1 *Unions should experiment with new approaches to represent workers and should address new issues of concern to workers. . . .* A two-fold response by unions is required.

First, unions must develop and put into effect multiple models for representing workers tailored to the needs and concerns of different groups. For example, in some bargaining units workers may not desire to establish a comprehensive set of hard and fast terms and conditions of employment, but may nonetheless desire a representative to negotiate minimum guarantees that will serve as a floor for individual bargaining, to provide advocacy for individuals, or to seek redress for particular difficulties as they arise. In other units, a bargaining approach based on solving problems through arbitration or mediation rather than through ultimate recourse to economic weapons may be most effective.

Second, and equally important, unions must continually seek out and address new issues of concern to workers. For example, the issue of pay inequity has become a proper concern of women workers; collective action provides the surest way of redressing such inequities. . . .

1.2 *Consideration should be given to establishing new categories of membership for workers not employed in an organized bargaining unit.*
. . . approximately 28% of all non-union employees—27,000,000 workers in all—are former union members; . . . There are hundreds of thousands more non-union workers who voted for a union in an unsuccessful organizing campaign or who are supporting or have supported efforts to establish a union in their workplace. . . . New categories of membership should be created by individual unions or on a Federation-wide basis to accommodate individuals who are not part of organized bargaining units, and affiliates should consider dropping any existing barriers to an individual's retaining his membership after leaving an organized unit.

SOURCE: *The Changing Situation of Workers and their Unions.* Report of the AFL-CIO Evolution of Work Committee, February 1985, pp. 18–19.

Nonunion workers in the Harris poll conducted for the AFL-CIO committee were about evenly divided in their responses to a question concerning whether problems are better resolved at the workplace by going to the employer as individuals or collectively. Specifically, 45 percent of the nonunion workers indicated a group response was more effective, while 43 percent indicated an individual response was better.

About 12 percent were either not sure or had no opinion. Younger, lower-wage, and lower-skilled workers were more likely to express a preference for the group option while older, higher-wage, management, professional, and sales employees tended to prefer the individual option. These data imply that interest in both individual and group expression is stronger than the preference for traditional union representation. (Recall that about one-third of the nonunion sample expressed a willingness to unionize.)

Further evidence of interest in alternative forms of representation was found when respondents were asked whether they were interested in receiving more individualized benefits and services (shown in table 8.5) that could transfer with them across jobs and employers. Majority support for such benefits and services as health insurance, labor-market information, legal services, and consumer discounts is understandable, given the increasing mobility of the labor force and an increasing employer preference for various part-time, temporary, contract, or other flexible (nonpermanent) hiring and employment relationships. The support voiced for these types of services led the AFL-CIO committee to recommend experimentation with an associate membership option that would allow individual workers to join unions and receive individual benefits even if no collective bargaining unit existed at their place of employment. It is clear that we will see some experimentation along these lines in the future. The question remains, however, whether the labor movement or any other employee organization can develop stable and effective strategies for providing these more individualized benefits and services.[17]

TABLE 8.5

Interest of Nonunion Workers in Various Benefits and Services

Interests in Joining an Employee Organization that Provided:	*Interested (Percentage)*	*Not Interested (Percentage)*	*Not Sure (Percentage)*
Counseling on Workplace Problems	42.2	56.6	1.1
Information on Job Opportunities and Training	59.8	39.1	0.9
Legislative Lobbying for Employee Interests	42.9	55.5	1.7
Medical or Dental Insurance	68.6	30.3	1.2
Legal Services	57.2	41.3	1.8
Buyers' Discounts	55.7	42.4	1.8
Day Care for Children	36.8	61.6	1.7

SOURCE: 1984 Harris poll conducted for the AFL-CIO Evolution of Work Committee.

223

Conclusions and Implications

The American public continues to see a need for unions, not only for blue-collar but also for white-collar and professional workers. Yet a majority of nonunion workers currently do not want to join a union because they see unions as unable to make a significant difference in the areas of traditional union activity and employee concern. The one-third of nonunion employees who do express an interest in traditional union representation face limited prospects of achieving it on their jobs because (1) union organizing activity currently covers only a minute fraction (less than 1 percent) of those eligible to organize, (2) it is unlikely that a majority of a given employee's peers agree that unionization is needed on their job, and (3) where there is majority interest and an organizing drive is started, employer opposition can reduce significantly the probability that a successful bargaining relationship will be established.

The benefits of the human resource innovations that serve as a partial alternative to unionization have diffused to only a limited number (at the most 25 percent) of employees. Moreover, an increasing number of workers at all occupational levels express declining confidence and satisfaction with employer policies and practices and behavior of top management. Another growing group of employees lacks the long-term attachment to an existing organization or employment relationship that is needed to build and support the mutual commitment and trust necessary to make the participatory processes embedded in the new human resource management models work, either because of the increasing trend toward temporary or flexible employment contracts or because of the increased percentage of professionals with greater attachments to their occupation than to their employers.

A central conclusion reached in earlier chapters was that the traditional models of representation and participation embedded in the New Deal industrial relations system are proving inadequate in meeting the contemporary needs of employers for efficiency, flexibility, and adaptability and of unions for organizing and representing workers. The data presented in this chapter suggest that the traditional system is also insufficient for meeting the current needs and expectations of the labor force. Nor are the participatory opportunities emphasized by the newer human resource management models sufficient or widely enough diffused to substitute for traditional union representation. Instead, what is needed is a blending of traditional representation and newer participatory processes, along with perhaps additional, more individualized forms of voice and representation. Moreover, all of these processes need to be diffused to a broader range of settings and employees. Thus employer, labor, and public policy decision makers are likely to be under pressure to adapt traditional practices and institutions to support a more varied and mutually reinforcing set of participation and representation procedures. The options facing each of these parties in addressing this challenge is discussed in the final chapter.

CHAPTER

9

Strategic Choices Shaping the Future

T HE HISTORY of U.S. industrial relations should caution anyone from making bold predictions about the future based on the trends of the recent past. We have documented how over the course of the past half century union and nonunion systems traded positions as the innovative force in industrial relations. Moreover, the points at which a transition in leader/follower relations occurred could never have been predicted based on previous trends. The union sector recaptured the lead in the 1930s as a result of the New Deal legislation, the explosion of industrial unionism, and an abrupt change in the economic, political, and social environment that undermined the confidence and trust American society had placed in the business community. The stability provided by the new labor legislation and its subsequent enforcement, along with the favorable economic environment, allowed unions to strengthen their leadership position by gradually improving wages, benefits, and working conditions through collective bargaining.

No one foresaw the rise of an alternative human resource management system that, over the course of the 1960s and 1970s, gradually overtook collective bargaining and emerged as the pacesetter by emphasizing high employee involvement and commitment and flexibility in the utilization of individual employees. Similarly, no one studying or practicing industrial relations in the 1970s foresaw the tumultuous changes that would take place in the union sector in the early 1980s at the workplace, in collective bargaining, or at the strategic level of decision making.

Given the strategic-choice perspective developed throughout this book, we are particularly unwilling to make predictions for the future based on projections of past trends. Indeed, because labor and management have initiated so much experimentation in recent years, we see the current period as one in which the parties have a special opportunity to shape the future patterns of industrial relations. That is, we see the current moment as one of those historic periods of transformation in which existing institutional structures have been challenged and opened up to experimentation in ways that allow considerable choice in how to reconstruct and modify them to best serve the interests of workers, employers, and society in general. The strategic choices made by employers, unions, workers, and public policy makers will have an important bearing on the shape and patterns of industrial relations in the future.

Given the importance of the choices that lie ahead, in this final chapter we shift our perspective from describing and interpreting past and current patterns of industrial relations activities to exploring the range of choices open to the parties. To anticipate the consequences of various choices and patterns of evolution we use the framework and evidence developed previously. In doing so, we hope not only to raise the level of public debate over the alternatives the parties face but also to test the theoretical power and practical utility of the strategic-choice model.

Future Environmental Conditions

Given our argument that effective industrial relations institutions need to be well matched to the environmental conditions they face, we need to make a number of broad assumptions about the future environment for U.S. industrial relations before we can go on to assess the range of choices and options facing the parties. While each individual worker, firm, labor market, and labor-management relationship will be exposed to diverse economic, technological, and social conditions, we shall assume, for discussion purposes, that the following broad patterns will dominate most industrial relations settings in the near future.

The majority of American firms can be expected to continue to face intense competition from foreign and domestic sources. One of the most important consequences for the parties to U.S. employment relationships in both union and nonunion settings will be that it will be difficult, if not impossible, to "take wages out of competition" by standardizing wages across competitors. In markets where the transfer of technology allows for global sourcing of production, American employers will find it difficult, if not impossible, to compete via a business strategy that depends on being the lowest labor-cost producer. To try to compete at the labor-cost levels of developing nations that do not share a commitment to protecting worker rights and that have standards of living considerably below that of the American labor force is likely to be self-defeating for the firm, for its employees, and, in the longer run, for American society. Firms will face a set of choices about how to find a competitive advantage in markets where labor costs not only vary across competitors but where American employers tend to be at or near the high end of the labor-cost distribution. Firms will have to identify high value-added opportunities (for example, extensive use of technology) as well as market niches that allow them to prosper with a high-wage/high-productivity combination. Where such a competitive strategy is not feasible, firms may have to abandon some segments of production and services. For this reason, we expect that the pace of economic and organizational restructuring that has characterized the U.S. economy over the past decade will continue for a long time to come. Indeed, for reasons to be outlined, rapid restructuring may become a permanent feature of the U.S. economy to which our industrial relations institutions will need to adapt.

One of the reasons that organizational restructuring and flexibility in the use of human resources will continue to be important is that along with increased competition, product-life cycles are becoming shorter. As they seek more varied and specialized niches, firms become more specialized and therefore smaller or they become more flexible in their ability to shift human and capital resources across multiple products and services.[1] Thus this recently developed premium on flexibility in the creation and use of human resources will continue to be important to employers and to the U.S. economy in the years ahead.

One implication of these market trends is that we can expect small firms and establishments dedicated to specialized products or services to continue to expand in numbers and in economic importance. This in turn will increase the proportion of the labor force employed in small and often temporary or flexible employment relationships that, as we noted, pose significant challenges to traditional industrial relations institutions and human resource management practices.

These market conditions interact with the potential for recent advances in information technology to produce additional restructuring and displacement of labor and to open a new range of choices for private and public decision makers as they manage the adaptation of new technology. We do not assume that massive job loss, displacement, and deskilling will inevitably result; nor will firms naturally and smoothly adjust to new technology by increasing productivity, creating new products and services, and increasing demand for a more highly skilled and analytically oriented labor force.[2] Instead, the potential for technological advances to create either of these outcomes will exist in a multitude of future situations. The parties and the institutions of industrial relations that structure and limit these choices will, therefore, play important roles in determining the circumstances under which the different scenarios will obtain.

The changing market and technological conditions will interact with equally important changes in the supply characteristics of the American workforce. Economic restructuring and technological adaptation will be an important challenge because a generation of older, higher-cost but less mobile and perhaps less technologically and socially adaptable workers will be at risk for some time to come. This is the group that will bear the greatest economic and social costs of the transitions that lie ahead. How their interests are dealt with will have an important bearing on the speed of technological adjustment and the ability of the larger society to enjoy the benefits of new technology.

While this adjustment process may be a more temporal challenge, responding to the broad expectations that most American workers have for their jobs and their careers will be a continuous challenge to the participation and representation processes and opportunities embedded in the industrial relations and human resource systems of the future. Compartmentalizing the rights of "workers" as being different from "supervisors" or "managers" conforms well to neither the shared expectations of people performing these roles nor to the reality of the roles in contemporary employment settings. Drawing tight boundaries around the scope of issues that can be legally discussed in negotiations between labor and management and excluding large numbers of affected employees within a firm from these discussions because they are not formally represented by a labor organization similarly makes less sense given that exposure to new technology, market changes, and new patterns of human resource management cut across employees at all levels of the organizational hierarchy.

Even though the political environment will influence the choices the parties make as they confront the demands posed by other elements in the environment, we do not find it easy or fruitful to predict future political trends. Instead, we prefer to focus on the choices that public and private decision makers will have to confront in the future regardless of the prevailing political climate or balance of power. Indeed, we believe that the challenges facing industrial relations have not received the attention they deserve in public policy discussions and in the various forums where leaders of labor and management meet to discuss long-term issues facing the economy and society. Therefore, what follows is less of a precise prescription for reform, since the scope and nature of any reforms that emerge will be heavily dependent on the political climate prevailing when these issues are joined. Instead we provide more of a menu of issues and options for further and more open debate and analysis.

Choices Facing Public Policy

This book has focused primarily on the changing practices of labor and management and, up to this point, has taken as given the public policy context in which changing practices are evolving. While we have explicitly noted that the legal environment has an important effect on management and union strategies, we have not sought to analyze in detail the historical evolution or contemporary status of labor law or its administration. Yet no analysis of the dynamics of U.S. industrial relations would be complete without considering the implications of changes in private practice for the future of public policy. Nor could we ever expect the private practices and experimentation that we have been describing to diffuse more widely without some sanctioning and institutionalizing role for public policy. Therefore, we shall begin our analysis of the choices facing the parties with a discussion of the challenges the private experimentation now underway poses for public policy.

UPDATING THE GOALS OF PUBLIC POLICY

The New Deal collective bargaining system that was given stability by the passage of the National Labor Relations Act and its subsequent administration and enforcement is no longer well matched to contemporary industrial relations. Therefore, the changes in U.S. industrial relations that erupted in the early 1980s could be described as a pre-public policy stage of private experimentation, much of which questions existing legal doctrines. At some point in the future, public policy makers most likely will seriously debate whether, as a 1984 report of a committee of the House of Representatives concluded, American labor law has "failed" or otherwise needs updating to support and institutionalize those practices needed to meet the economic and social needs of workers, employers, and the larger society.[3]

In the 1930s, the public policy challenge was to strengthen the power of workers in order to eliminate violence, regulate and institutionalize labor-management conflict, and thereby achieve the stability believed to be essential to economic progress. This produced a labor policy that endorsed collective bargaining and led to the institutionalization of a particular form of adversarial procedures and relationships. In the current environment, however, the economy demands flexibility more than stability. Effective representation requires planning and participation in decisions before they are made rather than just formal negotiations over their effects after the fact. And for competitive reasons employers need increased trust, commitment, and cooperation at the workplace rather than further institutionalization of adversarial relationships. Moreover, in a growing number of employment relationships employees will need more individualized due-process and representational procedures as much as collective forms of contract negotiations and enforcement.

Updating existing policy to meet these more complex contemporary goals will challenge many of the deeply held values and interests of employers and labor leaders. While the conflict over values has traditionally been played out over employer resistance to unions—and this resistance will require policy attention in the future as well—the central question policy makers will need to face will be whether to confer to individuals and groups of workers a broader and more varied set of rights to participation and representation in order to promote the mix of objectives noted earlier. The issue is one of how active a role federal and state-level policy makers should take in diffusing and institutionalizing the private practices now being experimented with.

PROCEDURES FOR UNION RECOGNITION

We choose to start our discussion of specific public policy choices with the issue of union recognition because this is the most visible and hotly debated labor policy issue of our time. Moreover, while the more complex set of objectives just noted needs to be addressed, the data reported in chapter 8 show that a significant number of the labor force still prefer and would likely benefit from traditional forms of union representation. Therefore, it is important for employees to be able to make effective and free choices on whether or not they would like to be represented by a union. Indeed, until the most obvious failures of current labor law to achieve its stated objectives are remedied, there is likely to be little support or enthusiasm among labor leaders for addressing the broader policy agenda.

Coping with Employer Strategies. By the 1980s the interplay of public policy and employer strategies had resulted in a situation where few representation elections were being held; where elections took place, fewer union victories and new contracts ensued. While it is hard to estimate the exact proportions, it is clear that a representation election was never held in the vast majority of new employment relationships created in the past two decades. Employer strategies of targeting employment expansion to new locations plus their introduction of the new human resource management model made employee choice a moot issue. In other words, employers were able to control the preconditions of the employment relationship so as to prevent unions from establishing a basis for holding representation elections.

For the small fraction of the workforce (less than 1 percent) exposed to the electioneering process in any given year, another set of employer tactics dominated the outcomes. As a result of the Taft-Hartley Act and subsequent decisions of the NLRB, employers have been able to engage in what some have labeled privileged electioneering[4] by pointing out the consequences of a union victory for the firm's economic viability. Moreover, an increasing number of employers have gone a step further and broken the law by engaging in a variety of coercive and intimidating actions. We shall have more to say about policy options for dealing with illegal employer behavior at the election stage of the union recognition process later. Setting this aside for now, policy makers need to recognize a more basic fact: the standard repertoire of employer strategies of reallocating investments to greenfield sites, use of sophisticated human resource management techniques, and aggressive albeit legal electioneering together have produced a result that is very different from the original premise of the NLRA, namely that collective bargaining would be preserved and strengthened by the use of representation elections to determine union status in new locations.

Whether or not public policy should (or could) address this unexpected outcome is complicated by the fact that the employer strategies reflect not just management's union-avoidance motives and values but also sound business decisions and innovations in human resource practices that are often beneficial and usually well received by employees. Thus the policy challenge is to continue encouraging innovation in human resource management practice but also to provide workers and union leaders with a fair opportunity to counter the union-avoidance elements that lie behind some of these employer strategies.

We do not believe that public policy can change underlying employer values or ideologies toward unions. Policy's role at this level of employer decision making may be to eliminate any legal obstacles that constrain the ability of unions and companies to discuss the competitive issues, human resource practices, and alternative forms of union representation that govern investment decisions and the design of new worksites. Encouraging more private dialogue and experimentation on this complex issue may be the appropriate direction for public policy at this time.

Reforming the Election Process. There is a growing consensus among industrial relations and labor-law researchers that the current law and procedures governing union certification are not fulfilling the intent of the act.[5] We share this view, based not only on our research but also on the empirical evidence from other studies that have demonstrated the (1) increased illegal conduct of employers during representation elections and initial contract bargaining processes; (2) significant effects illegal conduct has on the outcomes of elections and first contract bargaining; and (3) negative consequences of long delays in the appeal and enforcement procedures that characterize NLRA-based disputes that are not resolved informally by the parties and NLRB representatives. These findings are reinforced by the data presented in chapter 3, which show that the formal procedures provided in the law have not produced many new union members in those firms that assigned a high priority to union avoidance or in those firms opening new establishments in the 1970s and early 1980s. Thus, if American labor policy is to uphold the objectives stated in the National Labor Relations Act—to promote collective bargaining and provide employees with the opportunity to decide whether or not to be represented by labor organizations of their choosing—then the current law and its administration require substantial reform.

Specialists in labor law have suggested a number of changes in the law, ranging from reforms in NLRB administrative procedures to certification based on the signing of authorization cards or the arbitration of first contracts.[6] Our research suggests that minor changes will not have a significant remedial effect. To be effective, future procedures governing the process of union recognition must be based on the premise that American employers are strongly opposed to union representation and that the specific tactics used during representation elections reflect policies established at a much higher level of corporate decision making. Given the deep-seated managerial resistance to union organizing, statute and procedure revisions will need to be sufficiently comprehensive and strong to allow employee preferences to determine the outcome. This will require both major administrative reform to impose strong, certain, and speedy penalties on firms that encourage illegal union-avoidance policies and changes in the law that provide a means of resolving bargaining impasses in situations where employers have demonstrated their lack of commitment to the intent of the law.

PUBLIC POLICY AND BARGAINING PRACTICE

Correcting the serious problems in union representation election processes may be a necessary, but certainly not a sufficient, step in closing the gap between the stated objectives of public policy and contemporary practices. Indeed, our three-tier framework highlights a number of areas where the practices we describe challenge the assumptions built into U.S. labor policies. We start by discussing changes in practice at the workplace and move up to the levels of collective bargaining and strategic decision making.

New innovations at the workplace and strategic levels of industrial relations challenge at least four legal doctrines: (1) employer domination of labor organizations, (2) exclusive representation, (3) the legal distinction between workers and supervisors, and (4) the distinction among mandatory, permissive, and illegal bargaining subjects.[7]

In a number of nonunion workplaces, worker-participation processes and new forms of communication between management and the workforce violate or come very close to violating the NLRA's prohibition against company domination of labor organizations. That doctrine states that it is illegal for an employer to support or assist organizations of employees that represent workers in discussions over wages, hours, and working conditions. As we reported in chapter 6, despite stated policies to the contrary, quality-of-work-life discussions in unionized settings over time cannot be kept isolated from the issues covered by collective bargaining contracts. There is no reason to believe that successful participatory processes in nonunion settings will be any different. Indeed, as we observed, if participation programs are kept separate from the determination of basic work practices, then these programs will not reach their full potential as a means for introducing changes that can significantly improve organizational performance. The provision against company domination was inserted into the NLRA after considerable debate in response to a general concern that developed over company unionism in the 1920s. Policy makers now need to reconcile the desirability of informal means of employee participation in decision making and the need to protect against the potential abuses of company unions.

Where unions exist but are not significantly involved in worker-participation processes initiated by the employer, a challenge to the concept of exclusive representation may exist.[8] The same is true for some of the modern complaint and individual appeal procedures that are not part of any contractual grievance procedures. Yet it is not sensible to constrain the use of these practices simply because they violate the principle of exclusive representation. Again, policy makers need to reconsider how to preserve one of the original objectives of the law, in this case exclusive representation, while also encouraging innovative human resource management.

Those worker-participation programs that include semi-autonomous work groups or in other ways blur the distinction between workers and supervisors also conflict with existing labor law. Giving workers the power to make independent judgments regarding discipline, promotion, job assignment, hiring, and so forth would appear to qualify them as supervisors, based on the Taft-Hartley definition of a supervisor and the subsequent administration of the law. Moreover, in most modern organizations the role of the supervisor is quite different from the one envisioned in the law. New technology increases the analytical demands placed on many employees and requires increased teamwork and cooperation within and among work units. Furthermore, supervisory responsibilities will continue to filter into lower-level jobs as organizations decentralize decision making to employees traditionally categorized as nonsupervisory. Legal boundaries that attempt to draw a clear separation between workers and supervisors only inhibit development of new forms of work organization that are best suited to new technologies and new economic pressures, and are outmoded.

Decentralizing power to nonsupervisory workers threatens the job security and advancement of supervisory and middle-managerial employees. Under most worker-participation processes, supervisory employees tend to have less representation since they lack a union's organizational base and resources. It is not surprising, therefore, that numerous studies have documented the resistance of supervisors and middle managers to such processes. Thus questions concerning the legitimate job rights and employer expectations of supervisors and middle managers need to be reexamined based on the actual roles these groups perform in modern organizations. Indeed, the basic doctrines used to justify the exclusion of supervisors from NLRA protections should be reexamined.

In those settings where unions have achieved significant roles in strategic and business decision making, the old distinctions among mandatory, permissive, and illegal subjects of bargaining become impossible to discern and impractical. One of the messages of chapters 6 and 7 is that in many situations labor and management have chosen to broaden the bargaining agenda and informal discussions to subjects that actually are illegal or nonmandatory subjects. Moreover, if one underlying objective of our national labor policy is to provide employees with a means of participating in those decisions that most directly influence wages, hours, and working conditions, then we need to reconsider how far into the determination and modification of basic business decisions employees should be allowed and encouraged to go. Clearly, in the current environment some form of effective employee representation at the strategic level is required to meet the original goals of the NLRA. Yet not only does the prevailing public policy not actively encourage such a role, it provides a legal basis for employers to resist it.

These issues do not exhaust the choices policy makers will confront as they respond to the changes underway in the practice of industrial relations. Indeed, federal and state government decision makers will need to decide how active a role to play in the innovation process. To date, except for the efforts of selected divisions within the Department of Labor and the Federal Mediation and Conciliation Service, the federal government has not been involved in the diffusion or promotion of industrial relations reform. Government policy makers need to examine their role in this process as well as the changing roles of labor and management.

Choices for the Parties in Existing
Bargaining Relationships

In industrial relations, as in any social relationship, the parties focus their energies on those activities that have the potential to affect critical decisions. In recent years the locus of critical decision making in industrial relations and the power to influence events have shifted to activities above and below the level of negotiating collective agreements. Not surprisingly, what we have been witnessing in bargaining practice are the efforts of management and unions to respond to this shift.

In fact, management has adjusted more quickly than either labor unions or public policy. It was management that initiated the new nonunion personnel practices at the workplace and accelerated their expansion through strategic investment decisions. When management adjusted to economic pressures by broadening its activities to the workplace and strategic levels, it benefited from a significant power advantage and operated as the driving force in introducing change in industrial relations. The slow response of unions to management's broadened scope of activity has meant that their ability to influence critical events and, therefore, to effectively serve the needs of American workers, has declined.

It is not surprising that unions have begun searching for strategies to counteract the advantages employers have at higher and lower levels of industrial relations activity. Yet it has proven extremely difficult for unions to establish a meaningful role and achieve effective influence at strategic and workplace levels of decision making.

As analyzed in chapter 7, unions face particularly difficult problems when they try to expand their influence at the strategic level. For one thing, unions often confront strong resistance from management to their participation at this level. Opposition to union participation in business decision making also exists in the minds of many union leaders steeped in the American tradition of business unionism. Furthermore, American society historically has valued the entrepreneurial autonomy believed to be required for a dynamic and innovative economy. Government policy reflected this view by not regulating or otherwise intruding in strategic managerial decision-making except in periods of extreme economic or national security crises. Finally, rank-and-file workers have shown little interest in participation in broad managerial policies, except where strategic decisions are seen as influencing bread-and-butter job security concerns.

Unions face a somewhat different challenge at the workplace level. Here unions had historically achieved a significant role through job-control unionism. Enforcing detailed contracts through the grievance procedure gave U.S. unions a more powerful position at the plant level than any other labor movement. But it is precisely the key components of that base of power—the detailed contract, the uniformity in its administration, the constraints on communication, the narrowness of job designs, and the emphasis on stability—that are being challenged by new forms of employee participation, more flexible forms of work organization, and technological change. As outlined in chapter 6, unions are searching for ways to reorient practices at the workplace level so as to lower costs and increase flexibility in the deployment of human resources. The challenge confronting unions is how to define and sustain new roles in the midst of more flexible and less formal work practices. Developing these new roles is made more difficult by the legacy of mistrust that prevails between unions and employers as a result of employers' ideological resistance to unions.

Unions also face another dilemma in fashioning an effective role in representing workers on a day-to-day basis. On the one hand, the traditions of grievance handling, reinforced by the doctrine of fair representation, lead to more formalism and legalism (illustrated by the long delays and large backlog of grievances associated with the arbitration step in a number of industries). On the other hand, the new work systems and technologies require immediate problem solving and a clinical approach to issues. Just how this tension will be resolved remains to be seen. Clearly, however, part of the solution will lie in giving greater emphasis to continuous change and representation at the workplace, which involves multiple forums for solving problems and resolving conflicts.

The choices open to the parties in existing bargaining relationships will vary considerably depending on the current state of unionization in the firm and industry. Thus we shall discuss separately the choices facing parties in highly unionized and in partially unionized firms.

HIGHLY UNIONIZED FIRMS

Firms in which a large majority of the employees are organized and that operate in growing or stable markets are likely to continue to relate to their employees and unions in ways that approximate the traditional New Deal industrial relations pattern. The fact that these firms do not face severe environmental pressures makes it likely that they would choose to avoid the shifts in the locus of industrial relations activity and the innovations occurring in other sectors of the economy. As long as it is difficult for new competitors to enter these firms' markets, there is little incentive to change. However, outside of some public utilities, defense and aerospace contractors, and retail trade stores in highly unionized regions, few private-sector industries or firms currently enjoy these stable conditions or are likely to face them in the foreseeable future. Thus the stable, highly unionized sector represents a small and declining proportion of the total population of private sector union-management relationships.

In contrast, most highly unionized firms are likely to face severe external competition from domestic or foreign sources and/or mature rather than rapidly growing markets. In these settings, where union avoidance is not a viable short-run alternative for management, we expect to see continued vigorous efforts to innovate at all levels of industrial relations. Where unions still represent a majority of employees, they are less threatened by the fear that industrial relations innovations are merely a union-avoidance strategy. So it is in these settings that we expect to see the greatest union support for industrial relations innovation.

At the workplace level in highly organized firms there is likely to be a continuation of cooperative programs and other experiments that modify traditional work organization. As we observed in chapter 6, it is inevitable that QWL programs that were initially narrowly focused will expand to include more significant changes in work organization and broader forms of worker and union involvement in business decisions.

American unions will continue to be under intense pressure to move away from many of the job-control traditions associated with the New Deal model of collective bargaining. The highly detailed contract with uniform rules governing individual job rights fit a stable, high-volume, and mass-oriented production system. But the job control model is at a severe competitive disadvantage in a world of just-in-time inventories, short production runs, technologies that require greater analytical reasoning, and a workforce with greater interest in how work is conducted. For these reasons, we believe that while the fad of quality circles and the narrow forms of QWL programs may dissipate, efforts on the part of firms and local unions to foster greater employee participation and to adopt more flexible forms of work organization will be a constant feature of workplace industrial relations in the future. This in turn will require management and unions to train their professionals and elected leaders to facilitate problem solving while preserving employees' due-process rights.

Union support for new forms of work organization and worker-participation processes is likely to diffuse the fastest in settings where the union is accepted by management as a legitimate party to the employment relationship, the process is effective in producing tangible improvements in employment security and economic welfare, and the efforts at the workplace are reinforced and supported by decisions made at the collective bargaining and strategic levels of industrial relations.

We also expect that local union leaders will be more receptive to experimentation in new workplace activities than national union leaders. It is local union officers who most directly face employment losses when management shifts business to lower-cost locations. Thus it is local union leaders who are led to workplace experimentation as a pragmatic response rather than as part of a consciously planned national union strategy. Union leaders' response to quality-of-work initiatives generally followed this pattern. Those leaders who support reform efforts at the workplace, however, are likely to experience internal political opposition. The outcomes of these political conflicts will be influenced by such factors as the extent to which the reforms produce tangible gains and the degree of reinforcement received from union and management leaders at higher levels of decision making.

At the level of collective bargaining, pressures to moderate the growth in compensation and to adopt contingent compensation structures are likely to continue. Profit sharing, gain sharing, employee stock ownership plans, and bonus incentive and performance-based pay systems will take on added importance as managers search for ways to become more competitive while rewarding employees for helping them to do so. At the same time, we do not expect that unions, particularly those in highly organized firms, will eliminate the important role that contract negotiation plays in labor-management relations. In fact, union leaders will be under intense pressure in many situations to recoup the cuts in wages and fringe benefits that were made during the concessionary era. But the biggest challenge for unions by far will be to find ways to integrate collective bargaining activities with the expanding range of activities emerging at the workplace and strategic levels.

At the highest levels of strategic decision making, information sharing, consultation, and other forms of joint activity between union and management representatives over questions of long-term business strategies, investments in new plant designs, and employment stabilization policies are all likely to expand. It is in these highly unionized firms that we already see the most significant efforts by unions and employers to integrate their strategies across the different levels of their relationships.

Achieving this type of alignment of policies across levels will require a mixture of greater centralization and decentralization in management and union decision making. Greater centralization in the locus of union activities is needed for union leaders to engage line managers and executives at the level where strategic decisions are made. On the other hand, greater decentralization to support variation in the development and operation of work practices among workers in the same bargaining unit is needed to adapt compensation, work rules, and employee involvement processes to the reality of a more volatile and uncertain economic environment.

The success of these efforts will depend on the ability of the parties to identify and fill market niches that can support a high-productivity/high-wage strategy. This approach is unlikely to work in firms that seek to be the industry's low-cost/high-volume standard goods producer or service provider. This type of reform strategy also would be vulnerable to a deep economic recession, which would intensify cost pressures and perhaps tempt management to pursue an alternative non-union strategy. Moreover, the high-productivity/high-wage business strategy requires a matching union strategy. That is, it can succeed only if union leaders are willing and able to expand their roles to the strategic and workplace levels and integrate their policies across the three levels of the relationship.

Continued innovation along these lines will not go unchallenged by critics within union and management organizations. For example, as noted in chapter 7, some national and local union leaders in the UAW oppose the Saturn agreement and other steps underway by unions to get more heavily involved in strategic issues. Similarly, GM management has come under fire from many managers and some anti-union pressure groups, such as the National Right to Work Committee, who would prefer the firm to conform to the more pervasive union-avoidance strategy. While the outcomes of these political and internal power struggles cannot be predicted easily, it is clear that the failure of these innovative efforts would reinforce the determination of American management to contain or avoid unions in the future. Failure of the reform strategy also would produce a more rapid decline in U.S. manufacturing and other high-wage employment as management would accelerate the switch to offshore production or sourcing as an alternative cost-reduction strategy.

Just as the unions and companies in the auto industry served as pattern setters in industrial relations as the New Deal model was developing, in highly organized worksites they are currently involved in the widest experimentation. Their efforts will determine whether auto labor relations once again serve as a pattern setter for unions and companies in other industries or prove to be the last vestige of a model no longer suited to a highly competitive and open economy.

PARTIALLY UNIONIZED FIRMS

The internal contradictions in industrial relations policies and strategies are likely to be greatest among partially unionized firms. Yet in these settings the dominant management strategy of working cooperatively with union leadership where unions exist and avoiding unionization in new establishments is likely to continue as long as unions are unable to gain sufficient power to challenge management at the strategic level. This management strategy will be especially hard to change as long as the economic incentives facing management to reallocate resources from union to nonunion settings also remain strong.

In partially unionized firms management has been aggressive in shifting resources to new worksites while simultaneously deploying innovative human resource management systems. These new systems are offensive—they keep unions out—while they are also affirmative—they produce good economic performance outcomes. Indeed, there is some evidence that partially unionized firms have introduced more extensive innovations in human resource management than firms that are either highly unionized or totally unorganized.

While the degree of cooperation in labor-management relationships in these settings could vary from cooperative to highly adversarial, several factors are likely to be common. Management will continue to maintain as much decentralization in bargaining structures as possible in its attempt to achieve wage bargains that close the gap between its facilities and external competitors. High-cost, low-profit operations will be vulnerable to plant closings, sale to other firms, or gradual shrinkage as investment dollars are channeled to newer, more profitable, and generally nonunion alternatives.

Among the firms and unions in these settings, those most likely to develop relationship patterns that balance employers' needs for cost control and employees' need for employment security are firms that make a business strategy decision to stay in existing lines of business. The presence of large asset-redeployment costs or some other locational advantages will work in favor of existing sites in these firms.

It is difficult to predict how much innovation and worker participation will occur at the workplace and whether incremental innovations will eventually change managerial strategies and values at the corporate level. The range of discretion open to these parties is quite broad, since the environment does not dictate the choice or preordain the success of any particular industrial relations strategy. Our research shows that local union leaders are not likely to get much support or guidance from national unions when they face the decision of whether or not to participate in cooperative programs. National union leaders often oppose such programs on grounds that they are inconsistent with the simultaneous expansion in these firms of nonunion facilities, but these leaders rarely have an alternative strategy to recommend to hard-pressed local leaders.

In sum, in a large number of partially organized bargaining relationships, the future of industrial relations could develop along one of two very different paths, depending on whether the parties choose to continue evolving within their current state of internal contradiction or embark on a major realignment of policies and practices at the three levels of their relationship. Because this is such a large and pivotal sector of the U.S. economy and industrial relations system, we will sketch out what we see as the probable consequences of these distinct choices.

Continuing the current trends means that management will seek economic concessions in collective bargaining and labor-management cooperation at the workplace wherever local conditions will support them. However, it will continue to resist expansion of the union's role at the level of corporate strategy and will continue to channel new investments and human resource management innovations into nonunion alternatives. Union leaders will remain unsupportive of labor-management cooperation at the workplace; or those who support it will experience increasing political opposition both from an aging, shrinking, and more short-run-oriented rank and file and from national leaders who see negative long-term consequences for the union of the corporation's investment strategies. The spiral of low trust and high conflict described in chapter 4 is likely to intensify in these relationships, making it even more difficult for existing facilities to compete and speeding the process of employment decline and disinvestment. While this is a rather negative scenario, it is unfortunately the path that a very large number of partially unionized firms and their unions are following.

Thus, without some type of accord, we envision the parties in the partially organized sector to continue to choose those strategies that are producing the divergence of the two industrial relations systems. Management will continue to opt for an expansion of the human-resource system that operates without unions, while unions will stay fixed in their embrace of the philosophy and tactics of the New Deal system.

An alternative path would be one in which the parties choose to build on the incremental changes at the workplace and in collective bargaining that some have achieved in recent years and to extend these changes by overcoming the internal contradictions in their relationship. This in turn would involve broadening the scope of labor-management discussions, perhaps at first on selected topics or specific investment choices facing management, to see if new agreements can be found that trade union institutional security for a union commitment to continued innovation in work practices and rules that affect the firm's competitive performance. For this type of new bargain to work, however, will require the firm to commit resources to its unionized sector for the long term. It cannot work in settings where the firm is planning to redeploy its assets to activities and investments that cannot be carried out by its current workforce in its current locations. It also cannot work if the firm is committed to a low-wage or labor-cost minimization business strategy, because nonunion and/or foreign competitors will continue to underbid labor costs to levels unacceptable to American workers and their union leaders. In turn, this strategy cannot work unless the union leadership takes the initiative to both demand that the bargaining agenda be broadened to address the long-run strategic decisions that influence the economic future of relationship and demonstrate a clear and sustainable commitment to a new role at the workplace, in collective bargaining, and at the level of corporate decision making.

For labor and management to embark on this alternative path, both must see in it the prospect of tangible benefits and a reduction in risks. For management, this means that union representation will need to be seen as adding value or playing a positive role in managing the myriad of problems associated with introducing new technology, retraining and redeploying an existing workforce, and introducing human resource management practices that can equal or outperform nonunion alternatives. For union leaders, this path must offer the potential of more jobs at wages and working conditions that are equal to or better than those obtainable from traditional unionism.

But in addition to perceiving potential benefits, both management and union leaders will need to reduce the risks to each other associated with this alternative path. Managers, for example, fear that while creative union leaders might be able to produce the benefits just outlined, internal union politics is likely to produce a change in leadership that favors a return to the traditional system and its attendant problems. While this is a real possibility, our preliminary conclusions from some of our ongoing research is that union leaders who embrace these new strategies are more likely to succeed and survive than are those wedded to the traditional styles and tactics of the New Deal labor-management system. Their position is likely to further solidify over time as more of the rank and file who elect union leaders recognize the trade-offs associated with the two paths. National union leaders can, however, play an extremely important role in strengthening and reinforcing the political positions of those local leaders who embrace these new approaches and thereby reduce the risks to their continuity that management perceives.

On the union side, there are not only political risks but also risks that all of the cooperation or other innovations they support at the local level will not pay off unless they achieve access to strategic management decisions that affect the long-run security of the workforce and the institutional future of the union. That is, the path chosen must increase the chances of achieving the type of linkage in industrial relations practices across the strategic, collective bargaining, and workplace levels described in chapter 7.

It is clearly more difficult for management and labor leaders to embark on this alternative path than for them to maintain their current relationship patterns. Because, however, we see this option as one that more firms and unions need to take if the decline in both union jobs and the competitive performance of partially unionized firms is to be reversed, it deserves greater experimentation and support. More than any other illustration we have to offer, this demonstrates the important effect that the parties' strategic chocies will have on the future of industrial relations.

Choices in Nonunion Employment Relationships

Our emphasis on understanding the transformations occurring in union-management relations may seem to imply that the unorganized sector of the economy is in a state of equilibrium. This is no more true than was the case for the unionized sector during the postwar years, when labor-management relations appeared to be stable and unassailable. Nonunion firms are subject to the same market and technological pressures as are union firms, and nonunion employees do not have fundamentally different sets of values, expectations, or interests than do unionized employees. Moreover, throughout our analysis we have underscored the importance of understanding the interdependent character of the union and nonunion sectors. Thus in this section we examine the range of choices facing employers, workers, and unions that will affect the future course of industrial relations in nonunion employment relationships.

DYNAMICS OF MANAGEMENT HUMAN-RESOURCE POLICIES

Many of the totally unorganized firms that started up and grew rapidly in the 1960s and 1970s are now facing the challenge of adapting their human resource management practices to maturing, more price-competitive markets. Like their unionized counterparts, these firms will experience increased pressure to lower labor costs, streamline staffing levels, adopt labor-saving technologies, and redeploy workers and assets. Human-resource management professionals will be asked to adjust policies away from those that were designed to serve a business strategy that valued low turnover and high commitment to ones that better serve emerging strategies that depend on low labor costs. As these pressures increase, so does the potential for the emergence of conflict between employee expectations for employment continuity and career progression and management's efforts to contain costs. Moreover, these pressures are likely to affect employees at all levels of the firm, from hourly employees to middle managers and executives.

Whether firms reduce their commitment to the innovative human-resource policies that predominated during their startup and growth years will depend on the outcomes of the internal political debates and power struggles between the human resource executives responsible

246

for developing these policies and those line managers who stress short-term cost control and speedy adjustment to changed business conditions. We would expect that only in those firms where the human-resource policies are supported by deeply engrained values held by top executives will the human resource management staffs maintain sufficient power and influence to avoid abandonment of innovative policies. Moreover, we expect this to occur only in a limited number of large, highly visible firms where these values have already demonstrated their economic rationality and survival power through previous periods of economic adjustment.

An example is the manner in which IBM has responded to competitive pressures in such product areas as typewriters and memory chips by rebalancing the workforces involved—and achieving substantial manpower shifts without breaching its historic commitment to employment continuity. Precisely because the personnel function plays such a key role at all levels of the company and because top executives firmly value employment security, IBM fashioned transition plans that balanced the need to lower costs (redeployment of support personnel to work on the lines) with the need to implement a pro-employee redeployment plan (a transition period of several years was provided for).[9]

In firms whose top executives lack this deep commitment, strategies decided at the top of the organization will begin to produce the types of contradictions and mistrust among managers and employees that now prevail in many unionized firms that already faced economic and organizational restructuring. We expect this to be the predominant situation in the majority of midsize and smaller firms, and particularly in those firms that are most highly exposed to market pressures.

Moreover, to the extent that new technologies require higher degrees of consultation and participation in order to reach their full potential, nonunion employers will have to overcome their historic reluctance to establish formal structures that give employees voice and participation in strategic decisions (such as the introduction of new technology). The fear that formal structures for participation may lead to unionization may eventually limit the amount of participation nonunion employers are willing to extend to their employees and, ultimately, may limit the economic performance of these firms.

The pressure to shift to more cost-conscious human resource policies as businesses move to the mature stages of their life cycle is especially strong in those firms that adopt a business strategy that focuses on the high-volume–low-cost product segment of the market. Thus it is in these organizations that the tendency for internal contradictions and mistrust is greatest. In contrast, in firms that adapt to maturing product markets by seeking specialized niches, new products, and other business strategies that require high levels of employee expertise and autonomy, the pressures to shift to a human resource policy focused on cost reduction will not be as strong.

NEW START-UPS

Given our belief that new organizations tend to adopt the human-resource practices of the most visible and successful firms in their environment, we would expect that new organizations, or new units of existing organizations, will continue to follow the work organization and communication strategies of the most innovative nonunion firms. Moreover, given the growth strategies and strong values of the founders and entrepreneurs who lead new firms, employees in these new firms are likely to show little interest in forming traditional collective bargaining relationships. Thus, unless there is a significant shift in union-organizing strategies, there is every reason to believe that new firms will continue to be as successful in avoiding union organization in the future as they have been in the past two decades.

UNREPRESENTED WORKERS

Increased competition and changes in technology and in business and industrial relations strategies affect unrepresented employees as well as organized ones. Perhaps the overriding implication to draw from the diverse data summarized in chapter 8 is that workers in the future will seek a variety of direct and indirect representation strategies for pursuing their work-related interests. For example, professionals have a long tradition of forming occupational associations to enhance and protect their status. Some leaders from within the professional ranks may expand their efforts to influence the employment standards of their associates through such traditional strategies as salary surveys, career development and training programs, and occupational licensing. Others may follow the lead of such groups as nurses, teachers, and professional athletes and seek collective bargaining rights.

By contrast, clerical and blue-collar employees often lack a strong occupational or professional identity. Moreover, few of these workers can identify a particular occupational association that promotes their employment standards. These groups also have less individual bargaining power because they are more easily replaced by employers, their labor-market alternatives are generally less favorable, and their geographic mobility is more constrained. These are the employees, consequently, who are most dependent on the quality of the human-resource management practices provided by their employers, the positive threat effects of potential union organizing, and the labor standards provided via public policies. Whether these employees become more aggressive in seeking participation regarding decisions affecting their jobs will depend on how well they think employers are managing their interests and on the availability of viable options for formal representation.

Managers and supervisors not covered by the National Labor Relations Act are perhaps those whose employment prospects are most at risk due to changes in technology, decentralization of decision making to nonsupervisory employees, and the growing interest of top executives in cutting costs. At the same time, these employees have little legal or organizational protection, and often considerably less individual bargaining power. This group of most affected but least protected employees is likely to lead to an increased demand for stronger due-process rights and procedures for individual employees.

The most significant labor-market development of the 1980s has been the growth in temporary and part-time employment. At this point we know very little about the nature of these employment relationships or the people who fill these jobs. One thing that is clear is that the traditional union organizing and representation strategies found in the New Deal model (with the possible exception of craft-type representation for temporary workers who have a strong occupational identification, such as contract engineers) do not fit these employees and employment relationships. Yet it is possible that these types of employees eventually will seek some more organized form of representation, especially in light of their limited current involvement in decision making.

IMPLICATIONS FOR UNION ORGANIZING

Some industrial relations researchers and practitioners have argued that they have "great faith in the stupidity of American management." As soon as unions become too weak to be viewed as a viable threat and as soon as economic conditions require cutbacks in employment costs, management commitment to innovative human resource practices will weaken and unions will once again rebound. As the preceding discussion suggests, we do not agree with this simplistic view of managerial behavior. Human-resource practices have demonstrated their durability through ups and downs in a large number of firms precisely because they are not solely or primarily motivated by the goal of avoiding unions. Instead, many of these practices fit the economic needs of their firm and the expectations of employees. Nor do we believe that even if managerial commitment to human resource innovation diminishes, workers will automatically turn to unions as a response. Rather, for unions to organize a sufficient number of workers to reverse their declining membership will require that they both improve and modify their standard organizing strategies for those groups of employees who can benefit from traditional collective bargaining and expand the range of organizing and representational strategies to meet the needs of those groups for whom the traditional package of union services is not well suited. The individual membership option currently being developed by some unions, which includes labor-market information, fringe benefits, career counseling, and legal assistance, might provide one means of addressing the needs and interests of some professionals, temporary and part-time workers, and others not permanently attached to an identifiable employer. But much more than this will be required for a resurgence of the labor movement.

Alternative Scenarios for U.S. Industrial Relations

It should be clear by now that no single set of choices or pattern of evolution will capture the diversity of American industrial relations in the future any more than a single pattern characterized the past. The U.S. industrial relations system will continue to display considerable diversity across industries, firms, unions, and occupations. Moreover, there is every reason to expect that the future will continue to be characterized not only by the historic dynamic interplay between union and nonunion systems but also by an increasing variety of arrangements governing employment relationships. Unions and collective bargaining as envisioned by the New Deal are not likely to wither away or disappear completely, nor to quickly reestablish their dominance as the primary institutional mechanism governing employment relationships. Rather unions will continue to face intense pressure to modify their traditional strategies in order both to cope with changes in business and human resource management strategies and to give workers more say over the issues that affect their working lives. Meanwhile, those responsible for managing human resources in nonunion organizations will face challenges as their organizations age and move through later and more competitive stages of their life cycles.

Despite this diversity, certain broad patterns of evolution appear to be identifiable, given different assumptions about the nature of the future environment and the likely choices that will be made by management, labor, and public policy makers. Some of the plausible alternative scenarios are outlined in the following sections as a way of summarizing what we see as the overall consequences of the complex of choices reviewed in this chapter.[10]

SCENARIO 1: CONTINUATION OF CURRENT TRENDS

While we already have noted that past and current trends in industrial relations seldom can be counted on to last long, continuation of current trends is not only a distinct possibility, it is the most probable short-run outcome. Thus if we assume no major upheavals in the political and social environment, a continuation of competitive pressures at their current levels, no change in labor laws, and a continuation of current management and union strategies, we might expect:

1. Private-sector unionization will continue to decline while public-sector unionization will remain stable. By 1990 less than 15 percent of the labor force is likely to be unionized. The decline could be even steeper if we experience the intensified rate of technological change that many experts expect.
2. Unionization will not, however, continue to decline to zero. Instead unions will be more concentrated in selected sectors—the public sector; those industries that are currently very highly organized, such as automobiles; and those industries and firms that are more protected from foreign competition, such as utilities, defense contractors, and aerospace firms.
3. As the difference in age distributions of union and nonunion workers and establishments increases, unionized relationships will become less innovative, union-management relations will become more adversarial, managerial opposition will intensify, and management will speed the pace of outsourcing and technological change in order to further reduce vulnerability to unionization.
4. The threat effect of unions on nonunion employers will decline and slow the pace of innovation of human resource management practices, weaken the influence of human resource management professionals within nonunion firms, and lead to a weakened commitment to human resource management concerns in some organizations.

251

Under this scenario American society appears to be destined to relive its past history. That is, as unions decline to the point that their survival as a viable economic and social force is threatened, intensified labor-management conflicts will occur and eventually, when or if the political pendulum swings back to favor labor, a new set of legal and private institutions will emerge to govern employment relationships. This scenario suggests that events ultimately will overtake the ability of the parties to control their future. However, the pressures must intensify significantly before a crisis develops and new institutional forms emerge.

SCENARIO 2: LABOR-LAW REFORM

In a modest deviation from the preceding scenario, elected political leaders are convinced that the current problems in labor law require remediation but all other conditions just described prevail. Our best prediction is that if the rules governing union representation elections were to be reformed—for example, to eliminate delays, stiffen penalities for illegal conduct, and eliminate the problems experienced in achieving initial contracts—unions would increase their organizing success rates with low-wage workers in service industries and occupations and in small bargaining units. These changes would not, however, make any significant difference in the unionization rate of large firms or in the quality of the union-management relationship in existing bargaining units. Thus union membership would continue to decline, albeit at a somewhat slower pace, and the rest of scenario 1 would evolve, but again perhaps more slowly.

SCENARIO 3: DIFFUSION OF LABOR-MANAGEMENT INNOVATIONS

If labor-law reform were combined with a broader diffusion of innovations in existing bargaining relationships, particularly in partially unionized firms, the improvements in economic performance and the quality of labor-management relations might lead to a stabilization in employment and union membership around its current levels. Employment losses due to technological change in existing union sectors might be offset by more effective opportunities to organize workers in the low-wage service sector and in those new and existing manufacturing organizations where intensified competitive pressures could lead to a weakening of management's commitment to human resource management issues.

SCENARIO 4: NEW ORGANIZING STRATEGIES

By now it should be clear that to reverse the downward trend in worker representation we believe it will take all of the preceding changes plus the emergence of new strategies for organizing and representing individuals found in the growing occupations and industries. While all of these developments are possible, their realization requires the most fundamental shifts in the values, strategies, policies, and practices of all parties to industrial relations. For this reason, this scenario is perhaps least likely, yet the most interesting, to contemplate.

Predicting which of these views of the future will actually capture the evolutionary path of U.S. industrial relations is beyond our power. Determining which of these scenarios becomes the dominant path is, however, the central challenge facing the parties.

Notes

Chapter 1

1. Illustrative of these reports is the *New York Times* series "The Crisis of Trade Unionism," 15–22 January 1985.

2. "The New Industrial Relations," *Business Week,* 11 May 1981.

3. See "The Changing Situation of Workers and Their Unions," a report by the AFL-CIO Committee on the Evolution of Work, February 1985.

4. See, for example, the 1982 presidential address to the Industrial Relations Research Association by Milton Derber, "Are We in a New Stage?" *Proceedings of the Thirty-fifth Annual Meeting of the Industrial Relations Research Association* (Madison, Wis.: Industrial Relations Research Association, 1983), 1–9.

5. See John R. Commons, *A Documentary History of American Industrial Society,* vol. 5 (Cleveland: A. H. Clark Co., 1911), 19; and also Leo Wolman, *The Ebb and Flow in Trade Unionism* (New York: National Bureau of Economic Research, 1936).

6. John T. Dunlop, *Industrial Relations Systems* (New York: Holt, Rinehart, and Winston, 1958).

7. Ibid, 17. Dunlop's original statement on ideology allows for the possibility of the absence of a shared ideology. He notes that in such a case conflicts would arise over the very structure or organization of an industrial relations system. Unfortunately, this caveat was overlooked in most subsequent research. Indeed, the rest of Dunlop's analysis is predicated on the implicit assumption that a shared ideology prevailed in the post–New Deal environment in the United States. Yet, as we argue more fully throughout this book, it is the absence of a shared ideology that in part helps explain changes in the U.S. industrial relations system over time.

8. Clark Kerr, Frederick Harbison, John T. Dunlop, and Charles Myers, *Industrialism and Industrial Man* (Cambridge, Mass.: Harvard University Press, 1960).

9. This framework reflected a more general trend in social science that stressed concepts such as "industrial society," "modernization," "end of ideology," and so forth. For examples of this work, see Gabriel Almond and Sidney Verba, *The Civic Culture* (Princeton, N.J.: Princeton University Press, 1963); Daniel Bell, *The End of Ideology* (New York: The Free Press, 1960); and Seymour Martin Lipset, *Political Man* (Garden City, N.Y.: Doubleday, 1960).

10. See the discussion in chapter 2 and Larry T. Adams, "Changing Employment Patterns of Organized Workers," *Monthly Labor Review* 108, no. 2 (1985):25–31.

11. Representative of this view is the following passage from the most widely read textbook on collective bargaining in the 1960s:

> Collective bargaining today is to be distinguished from union-management relations in the past not only in its bilateral character (in contrast to the

earlier unilateral imposition of terms) but also in its incidence, its systematization, its continuity, and its acceptance. . . . Although collective bargaining relationships still have a mortality rating, they are becoming more and more entrenched, particularly in the larger companies, and the possibility that collective bargaining might pass from the industrial scene is no longer a live one. This is due partly to the fact that managements now recognize the need for collective bargaining for reasons of efficiency if for no others; bargaining through representatives freely selected by employees has been accepted by some, though not all, managers as a feasible and desirable method of meeting that need.

Neil W. Chamberlain and James W. Kuhn, *Collective Bargaining,* 2nd ed. (New York: McGraw-Hill, 1965):47.

12. See, for example, Richard Lester, *As Unions Mature* (Princeton, N.J.: Princeton University Press, 1958).

13. An initial description of the "shock effect" of unions is presented in Sumner Slichter, *Union Policies and Industrial Management* (Washington, D.C.: The Brookings Institution, 1941). For a follow-up study that discusses managerial responses to unions, see Sumner Slichter, James J. Healy, and E. Robert Livernash, *The Impact of Collective Bargaining on Management* (Washington, D.C.: The Brookings Institution, 1960). For a more recent discussion on the effects of unions on wages, see Richard B. Freeman and James L. Medoff, *What Do Unions Do?* (New York: Basic Books, 1984).

14. See Fred Foulkes, *Personnel Policies in Large Nonunion Companies* (Englewood Cliffs, N.J.: Prentice-Hall, 1980).

15. See, for example, Eric Batstone et al., *Unions in the Boardroom* (Oxford: Blackwell, 1983); James N. Baron and William T. Bielby, "Bringing the Firms Back In: Stratification, Segmentation, and the Organization of Work," *American Sociological Review* 45 (1980):737–65; and Keith Thurley and Stephen Wood, eds., *Industrial Relations and Management Strategy* (New York: Cambridge University Press, 1983).

16. See Alfred D. Chandler, Jr., *Strategy and Structure* (New York: Anchor Books, 1966).

17. For the classic exposition of this view, see ibid.

18. For a good description of this process, see Edgar H. Schein, "The Role of the Founder in Creating Organizational Culture," *Organizational Dynamics* (1983): 13–28. See also Edgar H. Schein, *Organizational Culture and Leadership* (San Francisco: Jossey Bass, 1985).

19. For more on this point, see Paul J. DiMaggio and Walter W. Powell, "The Iron Cage Revisited: Institutional Isomorphism and Collective Rationality in Organizational Fields," *American Sociological Review* 48 (1983):147–60; and Mark Granovetter, "Economic Action and Social Structure: A Theory of Embeddedness" (Department of Sociology, State University of New York at Stony Brook, 1983, manuscript).

20. See, for example, John R. Commons, *A Documentary History of American Industrial Society,* vol. 5; and Orley Ashenfelter and John H. Pencavel, "American Trade Union Growth, 1900–1960," *Quarterly Journal of Economics,* 83 (1969): 434–48.

21. Representative of this view are John T. Dunlop, *Industrial Relations System,* and Slichter, Healy, and Livernash, *Impact of Collective Bargaining on Management.* Interestingly, however, Slichter, Healy, and Livernash clearly recognized that management had resisted unionism quite vigorously over the years. They argued that "The American environment has produced strongly individualistic and highly competitive employers, who have been aggressively hostile to unions and who have

been willing to go to great extremes in order to destroy them." (p. 34).

22. Douglas V. Brown and Charles A. Myers, "The Changing Industrial Relations Philosophy of American Management," *Proceedings of the Ninth Annual Winter Meeting of the Industrial Relations Research Association* (Madison, Wis.: Industrial Relations Research Association, 1957), 92.

23. Reinhard Bendix, *Work and Authority in Industry* (New York: John Wiley & Sons, 1956).

24. For more on this, see Howell John Harris, *The Right to Manage,* (Madison, Wis.: University of Wisconsin Press, 1982), chap. 1.

25. See Harris, *The Right to Manage;* and Sanford Jacoby, *Employing Bureaucracy: Managers, Unions, and the Transformation of Work in American Industries, 1900–1945* (New York: Columbia University Press, 1985), for more on this point. For a more elaborate discussion of labor's force in the Civic Federation, see James Weinstein, *The Corporate Ideal in the Liberal State, 1900–1918* (Boston: Beacon Press, 1968); William Gomberg, "Special Study Committees," in John T. Dunlop and Neil W. Chamberlain, eds., *Frontiers of Collective Bargaining* (New York: Harper & Row, 1967), 235–51; Joel Cutcher-Gershenfeld, "Reconceiving the Web of Labor-Management Relations" (Paper presented at the 1985 spring meeting of the Industrial Relations Research Association, Detroit; and John R. Commons, *Myself* (Madison, Wis.: University of Wisconsin Press, 1964), 81–89 (originally published 1934).

26. John R. Commons, *Institutional Economics: Its Place in Political Economy* (New York: Macmillan, 1934), 311.

27. See James G. March and Johen P. Olsen, "The New Institutionalism: Organizational Factors in Political Life," *The American Political Science Review,* 78 (1984):734–49.

28. The classic statement of this view is Mancur Olson, *The Logic of Collective Action* (Cambridge, Mass.: Harvard University Press, 1960). For a good critique of this veiw, particularly as it applies to labor, see Claus Offe and Helmut Weisenthal, "Two Logics of Collective Action," in Maurice Zeitlin, ed., *Political Power and Social Theory* (Greenwich, Conn.: JAI Press, 1980), 67–115.

29. For a review of this literature, see Thomas A. Kochan, *Collective Bargaining and Industrial Relations,* (Homewood, Ill.: Richard D. Irwin, 1980), chaps. 4–7. See also Lee Dyer and Donald P. Schwab, "Personnel/Human Resource Management Research," in Thomas A. Kochan, Daniel J. Mitchell, and Lee Dyer, eds., *Industrial Relations Research in the 1970s: Review and Appraisal* (Madison, Wis.: Industrial Relations Research Association, 1982), 187–220.

30. For an earlier study of union-management relations that used a multiple-level model similar to our approach, see Neil W. Chamberlain, *The Union Challenge to Management Control* (New York: Harper and Row, 1948).

31. For some early research on workplace-level industrial relations, see Donald Roy, "Quota Restriction and Goldbricking in a Machine Shop," *American Journal of Sociology* 57 (1952):427–42; Leonard R. Sayles, *The Behavior of Industrial Work Groups* (New York: John Wiley & Sons, 1958); George Strauss, *Unions in the Building Trades* (Buffalo, N.Y.: University of Buffalo, 1958).

32. For a good discussion of the emergent industrial relations system of the 1930s, see Irving Bernstein, *The Turbulent Years: A History of the American Worker, 1933–1941* (Boston: Houghton Mifflin, 1969).

33. The experiences of the War Labor Board are described in *Termination Report of the War Labor Board* (Washington, D.C.: U.S. Government Printing Office, 1946) and by George W. Taylor, *Government Regulation and Industrial Relations* (New York: Prentice-Hall, 1948).

The process through which collective bargaining was extended and institutionalized in the auto and steel industries is described by Harold Levinson, "Pattern Bargaining: A Case Study of the Automobile Industry," *The Quarterly Journal of Economics,* 74 (1964):296–317; and George Seltzer, "Pattern Bargaining and the United Steelworkers," *Journal of Political Economy,* 59 (1951):319–31.

Chapter 2

1. For an alternative view of the role of public policy in the history of American workers, see Amy Bridges, "Becoming American: The Working Class in the United States Before the Civil War," in Ira Katznelson and Aristide Zolberg, eds., *Working Class Formation: Nineteenth Century Patterns in Western Europe and the United States* (Princeton, N.J.: Princeton University Press, forthcoming); and Victoria Hattam, "State Structure and Industrial Relations: American Labor and the Courts" (Ph.D. diss., Department of Political Science, MIT, in progress).

2. A thorough discussion of the historical evolution of economic theory in the late 1800s and early 1900s is presented in Joseph Dorfman, *The Economic Mind in American Civilization* (New York: Viking Press, 1949).

3. Illustrative of this view are John R. Commons, *Legal Foundation of Capitalism* (New York: Macmillan, 1924), and Selig Perlman, *A Theory of the Labor Movement* (New York: Macmillan, 1928). This view of the labor movement is compared with other theories in Mark Perlman, *Labor Union Theories in America* (New York: Row Peterson, 1958), and Philip Taft, "Theories of the Labor Movement," in IRRA, *Interpreting the Labor Movement* (Madison, Wis.: Industrial Relations Research Association, 1952), 1–38.

An alternative conception to both the neoclassical and pluralist views of labor is exemplified by Alan Dawley, *Class and Community: The Industrial Revolution in Lynn* (Cambridge, Mass.: Harvard University Press, 1976); Herbert G. Gutman, *Work, Culture and Society in Industrializing America* (New York: Vintage Books, 1977); and Sean Wilentz, "Artisan Republican Festivals and the Rise of Class Conflict in New York City, 1788–1837," in Michael H. Frisch and Daniel J. Walkowitz, eds., *Working Class America: Essays on Labor, Community, and American Society* (Urbana, Ill.: University of Illinois Press, 1983), 37–77.

For a good survey of this "new" labor history, see David Brody, "The Old Labor History and the New: In Search of an American Working Class," *Labor History* 20 (1979):111–26; and Jonathan Grossman and William T. Moye, "Labor History in the 1970s: A Question of Identity" in Thomas A. Kochan, Daniel J. B. Mitchell, and Lee Dyer, eds., *Industrial Relations Research in the 1970s: Review and Appraisal* (Madison, Wis.: Industrial Relations Research Association, 1982), 19–34.

4. A good summary of this view is presented in Jack Barbash, *The Elements of Industrial Relations* (Madison, Wis.: The University of Wisconsin Press, 1984), chap. 2. For a sociological discussion of the structural origins of social stratification and conflict, see Ralf Dahrendorf, *Class and Class Conflict in Industrial Society* (London: Routledge, 1959).

5. This pluralist view of the state as neutral mediator of societal groups contrasts with more recent neo-Marxist accounts that portray the state as a semi-autonomous actor promoting capitalist accumulation. Representative of this view are James O'Connor, *The Fiscal Crisis of the State* (New York: St. Martin's Press, 1973), and Nicos Poulantzas, *Political Power and Social Classes* (London: NLB and Sheed and Ward, 1973).

6. In Kenneth H. Parsons, "The Basis of Commons' Progressive Approach to Public Policy," in Gerald G. Somers, ed., *Labor, Management and Social Policy: Essays in the John R. Commons Tradition* (Madison, Wis.: University of Wisconsin Press, 1963), 20.

7. For the standard treatment of labor by neoclassical economists, see Milton Friedman, *Capitalism and Freedom* (Chicago: University of Chicago Press, 1962); Henry C. Simons, *Economic Policy for a Free Society* (Chicago: University of Chicago Press, 1948); and Charles E. Lindblom, *Unions and Capitalism* (New Haven: Yale University Press, 1949).

8. *First Annual Report of the National Labor Relations Board* (Washington, D.C.: National Labor Relations Board, 1936), 1.

9. Testimony of Senator Walsh, *Congressional Record of the U.S. Senate,* vol. 79, 1935, 7660.

10. For a good discussion of this point, see James A. Gross, "Introduction" to "The NLRA: A Symposium," *Industrial and Labor Relations Review,* 39 (1985): 10.

11. For an interesting discussion of this point, see analysis of the Twentieth Century Fund Report in Christopher L. Tomlins, "The New Deal, Collective Bargaining, and the Triumph of Industrial Pluralism," *Industrial and Labor Relations Review,* 39 (1985):19–34.

For a later statement of management's responsibility, see William Leiserson, *Right and Wrong in Labor Relations,* (Berkeley: University of California Press, 1938).

12. The earliest proponent of this view was Sumner Slichter. See his *Union Policies and Industrial Management* (Washington, D.C.: The Brookings Institution, 1941).

13. This view of the Depression continues to be debated. See, for example, Friedman, "The Role of Money Supply," in *Capitalism and Freedom,* 38. For a sample of divergent views on the causes of the Great Depression, see Karl Bruner, ed., *The Great Depression Revisited* (Boston: Kluwer-Nijhoff Publishing, 1981).

There are also several different interpretations of the postwar Keynesian system. For a sampling of alternative views, see Fred L. Block, *The Origins of International Economic Disorder* (Berkeley: University of California Press, 1977); Charles S. Maier, "The Politics of Productivity: Foundations of American International Economic Policy After World War II," *International Organization* 31 (1977):607–33; Alan S. Milward, *The Reconstruction of Western Europe, 1945–51* (Berkeley: University of California Press, 1984); and Donald Winch, *Economics and Policy, A Historical Study* (New York: Walker and Company, 1969).

14. Statement of Senate Committee on Education and Labor, 74th Congress, First Session, Hearings on a National Labor Relations Board, 1935, p. 218.

15. For an early formulation of this view, see John R. Commons, *The Economics of Collective Action* (New York: Macmillan, 1950).

16. A more elaborate discussion of this process is presented in Harry C. Katz, *Shifting Gears: Changing Labor Relations in the U.S. Auto Industry* (Cambridge, Mass.: MIT Press, 1985), and also in Michael J. Piore and Charles F. Sabel, *The Second Industrial Divide* (New York: Basic Books, 1984).

17. For an example of the traditional statement of this philosophy, see Robert F. Hoxie, *Trade Unionism in the United States* (New York: Appleton and Company, 1920).

18. An alternative view of the American labor movement is advanced by Dawley, *Class and Community,* and Gutman, *Work, Culture and Society in Industrializing America.*

19. For a good discussion of American labor's political activism, see David Brody, "The Uses of Power II: Political Action," in *Workers in Industrial America* (New York: Oxford University Press, 1980), 215–25; David J. Greenstone, *Labor in American Politics* (Chicago: University of Chicago Press, 1977); and Walter H.

Heller, *New Dimensions of Political Economy* (Cambridge, Mass.: Harvard University Press, 1966).

20. This process is described in detail in Piore and Sabel, *The Second Industrial Divide.* Comparing this process to European developments is quite interesting. For a good discussion of the postwar European labor movement, see Peter M. Lange, George Ross, and Maurizio Vannicelli, *Unions, Change and Crisis: French and Italian Union Strategy and the Political Economy, 1945–80* (London: George Allen & Unwin, 1982); and Peter Gourevitch, Andrew Martin, George Ross, Christopher Allen, Steven Bornstein, and Andrei Markovits, *Unions and Economic Crisis: Britain, West Germany and Sweden* (London: George Allen & Unwin, 1984).

21. A good discussion of this system is presented by Steven Fraser, "Dress Rehearsal for the New Deal: Shop Floor Insurgents, Political Elites, and Industrial Democracy in the Amalgamated Clothing Workers," in Frisch and Walkowitz, eds., *Working Class America*, 212–55; and in Piore and Sabel, *The Second Industrial Divide.*

22. For more on this point, see Slichter, *Union Policies and Industrial Management;* Sumner Slichter, James J. Healy, and E. Robert Livernash, *The Impact of Collective Bargaining on Management;* and Sanford M. Jacoby, *Employing Bureaucracy: Managers, Unions, and the Transformation of Work in American Industry, 1900–1945* (New York: Columbia University Press, 1985).

23. We are grateful to E. Robert Livernash for helping us develop the concept of eras in the United States over the post–New Deal period.

24. For a recent summary of differences in collective bargaining patterns across industries, see Gerald G. Somers, ed., *Collective Bargaining: Contemporary American Experience,* (Madison, Wis.: The Industrial Relations Research Association, 1980).

25. See James A. Gross, *The Making of the NLRB* (Albany: State University of New York Press, 1974).

26. See Frederick H. Harbison and Robert Dubin, *Patterns of Union-Management Relations* (Chicago: Science Research Associates, 1947).

27. For more on the War Labor Board's role in the evolution of collective bargaining procedures, see Howell John Harris, *The Right to Manage: Industrial Relations Policies of American Business in the 1940s* (Madison, Wis.: The University of Wisconsin Press, 1982).

28. See Steven Fraser, "Dress Rehearsal for the New Deal," in Frisch and Walkowitz, eds., *Working Class America;* and Harris, *The Right to Manage.*

29. "Work Stoppage Caused by Labor-Management Disputes in 1946," *Monthly Labor Review,* 64 (5) (1947):780–800.

30. Although management did not return to the aggressive union-busting strategies of earlier times, resistance to unionism nevertheless continued. Indicative of this persistent antiunionism is a *Business Week* article, "Resistance to Unions Grows," 11 January 1947:74. For a more elaborate discussion of this point, see Robert M. Collins, *The Business Response to Keynes* (New York: Columbia University Press, 1981), and Harris, *The Right to Manage.*

31. See Gross, "Introduction" to "The NLRA: A Symposium," *Industrial and Labor Relations Review* 39, no. 1 (1985):5–6.

32. See "Grievance Procedures in Union Agreements, 1950–51," *Monthly Labor Review* 73 (1951):36, and "Arbitration Provisions in Collective Bargaining Agreements, 1952," *Monthly Labor Review* 76 (1953):261. The expanding scope of collective bargaining agreements also is documented in *Basic Patterns in Union Contracts* (Washington, D.C.: Bureau of National Affairs, various years).

33. For further discussion of this event, see David Brody, "The Uses of Power I: Industrial Battleground," in *Workers in Industrial America;* Nelson Lichtenstein, *Labor's War at Home* (New York: Cambridge University Press, 1982); Katz, *Shifting*

Gears; and Piore and Sabel, *The Second Industrial Divide.*

34. Good descriptions of these internal battles are presented in Lichtenstein, *Labor's War at Home;* and in Ronald Schatz, *The Electrical Workers* (Urbana, Ill.: University of Illinois Press, 1983).

35. For more on this, see Melvyn Dubofsky, *American Labor Since the New Deal* (Chicago: Quadrangle Books, 1971); Roger Keeran, *The Communist Party and the Auto Worker* (Bloomington, Ind.: Indiana University Press, 1980); and Nelson Lichtenstein, "Conflict over Workers' Control: The Automobile Industry in World War II," in Frisch and Walkowitz, eds., *Working Class America.*

36. See Katz, *Shifting Gears,* chap. 2.

37. For a good description of the variety of responses by management to unionization, see Harris, *The Right to Manage,* chap. 1.

38. Jacoby, *Employing Bureaucracy,* 19.

39. James N. Baron, Frank R. Dobbin, and P. Devereaux Jennings, "War and Peace: The Evolution of Modern Personnel Administration in U.S. Industry" (Stanford University, February 1985, manuscript).

40. See Jacoby, *Employing Bureaucracy,* 19.

41. John T. Dunlop and Charles A. Myers, "The Industrial Relations Function in Management: Some Views on its Organizational Status," *Personnel* 31 (1955): 406–13.

42. Baron, Dobbin, and Jennings, "War and Peace," 37.

43. See Robert McKersie, "Structural Factors and Negotiations in the International Harvester Company" in Arnold Weber, ed., *The Structure of Collective Bargaining* (New York: Free Press of Glencoe, 1961).

44. See *The Personnel Executive: His Title, Functions, Staff, Salary, and Status* (Washington, D.C.: Bureau of National Affairs, 1952).

45. Dale Yoder and Roberta J. Nelson, "Industrial Relations Budgets—1950–1959," *Personnel* 27–56 (1950–59):279–306.

46. Jacoby, *Employing Bureaucracy.*

47. For more on this period, see various articles in the symposium "The Employer Challenge and The Union Response," *Industrial Relations* 2 (1962):9–56. See also the criticism and comment by George Strauss, "The Shifting Power Balance in the Plant," *Industrial Relations* 2 (1962):101–103.

48. Herbert N. Northrup, *Boulwarism,* (Ann Arbor Bureau of Industrial Relations, Graduate School of Business, University of Michigan, 1964).

49. This and other periods of concession bargaining are discussed in Daniel J. B. Mitchell, "Recent Union Contract Concessions," *Brookings Papers on Economic Activity,* 1 (1982):165–204.

50. Slichter, Healy, and Livernash, *Impact of Collective Bargaining on Management,* 960.

51. For the most recent BLS survey of the scope of these provisions, see U.S. Department of Labor, BLS (2013), *Characteristics of Major Collective Bargaining Agreements* (July 1, 1979). See also the biannual issues of BNA, *Basic Patterns in Union Contracts.*

52. For more on this point, see Clint Bourdon, "Pattern Bargaining, Wage Determination, and Inflation: Some Preliminary Observations on the 1976–1978 Wage Round," in Michael J. Piore, ed., *Unemployment and Inflation: Institutionalist and Structuralist Views* (White Plains, N.Y.: M. E. Sharpe, 1979), 115–33; Otto Eckstein and Thomas A. Wilson, "The Determination of Money Wages in American Industry," *Quarterly Journal of Economics* 75 (1962):370–414; and John E. Maher, "The Wage Pattern in the United States," *Industrial and Labor Relations Review* 15 (1961):1–20.

53. For a diagrammatic sketch showing the rise of contract rejections, see Thomas

A. Kochan, *Collective Bargaining and Industrial Relations* (Homewood, Ill.: Richard D. Irwin, 1980), 46; see also William E. Simkin, "Refusal to Ratify Contracts," in *Trade Union Government and Collective Bargaining* (New York: Praeger, 1970): 107–48.

54. See "Brushfires Plague Auto Industry," *Business Week,* 14 November 1964. For an interesting analysis of the rise of shop-floor militance in both the United States and Europe, see Charles F. Sabel, *Work and Politics* (New York: Cambridge University Press, 1982).

55. "Collective Bargaining in the Motor Vehicle and Equipment Industry," U.S. Department of Labor, Report 574. Washington, D.C.: Bureau of Labor Statistics.

56. These and the figures to follow are from unpublished GM files.

57. See William Serrin, *The Company and the Union* (New York: Knopf, 1973); and Katz, *Shifting Gears.*

58. Wallace Hendricks and Lawrence Kahn, "Wage Indexation in the United States: Prospects for the 1980s," *Proceedings of the 37th Annual Meeting of the Industrial Relations Research Association* (Madison, Wis.: Industrial Relations Research Association, 1985), 413.

59. For a more elaborate discussion of this point, see Daniel J. B. Mitchell, *Unions, Wages and Inflation* (Washington, D.C.: Brookings Institution, 1980); also Richard Freeman and James Medoff, *What Do Unions Do?* (New York: Basic Books, 1984), 53.

60. See Audrey Freedman, *Managing Labor Relations* (New York: The Conference Board, 1979); and Thomas A. Kochan, *Collective Bargaining and Industrial Relations,* 423–25.

61. Bert Spector, "General Motors Corporation-Detroit Plant," Case 9-676-072, Cambridge: Harvard Case Clearing House, p. 7. The history of QWL programs in the auto industry is discussed in more detail in chapter 6.

62. Allen R. Janger, *The Personnel Function: Changing Objectives and Functions* (New York: The Conference Board, 1977), 2.

63. John T. Dunlop, "The Limits of Legal Compulsion," *Labor Law Journal* 27 (1976):67–74. An interesting analysis of the evolution of the politics of the business community is presented by Thomas Byrne Edsall, *The New Politics of Inequality* (New York: Norton, 1984).

64. Janger, *Personnel Function.*

65. Ibid., 38.

66. For a more complete discussion of the evolution of union leaders' views toward worker-participation programs, see Thomas A. Kochan, Harry C. Katz, and Nancy R. Mower, *Worker Participation and American Unions: Threat or Opportunity?:* (Kalamazoo, Mich.: W. E. Upjohn Institute for Employment Research, 1984).

67. An interesting analysis of this development is presented by D. Quinn Mills, "Flawed Victory in Labor Law Reform," *Harvard Business Review* 57 (May–June 1979):92–102; and by David Brody, "The Uses of Power II: Political Action" in *Workers in Industrial America.*

68. This view was reflected by Slichter, Healy, and Livernash, *The Impact of Collective Bargaining on Management.*

Chapter 3

1. For a comprehensive review of the statistics on labor union growth and decline, see Richard B. Freeman and James L. Medoff, "New Estimates of Private Sector Unionism in the United States," *Industrial and Labor Relations Review* 32 (1979): 143–74.

Notes

2. See Larry T. Adams, "Changing Employment Patterns of Organized Workers," *Monthly Labor Review* (February 1985):25–31; and Paul O. Flaim, "New Data on Union Members and Their Earnings," *Employment and Earnings* 32 (January 1985):13–14.

3. See the Bureau of National Affairs, *Directory of United States Labor Organizations, 1984–85* ed. (Washington, D.C.: Bureau of National Affairs, 1985).

4. Herbert R. Northrup and Howard G. Foster, *Open Shop Construction* (Philadelphia: Industrial Relations Unit, Wharton School, University of Pennsylvania, 1975).

5. Estimates of the Research Department, International Brotherhood of Teamsters.

6. See Donald Scobel, *Creative Work Life* (Houston: Gulf Publishing Co., 1981).

7. See Noah M. Meltz, "Labor Movements in Canada and the United States," in Thomas A. Kochan, ed., *Challenges and Choices Facing American Labor,* (Cambridge, Mass.: MIT Press, 1985),

8. For an early exposition on this process, see Charles E. Lindblom, *The Intelligence of Democracy: Democracy Making Through Adjustment* (New York: The Free Press, 1965). A more recent elaboration of how incremental changes can produce the conditions necessary for more far-reaching structural transformations is presented in Michael J. Piore and Charles F. Sabel, *The Second Industrial Divide* (New York: Basic Books, 1984) chap. 7.

9. For various, more detailed descriptions of this process, see Arthur L. Sinchcombe, *Constructuring Social Theories* (New York: Harcourt, Brace and World, 1968); Paul J. DiMaggio and Walter W. Powell, "The Iron Cage Revisited: Institutional Isomorphism and Collective Rationality in Organizational Fields," *American Sociological Review* 48, no. 2 (April 1983):147–60; and Pamela S. Tolbert and Lynne G. Sucker, "Institutional Sources of Change in the Formal Structure of Organizations: The Diffusion of Civil Service Reform, 1880–1935," *Administrative Science Quarterly* 28 (1983):22–39.

10. See Henry S. Farber, "The Extent of Unionization in the United States" in Kochan, ed., *Challenges and Choices Facing American Labor,* pp. 15–44.

11. For an analysis that reaches a similar conclusion about the proportion of union decline from changes in the environment, see William T. Dickens and Jonathan S. Leonard, "Accounting for the Decline in Union Membership, 1950–1980," *Industrial and Labor Relations Review* 38 (1985):323–34. Another paper by Dickens and Leonard updates their earlier research, and estimates that perhaps as much as 58 percent of the decline in unionization from the 1950s through the 1970s can be attributed to the independent and interactive effects of structural change. See William T. Dickens and Jonathan S. Leonard, "Structural Changes in Unionization: 1973–1981," National Bureau of Economic Research Working Paper No. 1882, April 1986.

12. Charles McDonald, "Discussion, Part I" in Kochan, ed., *Challenges and Choices Facing American Labor,* 66.

13. The 1977 data are presented in Audrey Freedman, *Managing Labor Relations* (New York: The Conference Board, 1979). The data for 1983 are presented in Audrey Freedman, *A New Look in Wage Bargaining* (New York: The Conference Board, 1985).

14. See Thomas A. Kochan, Robert B. McKersie, and John Chalykoff, "Corporate Strategy, Workplace Innovation, and Union Members," *Industrial and Labor Relations Review* 39 (July 1986):487–501.

15. See Sumner Slichter, James J. Healy, and E. Robert Livernash, *The Impact of Collective Bargaining on Management* (Washington, D.C.: The Brookings Institution, 1960).

16. See Fred Foulkes, *Personnel Policies in Large Nonunion Companies* (Englewood Cliffs, N.J.: Prentice-Hall, 1980).

17. For more details on these statistics and other results from the Conference Board survey, see Kochan, McKersie, and Chalykoff, "Corporate Strategy, Workplace Innovation, and Union Members," *Industrial and Labor Relations Review.*

18. See Richard E. Walton, *The Impact of the Professional Engineering Study: A Study of Collective Bargaining Among Engineers and Scientists and its Significance for Management* (Boston: Division of Research, Graduate School of Business Administration, Harvard University, 1961); also see Robert L. Aronson, "Unionism Among Professional Employees in the Private Sector," *Industrial and Labor-Relations Review,* 38 (1985):352–64.

19. For further discussion of these changes, see Audrey Freedman, *A New Look in Wage Bargaining.*

20. See John Chalykoff, "Industrial Relations at the Strategic Level: Indicators and Outcomes" (MIT, 1985, manuscript).

21. See William K. Hall, "Survival Strategies in a Hostile Environment," *The McKinsey Quarterly* (1982):2–24.

22. Joseph A. Schumpeter, *Capitalism, Socialism and Democracy,* (New York: Free Press, 1950).

23. Roger W. Schmenner, *Making Business Location Decisions,* (Englewood Cliffs, N.J.: Prentice-Hall), 10.

24. Ibid.

25. Ibid, 88. See also Barry Bluestone and Bennett Harrison, *The Deindustrialization of America* (New York: Basic Books, 1982).

26. Based on field research notes.

27. See Schmenner, *Making Business Location Decisions,* 124–29.

28. Kidder-Peabody, "Company Comment on Cooper Industries" (New York: Research Department, Kidder-Peabody, 21 September 1983): 3.

29. "Emerson Electric: High Profits from Low Tech," *Business Week,* 4 April 1983: 58–62.

30. This case is excerpted from Anil Verma, "Relative Flow of Capital to Union and Nonunion Plants Within a Firm," *Industrial Relations* 24, no. 3 (1985): 395–405.

31. "Can Florida Steel Go It Alone?" *Financial World* 31 (March 1983):58–59.

32. Based on field research notes.

33. David Wessel, "Fighting Off Unions, Ingersoll-Rand Uses a Wide Range of Tactics," *Wall Street Journal,* June 13, 1985, p. 1.

34. Richard B. Freeman, "Why Are Workers Faring Poorly in NLRB Representation Elections," in *Challenges and Choices Facing American Unions,* ed. Thomas A. Kochan, 46.

35. William T. Dickens and Jonathan S. Leonard, "Accounting for the Decline in Union Membership," *Industrial and Labor Relations Review* 35 (1985):323–34.

36. See Richard B. Freeman and James L. Medoff, *What Do Unions Do?* (New York: Basic Books, 1984), 233–39.

Chapter 4

1. For more on this point, see Neil W. Chamberlain and James W. Kuhn, *Collective Bargaining* (New York: McGraw-Hill, 1965).

2. See Mary P. Rowe and Michael Baker, "Are You Hearing Enough Employee Concerns?" *Harvard Business Review* 62, no. 3 (1984):127–35.

Notes

3. See Alan Balfour, "Five Types of Non-union Grievance Systems," *Personnel* 61 (March–April 1984):67–76.

4. For further discussion of these procedures, see Richard E. Walton and Robert B. McKersie, *A Behavioral Theory of Labor Negotiations* (New York: McGraw-Hill, 1965); and Thomas Schelling, *Strategy of Conflict* (Cambridge, Mass.: Harvard University Press, 1960).

5. See Nancy Russell Mower, "The Labor-Management Relationship and Its Effects on Quality of Work Life: A Comparative Case Study" (M.S. thesis, Sloan School of Management, MIT, 1982).

6. A more elaborate discussion of these patterns is presented in Alan Fox, *Beyond Contract: Work, Authority, and Trust Relations* (London: Macmillan, 1974).

7. See Jack Barbash's Presidential Address to the Industrial Relations Research Association, "Values in Industrial Relations: The Case of the Adversary Principle," *Proceedings of the Thirty-third Annual Meeting of the Industrial Relations Research Association* (Madison, Wisc.: Industrial Relations Research Association, 1980).

8. For earlier work concerning work rules and productivity, see Sumner Slichter, *Union Policies and Industrial Management* (Washington, D.C.: The Brookings Institution, 1941); Sumner Slichter, James J. Healy, and E. Robert Livernash, *The Impact of Collective Bargaining on Management;* Paul T. Hartman, *Collective Bargaining and Productivity* (Berkeley: University of California Press, 1969); and Robert B. McKersie and Lawrence C. Hunter, *Pay, Productivity and Collective Bargaining* (London: Macmillan, 1973).

9. For various expositions on this point, see Donald Roy, "Quota Restriction and Goldbricking in a Machine Shop," *American Journal of Sociology* 57 (1952): 427–42; Leonard R. Sayles, *The Behavior of Industrial Work Groups* (New York: John Wiley & Sons, 1958); Melville Dalton, *Men Who Manage* (New York: John Wiley & Sons, 1959); and James W. Kuhn, *Bargaining and Grievance Settlement* (New York: Columbia University Press, 1961).

10. For a sample of this debate, see Arthur H. Brayfield and Walter H. J. Crockett, "Employee Attitudes and Employee Performance," *Psychological Bulletin* 50 (1955): 396–424; Frederick Herzberg, Bernard Mauser, and Barbara Snyderman, *The Motivation to Work,* 2nd ed. (New York: John Wiley & Sons, 1959); and Donald P. Schwab and Larry L. Cummings, "Theories of Satisfaction and Performance: A Review," *Industrial Relations* 9 (1978):408–30.

11. See Victor Vroom, *Work and Motivation* (New York: John Wiley & Sons, 1964).

12. For a summary of the Hawthorne experiments, see F. J. Roethlisberger, *Management and Morale,* (Cambridge, Mass.: Harvard University Press, 1941); see also P. S. Goodman and E. E. Lawler, *New Forms of Work Organization in the United States* (Geneva: International Labor Organization, 1977).

13. For one such case, see P. S. Goodman, *Assessing Organizational Change: The Rushton Quality of Work Experiment* (New York: Wiley-Interscience, 1979).

14. See Thomas A. Kochan, Harry C. Katz, and Nancy Mower, *Worker Participation and American Unions: Threat or Opportunity?* (Kalamazoo, Mich.: W. E. Upjohn Institute for Employment Research, 1984).

15. See Michael J. Piore and Charles F. Sabel, *The Second Industrial Divide* (New York: Basic Books, 1984).

16. See Slichter, Healy, Livernash, *Impact of Collective Bargaining on Management.*

17. Harry C. Katz, Thomas A. Kochan, Mark Weber, "Assessing the Effects of Industrial Relations Systems and Efforts to Improve the Quality of Working Life on Organizational Effectiveness," *Academy of Management Journal* 28 (1985): 509–26.

18. See J. R. Norsworthy and Craig Zabala, "Worker Attitudes, Worker Behavior, and Productivity in the American Automobile Industry, 1959–1976," *Industrial and Labor Relations Review* 38 (1985):556.

19. For further discussion of this analysis, see Casey Ichniowski, "How to Labor Relations Matter? A Study of Productivity in Eleven Manufacturing Plants" (Ph.D. diss., Sloan School of Management, MIT, 1983).

20. For an overview of work motivation and work design, see Richard Hackman and Greg Oldham, *Work Redesign* (Reading, Mass.: Addison-Wesley, 1980).

21. See Douglas McGregor, *The Human Side of Enterprise* (New York: McGraw-Hill, 1959).

22. See Charles L. Hulin and Milton R. Blood, "Job Enlargement, Individual Differences, and Worker Responses," *Psychological Bulletin* 69 (1968):41–55.

23. See Eric Trist, *The Evolution of Socio-Technical Systems* (Toronto: Ontario Quality of Working Life Center, 1981).

24. See Donald Scobel, *Creative Work Life* (Houston, Tex.: Gulf Publishing Co., 1981).

25. See Richard E. Walton, "Work Innovations in the United States," *Harvard Business Review* 57 (July–August 1979):88–98.

26. See the discussion of personnel policies at IBM in Thomas A. Kochan and Thomas A. Barocci, *Human Resource Management and Industrial Relations,* (Boston: Little, Brown, 1985).

27. See Rowe and Baker, "Are You Hearing Enough Employee Concerns?"

28. This case was excerpted from Anil Verma, "Union and Nonunion Industrial Relations at the Plant Level" (Ph.D. diss., Sloan School of Management, MIT, 1983).

29. See Richard B. Freeman and James L. Medoff, *What Do Unions Do?* (New York: Basic Books, 1984).

30. Robert B. McKersie and Janice Klein, "Productivity: The Industrial Relations Connection," in William J. Baumol and Kenneth McLennan, eds., *Productivity Growth and U.S. Competitiveness* (New York: Oxford University Press, 1985), 119–59.

Chapter 5

1. For a sampling of this debate see Audrey Freedman, "A Fundamental Change in Wage Bargaining," and John T. Dunlop, "Working Toward a Consensus," *Challenge* 25, no. 3 (1982):14–17 and 26–34. See also Milton Derber's 1982 presidential address to the Industrial Relations Research Association, "Are We in a New Era?" *Proceedings of the Thirty-fifth Annual Meeting of the Industrial Relations Research Association* (Madison, Wis.: Industrial Relations Research Association, 1983), 1–9; and Daniel J. B. Mitchell, "Recent Union Contract Concessions," *Brookings Papers on Economic Activity,* 1 (1983):189–92.

2. For a wide-ranging discussion and diverse views on collective bargaining developments in the early 1980s, see *Proceedings of the Industrial Relations Research Association,* (Madison, Wis.: Industrial Relations Research Association, 1985). These proceedings are also reprinted in the August 1985 issue of *Labor Law Journal.*

3. See John T. Dunlop, "Policy Decisions and Research in Economics and Industrial Relations," *Industrial and Labor Relations Review* 30 (April 1977): 275–82.

4. Henry Farber, Beverly Hirtle, Thomas A. Kochan, and Wayne Vroman, "Wage Determination Under Collective Bargaining: Preliminary Evidence on a Structural

Shift in the 1980s" (Unpublished manuscript, Sloan School of Management, MIT, 1986).

5. See Daniel J. B. Mitchell, "Shifting Wage Norms and Bargaining," *Brookings Papers on Economic Activity,* in press.

6. Ibid., table 3.

7. Median voter models are discussed in Richard B. Freeman and James L. Medoff, *What Do Unions Do?* (New York: Basic Books, 1984).

8. See Paul O. Flaim and Ellen Sehgal, "Displaced Workers of 1979–83: How Well Have They Fared?" *Monthly Labor Review,* (1985):3–16.

9. See *Employment and Earnings* (Washington, D.C.: Bureau of Labor Statistics, various years).

10. See Robert S. Gay, "Union Settlements and Aggregate Wage Behavior in the 1980s," *Federal Reserve Bulletin,* 70 (1984):843–56.

11. See Peter Cappelli, "Concession Bargaining and the National Economy," in *Proceedings of the Thirty-fifth Annual Meeting of the Industrial Relations Research Association, 1982,* (Madison, Wis.: Industrial Relations Research Association, 1983), 362–71.

12. For further statistical analysis of the connection between employment loss and the occurrence of concession bargaining, see ibid., 364–69.

13. See John Chalykoff, "Industrial Relations at the Strategic Level: Indicators and Outcomes" (Sloan School of Management, MIT, 1985, manuscript).

14. These figures are derived from *Current Wage Developments* (Washington, D.C.: Bureau of Labor Statistics, various issues); and are reported in Gay, "Union Settlements and Aggregate Wage Behavior in the 1980s." For similar calculations, see Robert J. Flanagan, "Wage Concessions and Long-Term Union Wage Flexibility," *Brookings Papers on Economic Activity,* 1 (1984):183–216.

15. See Daniel Mitchell, "Shifting Norms in Wage Bargaining," table 1.

16. See Flanagan, "Wage Concessions and Long-Term Union Wage Flexibility," 189, table 2.

17. See Chalykoff, "Industrial Relations at the Strategic Level."

18. See Thomas A. Kochan, *Collective Bargaining and Industrial Relations* (Homewood, Ill.: Irwin-Dorsey, 1980), 322–23.

19. For a more elaborate discussion of this relationship, see Robert J. Flanagan, "Wage Concessions and Long-Term Union Wage Flexibility."

20. See Sumner Slichter, *Union Policies and Industrial Management* (Washington, D.C.: The Brookings Institution, 1941).

21. See the symposium "The Employer Challenge and the Union Response" in *Industrial Relations* (1961). See also George Strauss, "The Shifting Balance of Power in the Plant," *Industrial Relations* 2 (1962):65–96.

22. For a good summary of the productivity bargaining developments during this period, see George P. Shultz and Robert B. McKersie, "Stimulating Productivity: Choices, Problems and Shares," *British Journal of Industrial Relations* 5 (1967):3–18.

23. Peter Henle, "Reverse Collective Bargaining: A Look at Some Union Concession Situations," *Industrial and Labor Relations Review* 26 (1973):956–68.

24. This figure was derived in our own analysis of the Conference Board data. For related figures see Audrey Freedman, "The New Look in Wage Policy and Employee Relations," (New York: The Conference Board, 1985).

25. A more complete discussion of this point is presented in Thomas A. Kochan and Harry C. Katz, "Collective Bargaining, Work Organization and Worker Participation: The Return to Plant-Level Bargaining," in *Paper and Proceedings,*

Spring Industrial Relations Research Association Meeting, 1983, (Madison: Wis.: Industrial Relations Research Association, 1983), 524–29.

26. For a description of the most famous of these, see George P. Shultz and Arnold R. Weber, *Strategies for Displaced Workers* (New York: Harper & Row, 1966).

27. Most carriers experienced several rounds of negotiations with different craft unions in this period; some may also have altered their business strategies over time. The relations outlined here represent the average or general experiences over the deregulation period. Information on business strategies was obtained by interviews with management, from corporate reports, and from the business and industry press. Information on collective bargaining was obtained from these sources as well as from Airline Industrial Relations Conference, the major trade association in the industry. Table 5.2 and the discussion draw heavily from Peter Cappelli, "Competitive Pressures and Labor Relations in the Airline Industry," *Industrial Relations* 24 (1985):316–38.

28. See "Rewarding Route," *Barrons,* July 19, 1982:13.

29. For an elaboration on this point, see Herbert R. Northrup, "The New Employee-Relations Climate in Airlines," *Industrial and Labor Relations Review,* 36 (1983):167–82.

30. See "How American Mastered Deregulation," *Fortune,* 11 June 1984:38.

31. Two-man crews saved $75 million per year, but the costs of carrying laid-off pilots when business turned down was $20 million per year. For more on this point, see "The Upstarts Hit a Downdraft," *Business Week,* 26 October 1981:186.

32. See "An Even Better Deal" (American Airlines newsletter to union members, 1983).

33. See "TWA: The Incredible Shrinking Airlines," *Business Week,* 25 July 1983:86.

34. Ibid.

35. See "Eastern's Revolutionary Treaty with Its Unions," *Business Week,* 26 December 1983:22.

36. This double-breasted operation took the Texas International/New York Air example further because Frontier and Horizon would be operated in a coordinated fashion with employees working side by side. For a more elaborate description of this phenomenon, see "Can Frontier's Nonunion Airline Fly?" *Business Week,* 22 August 1983:30.

37. For a more elaborate discussion of these events, see "Continental Is Coming Out a Winner," *Business Week,* 30 January 1984:21; and "The Trying Times for Continental Aren't Over Yet," *Business Week,* 19 March 1984:44–46.

38. See "Pilots End Two-Year Strike at Continental Accept Terms Awarded by Bankruptcy Court," *Daily Labor Report,* 213 (4 November 1985).

39. By "formal bargaining structure" we mean the actual bargaining unit covered by a contract. "Informal bargaining structure" refers to situations where through pattern following, settlements covering one bargaining unit influence the terms agreed to in another unit.

40. See "Steel Companies Will End 30-Year Practice of Joint Negotiations with Steelworkers," *Daily Labor Report,* 87 (6 May 1985):A-10–A-11.

41. For an insider's view of these changes, see William B. Solomon, "Discussion," in *Proceedings of the Thirty-seventh Annual Meeting of the Industrial Relations Research Association* (Madison, Wis.: Industrial Relations Research Association, 1985), 352–59.

42. For more on this point, see Harry C. Katz, *Shifting Gears* (Cambridge, Mass.: MIT Press, 1985), chap. 3.

43. See Harold M. Levinson, "Trucking," in Gerald B. Somers, ed., *Collective Bargaining: Contemporary American Experience* (Madison, Wis.: Industrial Relations Research Association, 1981), 99–150.

44. For a discussion of this, see Audrey Freedman, *The New Look in Wage Policy and Employee Relations.*

45. In a study of corporate strategy and labor relations, Christiansen concluded: "Labor relations staff were quite isolated throughout the six successful companies and labor relations procedures reflected this fact. . . . Where labor relations was most isolated from management were precisely those companies where labor relations and unions were most adversarial." E. Tatum Christiansen, "Corporate Strategy and Labor Relations (Ph.D. diss., Harvard Business School, 1982), 228, 234.

46. Letter of understanding to Donald F. Elphin from Peter Pestillo, 12 February 1982.

47. See Audrey Freedman, *The New Look in Wage Policy and Employee Relations.*

48. Flanagan, "Wage Concessions and Long-Term Union Wage Flexibility," 193. See also "Major Work Stoppages: 1984," *Bureau of Labor Statistics* (27 February 1985).

49. See Thomas A. Kochan, *Collective Bargaining and Industrial Relations,* 320–24; see also Cynthia L. Gramm, "The Determinants of Strike Incidence and Severity: A Micro-level Study," *Industrial and Labor Relations Review* 39(1986): 361–76.

50. See "The Pork Workers' Beef: Pay Cuts That Persist," *Business Week,* 15 April 1985:75–76.

51. The decertification vote and the United Steelworkers efforts to challenge that vote are discussed in "Steelworkers to Challenge Vote Results," *AFL-CIO News,* 16 February 1985:2.

52. See "If Anyone Won the Strike, Greyhound Did," *Business Week,* 19 December 1983:39–40.

Chapter 6

1. Union resistance to early QWL programs and the way they were presented by organizational development specialists is discussed in Thomas A. Kochan, Harry C. Katz, and Nancy Mower, *Worker Participation and American Unions: Threat or Opportunity?* (Kalamazoo, Mich.: W. E. Upjohn Institute for Employment Research, 1984), chap. 1.

2. For a more complete discussion of these developments, see Harry C. Katz, *Shifting Gears* (Cambridge, Mass.: MIT Press, 1985), chap. 4.

3. See GM Corporation, "Agreement between General Motors and the UAW," (GM Corporation publication, 1982):265–76.

4. See Robert H. Guest, "Quality of Work life—Learning from Tarrytown," *Harvard Business Review* 57 (1979):76–87.

5. S. William Alper, Bruce N. Pfau, and David Sirota, *The 1985 National Survey of Employee Attitudes* (New York: Sirota and Alper Associates, 1985).

6. See Harry C. Katz, Thomas A. Kochan, and Kenneth Gobeille, "Industrial Relations Performance, Economic Performance, and Quality of Working Life Efforts: An Inter-Plant Analysis," *Industrial and Labor Relations Review* 37 (1983): 3–17; and Harry C. Katz, Thomas A. Kochan, and Mark Weber, "Assessing the Effects of Industrial Relations and Quality of Working Life Efforts on Organizational Effectiveness," *Academy of Management Journal* 28 (1985):509–27.

7. QWL involvement has a statistically insignificant effect on the divisionwide data sample for the years 1970 to 1980. A subset of these data is analyzed in Katz, Kochan, and Weber, "Assessing the Effects of Industrial Relations."

8. See, for example, Irving Bluestone, "How Quality of Worklife Projects Work for the United Auto Workers," *Monthly Labor Review* 103, no. 7 (1980):39–40; and Stephen Fuller, "How Quality of Worklife Projects Work for General Motors," *Monthly Labor Review* 103, no. 7 (1980):37–38.

9. In the 1980 *Monthly Labor Review* statement, Irving Bluestone claimed that the guiding principle of QWL programs is "the provision of the national agreement and of the local agreements and practices remain inviolable" (p. 40). Bluestone went on to state that where QWL is introduced, "The local understands that normal collective bargaining continues" (p. 40).

10. The two Packard Electric plants in Mississippi discussed later are examples of this process.

11. The competitive problems the U.S. auto industry faces are discussed more fully in Alan Altshuler et al., *The Future of the Automobile* (Cambridge, Mass.: MIT Press, 1984); and in William J. Abernathy, Kim B. Clark, and Alan M. Kantrow, "The New Industrial Competition," *Harvard Business Review* 59 (1981): 68–81.

12. These changes are discussed in more detail in Katz, *Shifting Gears,* chap. 3.

13. The 1982 agreements are described in more detail in ibid.

14. An early example where the team system was introduced in the North is GM's Cadillac engine plant in Livonia, Michigan.

15. For more on this point, see Kochan, Katz, and Mower, *Worker Participation and American Unions.*

16. Note that the Packard Electric division was the first of the General Motors' component divisions to follow this route of opening nonunion plants in the South.

17. Note that this practice was later greatly expanded inside General Motors and other American manufacturers. Packard Electric was the first division in GM to extensively utilize such dedicated suppliers.

18. See John Russo, "General Motors Local Votes for Lifetime Job Security and a Three-Tier Wage Plan," *Labor Notes* (1985):5; and "A Pioneering Pact Promises Job Security for Life," *Business Week,* 31 December 1984:48–49.

19. "The Quality of Work Life Process at AT&T and the Communications Workers of America: A Research Study After Three Years" (Report prepared for the U.S. Department of Labor by AT&T and the Communications Workers, January 1984).

20. Ibid, p. 7.

21. See Kochan, Katz, and Mower, *Worker Participation and American Unions.*

22. See, for example, Paul S. Goodman, *Assessing Organizational Change: The Rushton Quality of Work Experiment,* (New York: Wiley-Interscience, 1979); and Michael Schuster, "The Impact of Union-Management Cooperation on Productivity and Employment," *Industrial and Labor Relations Review,* 36 (1983): 415–30.

Chapter 7

1. For more on this point, see Milton Derber, *The American Idea of Industrial Democracy, 1865–1965,* (Urbana, Ill.: University of Illinois Press, 1970).

For a discussion of the role of unions in entrepreneurial decision making, see Robert B. McKersie, "Union Involvement in Entrepreneurial Decisions of Business," in Thomas A. Kochan, ed., *Challenges and Choices Facing American Labor,* (Cambridge, Mass.: MIT Press, 1985), 149–166.

2. For an interesting discussion on this period, see Walter Galenson, *The CIO Challenge to the AFL* (Cambridge, Mass.: Harvard University Press, 1960).

3. These examples are excerpted from Kochan, ed., *Challenges and Choices Facing American Labor,* 167–72.

4. See Albert Rees, "Tripartite Wage Stabilization in the Food Industry," *Industrial Relations* 14 (1975):250–58.

5. See "Original Agenda, Joint Labor-Management Committee of the Retail Food Industry," Committee Memorandum, (29 March 1974), p. 1.

6. For a more elaborate discussion of this point, see William T. Moye, "Presidential Labor-Management Committees: Productive Failures," *Industrial and Labor Relations Review* 34 (1980):51–66.

7. For a good discussion on this point, see Jesse Thomas Carpenter, *Competition and Collective Bargaining in the Needle Trades, 1960–67* (Ithaca, N.Y.: New York State School for Industrial and Labor Relations, Cornell University, 1972); see also Steven Fraser, "Dress Rehearsal for the New Deal; Shop Floor Insurgents, Political Elites, and Industrial Democracy in the Amalgamated Clothing Workers," in Michael A. Frisch and Daniel J. Walkowitz, eds., *Working Class America* (Urbana, Ill.: Univ. of Illinois Press, 1983): 212–55. For examples of this phenomenon in other sectors, see Charles Sabel and Jonathan Zeitlin, "Historical Alternatives to Mass Production: Politics, Markets and Technology in Nineteenth-Century Industrial Relations," *Past and Present* 108 (1985):133–76.

8. For a description of the results of the J. P. Stevens corporate campaign, see "Stevens and Textile Union Halt 17-Year Labor Dispute," *Daily Labor Report,* 204, (20 October 1980):AA1–AA3, D1–D3.

9. For a discussion of the report and the origins of the committee, see John T. Dunlop, *Dispute Resolution: Negotiations and Consensus Building* (Dover, Mass.: Auburn House, 1984), 247–51.

For more on this project, see Marshall Goldman, "Bringing Manufacturing Jobs Back Home," *Technology Review* 88 (February-March 1985):10–11; and Richard Kazis, "The Tailored Clothing Technology Corporation: A Case Study in Collaborative Research and Development" (MIT, January 1985, manuscript).

10. This case is drawn from Tove H. Hammer and Robert N. Stern, "A Yo-Yo Model of Union-Management Cooperation," *Industrial and Labor Relations Review* 39 (1986):337–49.

11. This case is reported in full in Kirsten Wever, "Union Strategy and Vision: Changes in Airline Industrial Relations," (Ph.D. diss., Department of Political Science, MIT, 1986).

12. For more on this, see "Statement" of Norman A. Weintraub, Chief Economist and Director, International Brotherhood of Teamsters, before the Surface Transportation Subcommittee on Commerce, Science and Transportation, U.S. Senate, 27 September 1985.

13. Testimony of Norman Weintraub before the Surface Transportation Subcommittee on Commerce, Science, and Transportation, U.S. Senate, 9 September 1985. The subsequent bankruptcy of McLean Trucking Company in January 1986 raised the estimate of the percentage of general freight industry that went into receivership to 25 percent. This affected approximately 87,000 workers. See "Shutdown at McLean Trucking," *New York Times,* 11 January 1985:36.

14. See "Report of Joint IUD-Litton Committee to Mr. Fred O'Green—Chairman and Chief Executive Officer, Litton Industries" (pamphlet, 20 November 1984):1.

15. Ibid., 5.

16. Ibid., 3.

17. For a discussion of the development and operation of the operating team system in GM, see Katz, *Shifting Gears,* and chap. 4 above.

18. Saturn will also operate with a number of other novel contractual features. For instance, all workers will be salaried employees (work without time clocks), and their pay will be partially linked to the financial performance of their work units and the overall Saturn project.

19. See, for instance, William Serrin, "Saturn Pact Assailed by UAW Founder," *New York Times,* 28 October 1985, p. 21. For a more complete discussion see Harry C. Katz, "The Debate over the Reorganization of Work and Industrial Relations Within the North American Labor Movements (Paper presented at the conference on Trade Unions, New Technology, and Industrial Democracy, University of Warwick, 6–8 June 1986.

20. Japanese companies, including Honda and Nissan, recently opened nonunion plants in the United States, so the industry is no longer completely organized. But the share of these unorganized firms is, and has been, so small as to not significantly affect the bargaining leverage held by the UAW and the IUE.

Chapter 8

1. For a discussion of the concept of worker needs and the influence of their social context, see Gerald R. Salancik and Jeffrey Pfeffer, "An Examination of Need Satisfaction Models of Job Attitudes, *Administrative Science Quarterly* 22 (1977):427–56.

2. See Rosabeth Moss Kanter, "Work in America," *Daedalus* 107 (1978):53–54. For additional data on worker values and attitudes, see Graham L. Staines and Robert P. Quinn, "American Workers Evaluate the Quality of Their Jobs, *Monthly Labor Review* 102 (1974):3–12. These authors report the complete survey results in *The 1977 Quality of Employment Survey* (Ann Arbor: University of Michigan Survey Research Center, 1978).

3. William A. Schiemann, ed., *Managing Human Resources: 1985 and Beyond* (Princeton, N.J.: Opinion Research Corporation, 1984).

4. A complete discussion of these survey data is provided in Thomas A. Kochan, Harry C. Katz, and Nancy Mower, *Worker Participation and American Unions: Threat or Opportunity?* (Kalamazoo, Mich.: W. E. Upjohn Institute for Employment Research, 1984).

5. Further discussion of this point is provided in ibid., 13–96.

6. For similar results from worker samples in twelve countries, see *Industrial Democracy in Europe* (Oxford: Oxford University Press, 1981). For similar results from two samples of U.S. workers, see John F. Witte, *Democracy, Authority and Alienation in Work* (Chicago: University of Chicago Press, 1980), 32.

7. S. William Alper, Bruce N. Pfau, and David Sirota, *The 1985 National Survey of Employee Attitudes* (New York: Business Week and Sirota and Alper Associates, 1985), 13–15.

8. Ibid., p. 16.

9. Thomas A. Kochan, "How American Workers View Unions," *Monthly Labor Review* 102 (April 1979):24.

10. James L. Medoff, "The Public's Image of Labor and Labor's Response" (Harvard Univ., Department of Economics, 1984, p. 16, manuscript).

11. Henry S. Farber., "The Extent of Unionism in the United States," in Thomas A. Kochan, ed., *Challenges and Choices Facing American Labor* (Cambridge, Mass.:

Notes

MIT Press, 1984), p. 35. See also Kochan, "How American Workers View Unions,"
26.

12. The results from the AFL-CIO/Harris poll reported here are derived from
our own analysis of these data. We wish to thank the AFL-CIO Evolution of Work
Committee and Louis Harris and Associates for making these data available to
us.

13. Richard B. Freeman and James L. Medoff, *What Do Unions Do?* (New York:
Basic Books, 1984), 48–51.

14. Stephen M. Hills, "The Attitudes of Unions and Non-Union Male Workers
toward Union Representation," *Industrial and Labor Relations Review* 38 (1985):
183.

15. Kochan, Katz, and Mower, *Worker Participation and American Unions,*
13–64.

16. See Garth Mangum, Donald Mayall, and Kristen Nelson, "The Temporary
Help Industry: A Response to the Dual Internal Labor Market," *Industrial and
Labor Relations Review* 38 (1985):599–611.

17. For a more comprehensive and far-reaching discussion of types of alternative
forms of worker representation that may evolve see Charles Hecksher, "Multilateral
Negotiation and the Future of American Labor," *Negotiations Journal* 2 (1986):
141–55.

Chapter 9

1. See Michael Piore and Charles Sabel, *The Second Industrial Divide* (New
York: Basic Books, 1984).

2. There is a great deal more debate and speculation on the effects of technology
on the level of skills and employment than there are actual data. For a statement
supporting the argument that new technology will lead to lower skill content, see
Harley Shaiken, "The Automated Factory: The View from the Shopfloor, *Technology Review* 88, no. 1 (1985):16–27. For a view that new technology introduces
a need for greater analytical ability and therefore will have the net effect of increasing skill levels, see Shoshana Zuboff, "New Worlds of Computer-oriented
Work," *Harvard Business Review,* 60, no. 5 (1982):142–52. For the most careful
forecast of the effects of new technology in the auto industry on both the number
and mix of jobs, see Allan Hunt and Timothy L. Hunt, *Human Resource Implications of Robotics* (Kalamazoo, Mich.: W. E. Upjohn Institute, 1983).

3. The most comprehensive compilation of criticisms of the current law and
procedures governing representation elections is contained in the record of the
Hearings of the Subcommittee on Labor Management Relations of the House of
Representatives held on June 21, 25, and 26, 1984, on the subject "Has Labor
Law Failed?"

4. See Janice A. Klein and E. David Wanger, "The Legal Setting for the Emergence of the Union Avoidance Strategy," in Thomas A. Kochan, ed., *Challenges
and Choices Facing American Labor* (Cambridge, Mass.: MIT Press, 1985), 82.

5. Hearings of the Subcommittee on Labor Management Relations of the House
of Representatives, June 21, 25, 26, 1984.

6. See, for example, the statements in the Hearings cited in note 4 of Professors
Paul Weiler, Clyde Summers, William Gould, James Atelson, and Dan Pollitt.
For a study of the experience of unions in negotiating initial contracts after winning
representation elections, see William N. Cooke, *Union Organizing and Public Policy:*

272

Failure to Secure First Contracts (Kalamazoo, Mich.: W. E. Upjohn Institute, 1985).

7. For a discussion of these legal doctrines and the reasons why they need to be modified as part of the updating of public policy, see Stephen I. Schlossberg and Steven M. Fetter, "U.S. Labor Law and the Future of Labor-Management Cooperation" (U.S. Department of Labor, June 1986).

8. See Donna Sockell, "The Legality of Employee-Participation Programs in Unionized Firms," *Industrial and Labor Relations Review,* 37 (1984):541–56.

9. See Leonard Greenhalgh, Robert B. McKersie, and Roderick Gilkey, "Rebalancing the Workforce at IBM: A Case Study of Redeployment and Revitalization," MIT Sloan School of Management Working Paper No. 1718–85, October 1985.

10. These scenarios were initially developed to facilitate discussions over the future of unions in American society among members of the Collective Bargaining Forum, a private labor-management committee that has been meeting to discuss the future of union-management relations in the United States. A more complete discussion of the scenarios will be presented in the final report of the forum scheduled for release in 1987. We would like to thank Malcolm Lovell, the chairman of the Collective Bargaining Forum, for encouraging the development of these scenarios.

Index

absenteeism, 89; in auto industry, 151; QWL programs and, 156
ACF Industries, 71
affirmative action, 43
airlines industry, 38; concessions in, 121–127; deregulation of, 121, 138, 267n27; industrial relations professionals in, 131; job security in, 125–126; pay criteria in, 134; product-market strategies in, 121–122; union avoidance in, 126–127; workers' equity in, 126
Alcoa, 70
all salaried pay plans, 99, 100, 102
Amalgamated Clothing and Textile Workers Union (ACTWU), 163–168; in corporate decision making, 188; in Tailored Clothing Technology Corporation (TC)² program, 187–189
American Airlines, 119, 123, 124, 125, 132–134
American Federation of Labor and Congress of Industrial Organizations (AFL-CIO), 58; Industrial Union Department (IUD) of, 195–197; jurisdictional disputes under, 38; on strategic-choice participation, 182
American Federation of Labor and Congress of Industrial Organizations Committee on the Evolution of Work report: new membership categories proposed by, 222; on part-time and temporary workers, 221; public opinion polls for, 216; recommendations of, 221–222; as response to membership decline, 3–4
American Motors, 151

American plan, 25
anti-union activities, *see* union-avoidance strategies
anti-union pressure groups, 241
arbitration of first contracts, 234
arbitration procedures, 83
arbitrators, 32
AT&T, 149, 174–175
authorization cards, 234
Automation Funds, 120
automobile industry: concession bargaining in, 115, 119; economic decline in, 159; employment decline in, 115; information sharing in, 133; Japanese competition in, 159; labor relations performance in, 93; plant-level agreements in, 129; QWL programs in, 150–152, 154–157; shop-floor problems in, 39, 151; strikes in, 32, 33, 40; unemployment in, 159; union officials' role in, 159; union organizing in, 30–31; wage formula adopted in, 26, 40; as workplace innovation trend setter, 242
autonomous work groups, 96, 99, 100, 174, 211
auto parts industry, 34, 50

bankruptcy: under Chapter 11, 127; at Rath Meatpacking, 190; threat of, 122–124; in trucking industry, 193
bargaining relationships: anti-union pressures on, 241–242; choices in, 237–245; competitive pressures on, 240–241; cost

Index

bargaining relationships: *(continued)*
control and, 242–243; decentralization and, 241, 242; diverging scenarios for, 243–245; at highly unionized firms, 238–242; high-productivity/high-wage strategy in, 241; human resource management strategies in, 242; at partially unionized firms, 242–245; at strategic level, 237–238, 240–241; at workplace level, 238–240
Baron, James N., 36
Basic Steel Agreement, 128
behavioral science theories, 62, 94–95, 101, 150
Bendix, Reinhard, 14–15
Bendix auto parts company, 50
benefits: in 1950s, 38; nonunion workers' interest in, 223; perceived effects of unionization on, 218, 219; union/nonunion differentials in, 103
Bennett, Michael, 182
Bethlehem Steel, 174
"Big Labor" stereotype, 216
blue-collar workers: bargaining power of, 248–249; interest in worker participation among, 212; occupational identity of, 248; union coverage of, 216; union wages set for, 30
Bluestone, Irving, 42, 44, 151, 269n9
Boeing, 120
bonus incentives, 240
Boulware, Lemuel R., 37
Boulwarism, 37–38
Braniff Airlines, 123, 134
Bricklayers union, 182
Brown, Douglas, 14
Brown and Williamson Tobacco, 26
Bureau of Labor Statistics (BLS), 48, 115
Bureau of National Affairs, 37
Burlington Mills, 56
business unionism, 17, 23; managerial control under, 27, 28, 178, 179; narrow scope of bargaining under, 27–28; NLRA institutionalization of, 178
Business Week, 216

Camens, Sam, 181
Canada, 51
capital investments, *see* investment decisions
capitalistic system of production, 22
Cappelli, Peter, 115, 121
Carmichael, John, 181
Carter, Jimmy, 44
Champion International, 71
Chandler, Alfred, 10
chemical industry, 58
chief executive officers (CEOs): on bargain-ing teams, 131; in human resource man-agement, 62–64
Chrysler Corporation, 151, 190
civil rights legislation, 40
civil rights movement, 38–39
clerical workers, 248–249
clothing industry, 32; new technology in, 187–189; union organizing in, 31
coal industry, 32, 34, 49
collective bargaining: communication strat-egies in, 132–134; contingent compensa-tion structures and, 240; decentralization of, 34, 113–114, 128–130; economic pres-sures on, 111–112; employment conditions influenced by, 30; expanded agenda for, 118–121; formal vs. informal structures in, 267n39; incremental vs. fundamental changes in, 30, 109–110; information sharing and, 133–134; institutional view of, 22–24; management accommodation to, 14–15; managerial decisions under, 178; mandatory, permissive, and illegal subjects of, 236; as means to increase purchasing power, 26; narrow interpretations of, 27–28; national vs. company levels of, 129; as New Deal system center, 25–27; under NLRA, 7–8; NLRB clarification of scope of, 31; QWL programs and, 148–150; sta-bility in, 26–27; strategic business decisions and, 178–179; in three-tier framework, 16–17; union officials bypassed in, 132–133; worker expectations and, 220; *see also* bar-gaining relationships, choices in; conces-sion bargaining; contract negotiations; New Deal industrial relations system
Collective Bargaining Forum, 273n10
Commerce Department, U.S., 188
Commons, John R., 15, 23
communications programs, 57, 95, 132–134; at American Airlines, 132–133; in auto in-dustry, 159; as bargaining strategy, 132–134; in contract ratification, 142–143; at GM, 151–152; Mutual Growth Forums in, 133–134; at Schneider Transport, 142–143
Communication Workers of America (CWA), 174–175
communist union leaders, 33
company domination prohibition, 234–235
company unionism, 9, 235
comparison pay, 137–138
competition, foreign and domestic, 40, 228
Competitive Action Plan (CAP) (Western Airlines), 192
computer-aided design (CAD), 120
computer-aided manufacturing (CAM), 120
concession bargaining: in airlines industry, 121–127; bankruptcy threat in, 122–124; board representation in, 190–91; as break-down of New Deal system, 21; COLAs in,

116; communications strategies in, 132–134; contingent pay procedures in, 134; in early 1980s, 3–4; employment loss and, 115; environmental forces and, 113; in highly unionized firms, 116–117; job security in, 119–121; management structure in, 131–132; noncash benefits in, 112; at partially unionized firms, 243; pay cuts and freezes in, 116–117; pressures to recoup losses in, 240; quid pro quos in, 118–119; during recessions, 117–118; at Schneider Transport, 137–143; theoretical framework for analysis of, 112–114; in trucking industry, 193–195; union coverage in, 113; worker ownership in, 126; work rules in, 112, 113, 117–118

Conference Board surveys, 41–42, 43, 56, 59, 61–64, 67, 77–78, 99, 100, 115, 116–117, 118, 134

conflict management systems, 82–85; communication procedures in, 95; empirical illustrations of, 89–93; grievance rates and, 89–93; at IBM, 95; in nonunion systems, 83, 94–95; ombudspersons in, 95; organizational effectiveness and, 83–84; production costs and, 93; union vs. nonunion forms of, 83

Congress, U.S., 32–33, 44, 231

Congress of Industrial Organizations (CIO), 33

construction industry, 34, 49

consumer price index (CPI), 117

Continental Airlines, 123, 127, 135

contingent pay procedures, 134

contract, freedom to, 24

contract administration, 17, 29

contracting out, see subcontracting

contract negotiations: financial executives in, 131; grievances and, 84, 85; local issues in, 39; management teams for, 131–132

contract ratification process, 132; rejection rate in, 39; at Schneider Transport, 142–143

contracts: GM-UAW 1948 model for, 33–34; industry-wide, 38; under job control unionism, 28–29; multiyear, 33–34, 38; national, 38; under NLRA, 24–25; workplace practices under, 88–89

cooperative unions, 58

Cooper Industries, 73–74

copper mining industry, 115, 136

Corning Glass, 71

corporate board representation for unions, 189–193; concessions exchanged for, 190–191; nonunion appointees in, 194; rank-and-file attitudes towards, 191, 192; at Rath Meatpacking, 190–191; at Western Airlines, 191–193

corporate campaigns, 188; communications opened through, 196–197; at Litton Industries, 195–197

cost-of-living adjustments (COLAs), 26; in auto contracts, 160; concessions in, 116; contingent pay provisions and, 134; 1970s expansion of, 40

counseling on workplace problems, 223

craft unions, 25, 34

creative destruction of capital concept, 65

Cummins Engine company, 71, 132

Dana Corporation, 50, 75–76

day-care benefits, 223

Delta Airlines, 56, 123, 124, 125

dental insurance benefits, 223

deregulation: in airlines industry, 121, 138, 267n27; cost competition increased in, 114–115; in 1970s, 40; in trucking industry, 49, 129–130, 138–139

developing nations, 228

Dickens, William, 77

discipline cases, 89–93

disinvestment, 72–75; in 1980s, 75–76; in partially unionized firms, 243–244; planned, 73–74; rapid, 74–75; slow, 72–73; see also investment decisions

Dobbin, Frank R., 36

Draper Laboratories, 188–189

due process, 82–85, 231

dues check-off procedures, 33, 36

Dunlop, John, 7, 36, 42–43, 188

Du Pont, 34, 68–69

Eastern Airlines, 123, 125–126, 134, 190

Eaton auto parts company, 50

economic restructuring, 228–229

economics: classical, 22, 23; institutional, 22–24; Keynesian, 26; neoclassical, 15–16

Education and Labor Subcommittee, U.S. House of Representatives, 196

electoral politics, unions in, 216

electrical products industry, 34, 38, 119

Emerson Electric, 73–74

employee involvement (EI) programs, see quality of working life

employee stock ownership plans (ESOPs), 192; at Rath Meatpacking, 190; in trucking industry, 193–195; voluntary participation in, 194; at Western Airlines, 191–192

employment: decision-making power shift in, 9–10; internal vs. external pressures on, 120; in manufacturing, 115; wages and, 114

engineers, professional, 61

environmental forces: concession bargaining and, 113; in Dunlop's system model, 7; economic restructuring in, 228; in future developments, 227–230; increased competition in, 228; managerial strategic decisions and, 112–113; market trends in, 228–229; on New Deal system, 45–46, 109–110, 114–115; new technology in, 229; in 1970s, 40; in 1980s, 109–110; organizational hierarchy and, 229–230; political climate and, 230; in strategic perspective, 4–5, 12, 13–14; union response to, 12–13; in workers' attitudes, 207–208
Ephlin, Donald, 160, 181
equal employment opportunity, 43
equal pay for equal work, 40
exclusive representation principle, 235
Experimental Negotiating Agreement, in the steel industry, 40

fair representation doctrine, 238
Farah Company, 188
Farber, Henry, 53–54, 55, 76
farm machinery industry, 115
Federal Mediation and Conciliation Service, 236
federal pay guidelines, 40
Firestone, 71
Flanagan, Robert, 134–135
flexible work schedules, 99, 100
Florida Steel, 75
Ford Motor Company, 61, 119, 120, 121; Mutual Growth Forums at, 133–134; QWL programs at, 151; worker participation programs at, 159–160
foreign competition, 40, 228
foremen, 89
Freeman, Richard, 77
fringe benefits, see benefits
Frontier Airlines, 123, 127
Fuller, Stephen, 42, 151

gain-sharing plans, 69, 167
garment industry, 40; import restrictions in, 187, 188; new technology in, 187–189; TC program in, 187–189
General Dynamics, 71
General Electric (GE), 37–38, 49
General Mills, 71
General Motors (GM), 33, 39; administrative teams at, 198; anti-union pressure groups and, 241; conflict management at, 89–93; Fiero plant at, 161–162, 197–199; industrial relations staff at, 131; job bank negotiated at, 170; Lordstown strike at, 151; 1960s shop-floor unrest at, 39; operating teams at, 151, 158, 161–162, 199, 201; Packard Electric subsidiary of, 149, 158, 168–172, 176, 199–200, 202, 203; pilot employment guarantee at, 121; painting committees at, 201; QWL programs at, 42, 151–152, 154–157; in representation elections, 159; Saturn project at, 199, 201, 202, 271n18; southern strategy of, 59, 61, 158–159, 269n16; strategic business decisions at, 198–199; UAW's 1948 contract with, 33; union-avoidance strategies at, 59; white-collar workers at, 61
General Tire, 71
Germany, Federal Republic of (West Germany), 169
Gompers, Samuel, 23
good faith bargaining, 25, 37–38
Goodyear, 69, 71
Great Depression, 25, 26, 118
greenfield sites, 67, 94
Greyhound, 135–136
grievance procedures: in conflict management, 83; contract negotiations and, 84, 85; contractual, 85; under job control unionism, 28; under New Deal system, 27, 28; new technology and, 238; at nonunion firms, 83, 95, 99, 100; organizational effectiveness and, 83–84; as organizing tools, 36; perceptions of union performance on, 219; productivity and, 93; QWL programs and, 155, 156; rate of filings under, 89–93; shop-floor unrest and, 39; union plant-level power and, 238; volume of complaints under, 83–84; under WLB, 32; workers' attitudes on, 211
Gross, James, 33
Grumman Aircraft, 56
guaranteed income stream programs, 119, 160

Hammer, Tove, 190
Harbison, Frederick, 7
Harris, Howell John, 15
Harris polls, 216–217, 221, 222–223
Hawthorne experiments, 87
health care benefits, 38, 223
Healy, James J., 38, 88–89, 255n21
Henle, Peter, 118
high-productivity/high-wage business strategy, 241
high technology industries, 39
high-volume/low-cost business strategy, 247–248
Hoffa, Jimmy, 129

Honda, 271n20
House of Representatives, U.S., 231
human resource management system, 5; chief
  executive officers in, 62–64; durability of,
  249–250; at high-volume/low-cost firms,
  247–248; at IBM, 95; as innovation pacesetter, 226–227; line and staff responsibilities in, 62–64; management commitment
  to, 249–250; managerial values in, 55–56;
  market pressures on, 246–247; model for
  diffusion of, 52–53; New Deal system and,
  21, 45–46; nonunion innovations in, 9; in
  partially unionized firms, 242; at Schneider
  Transport, 139–142; temporary workers
  and, 221; in unionized workplaces, 9
human resource specialists, 43; industrial
  relations professionals vs., 43, 62–64; line
  managers and, 62–64; in union-avoidance
  strategies, 62

IBM, 56, 68, 95, 247
Ichniowski, Casey, 93
ideology: consensus or shared, 7, 8–9, 254n7;
  in Dunlop's system model, 7, 254n7; in
  managerial values, 8–9
immigration, 35
imports: in garment industry, 187, 188; in
  immediate postwar years, 34
income security provisions, 38
independent unions, 34; at Du Pont, 69; local,
  58; management encouragement of, 58
industrial commissions, 25
industrial engineering, 29, 89
industrial espionage, 35
industrial relations, strategic perspective on:
  defined, 4–5; environmental forces in, 4–
  5, 12, 13–14; on future of industrial relations, 226–227; general framework for, 11;
  management structures and, 9–10; 1980s
  shifts analyzed with, 112–114; organizational responses in, 13; role of choice in,
  13–15; three-tier framework in, 16–20;
  traditional theory in, 11–12, 13; on workplace innovations, 81–82
industrial relations professionals: concession
  bargaining and, 131; human resource specialists vs., 43, 62–64; importance attached
  to, 37; 1970s status quo orientation of, 41–
  42; personnel department growth and, 35–
  36; in search for stability, 36–37, 41–42;
  training and development of, 16; union
  leaders' symbiotic relations with, 36;
  union membership decline and, 43–44;
  worker participation and, 42
industrial relations systems: defined, 7;

Dunlop on, 7; environmental pressures on,
  4–5; European, 17; fundamental change in,
  3–4, 20; management structure and, 9–10;
  managerial adjustments in, 9; union vs.
  nonunion dynamic in, 5; see also New Deal
  industrial relations system
Industrial Relations Systems (Dunlop), 7
industrial relations theories: anomalies
  unexplained by, 6, 7; current developments
  and, 4; environmental forces in, 7, 12–14;
  general social sciences theories vs., 15–16;
  institutional, 15–20; managerial values
  and, 8–9; neoclassical economics vs., 15–
  16; strategic inconsistencies within firms
  and, 19; workplace policy research in, 18
industrial unionism, 20, 35, 88
inflation, 41, 117
information-processing technology, 96, 229
Ingersoll-Rand, 76
institutional labor economists, 22–24
institutional structure: broad normative
  perspective and, 19–20; defined, 15–16;
  managerial inconsistencies identified in,
  19; three-tier framework for, 16
International Association of Machinists
  (IAM), 120
International Brotherhood of Electrical
  Workers (IBEW), 58
International Brotherhood of Teamsters,
  129–130; contract ratification in, 142–143;
  in corporate board representation, 192; in
  ESOPs, 193–195; limited engagement
  strategy of, 193; at Schneider Transport,
  137–143
International Chemical Workers (ICW), 69
International Harvester, 36–37
International Ladies Garment Workers
  Union (ILGWU), 187
International Paper, 71
International Union of Electrical Workers
  (IUE), 58, 158, 168–171, 199–200, 202
International Union of Mine, Mill and
  Smelter Workers, 136
Interstate Commerce Commission, U.S., 130,
  138
investment decisions, 72–76; labor-cost dif-
  ferentials in, 103–104; as top tier strategy
  decisions, 17, 18; workers' attitudes on,
  211–213; see also disinvestment
Ireland, 169

Jacoby, Sanford M., 35–36
Japan, 150, 159
jawboning, 40
Jennings, P. Devereaux, 36
job banks, 119, 171

job classifications, 28, 97, 101; concessions in, 118; operating teams and, 160, 162; at union vs. nonunion plants, 102
job control unionism, 28–29, 88, 94; at competitive disadvantage, 239; economic context for, 88; QWL programs and, 148, 161; at workplace level, 88–89
job design, 17; flexibility in, 96; new models for, 94
job enlargement theories, 94
job evaluation procedures, 89
job satisfaction, 86–87; decline in, 214–215; surveys on, 214; workers' views on unions and, 216–217
job security: in airlines industry, 125–126; in concession bargaining; 119–121; under job control unionism, 29; at Packard Electric, 200; perceived effects of unionization on, 218; QWL programs and, 121; specialized training and, 119–120; for supervisory employees, 236; training programs and, 120–121
Johnson, Lyndon, 40
Joint Labor-Management Committee of the retail food industry (JLMC), 183–187; accomplishments of, 185–186; in collective bargaining disputes, 186; communications enhanced through, 185; limitations of, 186–187; management resistance to, 184; objectives of, 183–184; research projects conducted by, 185–186
Jones and Laughlin Company, 172–173
J. P. Stevens, 188
just-in-time inventories, 239

Kanter, Rosabeth Moss, 209–210
Kennecott Copper Corporation, 136
Kennedy, John F., 39, 40
Kerr, Clark, 7
Keynesian theory, 26

Labor Committee, U.S. Senate, 24–25
labor costs: in developing nations, 228; market pressures on, 246; productivity and, 103–104; product market competition and, 65–66, 228; QWL programs and, 157; at Schneider Transport, 139; turnover rates and, 104; union/nonunion differential in, 103–104; work rules and, 86
Labor Department, U.S.: in clothing industry training program, 188; growth of regulations administered by, 42–43; in industrial relations reform, 236

labor efficiency index, 155–156
labor law, 17; company domination prohibition in, 234–235; 1977 bill on, 44; as outdated, 231; reform needed in, 233–234; scenario for reform in, 252; on union recognition, 232–234; worker/supervisor distinction in, 235–236
labor-management committees, 183–187; basic issues in, 184; at Litton Industries, 196–197; threats to survival of, 184–185; union leaders in, 184–185; see also Joint Labor-Management Committee of the retail food industry (JLMC)
labor-management discussion groups, 15
labor-management participation teams (LMPTs), 147, 172–173
Labor-Management Reporting and Disclosure Act (1959), 38
labor markets: classical view of, 22, 23; institutional view of, 22–24; during World War II, 35
Lackey, Doris, 182
layoffs, 115, 119–120, 169–171
legal services benefits, 223
Leonard, Jonathan, 77
limited engagement strategy, 193
line managers, 62–64, 96, 150
Litton Industries, 195–197, 202
Livernash, E. Robert, 38, 88–89, 255n21
lobbying, 223
longshore industry, 40, 119
LTV steel company, 174

McClellan hearings, U.S. Senate, 38
McDonald, Charles, 55
maintenance workers, 101, 102, 105
management: centralization of industrial relations function by, 41; foreman-driven system of, 88–89, 93; "hard line" policies of, 37–38; scientific, 29, 89; stability sought by, 35–37
Management Assessment Program (MAP), 141
managerial strategies: environmental forces in, 12–14; market forces in, 13; union-free preference in, 12, 14–15
managerial values: broader social values and, 14–15; consensus ideology in, 8–9; cooperative unions and, 58; in firms never organized, 56; historic hostility to unions in, 14–15; inconsistency in, 15; NLRA and, 25–26; in plant location decisions, 68; public policy and, 233; strategic adaptations vs., 15; in union-avoidance strategies, 65; "union-free" preference in, 9; in union membership decline, 55–58

managers: job security of, 249; lack of NLRA coverage for, 249; middle, 236; work values of, 210
Manufacturers Hanover Trust, 136
mass production, 29, 88
Mead paper company, 71
meatpacking industry, 32, 34, 40, 119
mediators, 32
medical insurance benefits, 38, 223
Mexico, 168, 169, 203
minimum wage laws, 28
minorities, 217, 218
Mitchell, Daniel, 111, 116
Mobil Oil, 71
Monsanto, 49–50
Morris, George B., 42
motivation theories, 94
Motor Carrier Act (1980), 130
Motorola, 56
multiemployer pension funds, 186
multifiber agreement, 188
Murray, Philip, 33
Mutual Growth Forums, 133
Myers, Charles, 7, 14, 36

National Civic Federation, 15
National Industrial Recovery Act, 24
National Labor Board, 24
National Labor Relations Act (NLRA), 7–8; bargaining subjects under, 236; in broader social ethos, 24–25; business unionism under, 178; collective bargaining advanced by, 7, 8; company domination of unions banned under, 234–235; constitutional ruling on, 35; framers' assumptions in, 17; institutionalist view in, 23–24; managerial values and, 25–26; managers and supervisors not covered by, 249; organizing efforts under, 25–26; as outdated, 231; previous policies embodied in, 25; reform needed in, 233–234; Taft-Hartley amendments to, 32–33
National Labor Relations Board (NLRB), 67; administrative reform needed in, 234; bargaining scope defined by, 31; creation of, 24; delays in appeals to, 233; Litton case in, 196; privileged electioneering under, 232
National Longitudinal Survey, 218
National Master Freight Agreement (NMFA), 118, 128, 129–130, 137, 141, 142, 143
National Right to Work Committee, 241
National Steel, 174
National Survey of Employee Attitudes, 215
National War Labor Board (WLB), 24; collective bargaining institutionalized through, 20; job control unionism supported by, 88; mediation role of, 32; membership maintenance policies supported by, 31; personnel departments encouraged by, 35; as training ground for labor professionals, 32; wage standardization promoted by, 26
New Deal industrial relations system, 5, 13, 21–46; collective bargaining as center of, 25–27; environmental pressures on, 45–46, 109–110, 114–115; highly unionized firms and, 238–239; human resource management and, 45–46; incremental changes in, 30, 45–46; institutional view in, 22–24; job control unionism in, 28–29; key industries organized under, 30–31, 34–35; Keynesian theory in, 26; labor's political program under, 27–28; in 1940s, 30–37; in 1950s, 37–38; in 1960s, 38–40; in 1970s, 40–45; nonunion pressures on, 114; normative foundations for, 22–25; part-time and temporary workers and, 249; QWL programs and, 148; strategic level of, 27–28, 179; Taft-Hartley and, 33; workers' attitudes and, 206–207, 208; workplace policies in, 28–29; see also job control unionism
Newspaper Guild, 181
new technology, 185; ACTWU involvement in, 187–189; clinical approach required by, 238; employment impact of, 229, 272n2; job control unionism and, 239; market conditions and, 228–229; in nonunion firms, 247; older workers and, 229; organizational hierarchy and, 229–230; workers' attitudes on, 212, 213; worker/supervisor distinctions blurred by, 235–236
Nissan, 271n20
nonunion industrial relations system, 47–80; causal forces in rise of, 51–53; compensation innovations in, 102; complaint procedures in, 83; conflict management in, 83, 94–95; diffusion of, 47–48, 99–100; disinvestment and, 72–76; economic incentives and, 70–72; existing unionization and, 59–62; human resources management in, 5; individual employee concerns in, 89, 93–94; in industrial relations dynamic, 5; innovations threatened in, 247; labor costs in, 103–104; labor-market changes and, 53–55; management dynamics and, 62–65; managerial values and, 55–59; new plants opened in, 66–67, 71, 248; organized sector's impact on, 21; partially organized firms and, 68–70; plant age associated with, 100; plant location and, 66–68; political debates within, 246–247; in price-competitive markets, 246–247; product markets and, 65–66; representation elections and, 76–79; strategic choices in, 246–248; theo-

Index

nonunion industrial *(continued)*
retical framework for, 51–53; union decline and, 48–51; worker allocation in, 102; at workplace level, 81–82, 100–108

nonunion workers: alternative forms of representation for, 223; benefits and services desired by, 223; as former union members, 222; on group vs. individual action, 222–223; individual bargaining power of, 248–249; in newer industries, 8; professionals, 248; unions as viewed by, 217

Norsworthy, J. R., 93

Northwest Airlines, 123

no-strike pledges: in steel industry, 40; during World War II, 31, 32

occupational accident and injury rates, 93

occupational associations, 248

occupational licensing, 248

occupational safety and health, 28, 44, 185, 218

offshore production, 242

Oil, Chemical and Atomic Workers (OCAW), 69

oil industry, 58

ombudspersons, 83, 95

open-door programs, 95

operating teams, *see* team work systems

Operation Handshake, 140

Opinion Research Corporation (ORC), 210, 214–215

organizational development consultants, 148, 150

organizational psychology, 86, 87

outsourcing, *see* subcontracting

Ozark Airlines, 123

Packard Electric, 149, 158, 168–172, 176, 269n17; job security at, 200; strategic business issues at, 197, 199–200, 202, 203

paid holidays, 160

Pan Am, 122, 123, 124–125, 126, 190

paper industry, 34

Partnership Plan (Western Airlines), 191–192

part-time workers, 171, 221, 249

pattern bargaining, 27; contingent pay provisions vs., 134; erosion of, 128–130; as stabilizing force, 34; in steel industry, 128–129; in trucking industry, 129–130; union coverage and, 129; wages in, 111

pay-for-knowledge systems, 96, 98–99, 100, 102; at GM, 158; in team work systems, 162

pension benefits, 38

Pepsi Cola, 71

performance-based pay systems, 240

Performance Recognition Program (PRP), 140

personnel departments: creation of, 35; equal employment opportunity units in, 43; formalization of procedures for, 35–36; government regulations and, 42–43; human resource specialists in, 43; importance attached to, 37

Persons, W. R. "Buck," 74

Pestillo, Peter, 160

petroleum refining industry, 49

Phelps Dodge, 135–136

Piedmont Airlines, 123

pilot employment guarantee, 121

Piper Aircraft, 71

plant age, 100–101

plant closings, 72–76, 115, 119

plant location decisions: for firms never organized, 68; large asset-redeployment costs and, 243; onsite expansion vs. new plant construction in, 66–67, 71; for partially organized firms, 69–70; in union-avoidance strategies, 54–55, 58, 67–68, 70

Portugal, 169

Pratt & Whitney, 71

privileged electioneering, 232

Procter and Gamble (P&G), 69

production costs, 93

productivity, 42, 65; grievance rates and, 93; industrial relations performance and, 92–93; injury rates and, 93; job security and, 120; perceptions of union performance in, 219–220; QWL programs and, 150; in union vs. nonunion plants, 103–104; work rules and, 86, 104–107

product-life cycles, 10, 228

product markets: for high-wage producers, 230; increased competition in, 65–66, 228; plant location decisions and, 65, 66–67; wage standardization and, 26

product quality, 92–93; at GM Fiero plant, 199; QWL programs and, 156–157; workers' attitudes on, 211

professionals, 248

profits: grievance rates and, 93; at union vs. nonunion plants, 103–104, 107–108; wage demands and, 33

profit-sharing plans, 99, 100, 134; as continuing trend, 240; at Western Airlines, 191, 192; worker attitudes towards, 192

property rights, 15, 22, 24

Prosten, Richard, 182

public policy: on bargaining practice, 237–237; classical economic theory in, 22; em-

ployer anti-union activities and, 232–233; environmental changes and, 12–13; on exclusive representation, 235; flexibility needed in, 231; institutional view of, 23–24; market forces and, 13; in New Deal system, 22; private experimentation and, 230–231; on union recognition, 232–234; updated goals for, 231; on worker participation, 17–18; on worker rights, 231
public sector unions, 39

quality circles (QCs), 147
Quality of Employment Survey, 216, 217
quality of working life (QWL) programs, 42, 147–177; absenteeism and, 156; at AT&T, 174–175; attitudinal relations improved by, 174; in auto industry, 150–152, 154–157; collective bargaining vs., 148–150; company domination prohibition and, 235; contractual language and, 167–168; diffusion of, 150–151, 152–153; economic effects of, 154; employment security and, 121; external pressures for, 152; financial information in, 161; at GM, 42, 151–152, 154–157; grievance procedures and, 155, 156; at highly unionized firms, 239; housekeeping issues addressed in, 157–158; individual needs stressed in, 148; integrated effort required in, 204–205; labor efficiency index for, 155–157; at large vs. small firms, 153–154; line managers in, 150; local union leaders' support for, 240; in nonunion firms, 150, 153; organizational effectiveness of, 153–157; at Packard Electric, 168–172, 176; performance improvements through, 87; product quality and, 156–157; rank-and-file acceptance of, 168; scope of, 147; shared labor/management commitment in, 168; types of, 147–148; as union-avoidance strategy, 150; at union firms, 150, 153; union performance evaluated in, 220; worker attitudes and, 174, 211; workers covered under, 152–153; worker-supervisor relations under, 157–158; workplace changes brought by, 153–154; work reorganization and, 158; at Xerox Corporation, 163–168, 171–172, 176

railroad industry, 32, 38
Railway Labor Act, 38
Rath Meatpacking, 190–191
Reagan administration, 188
recessions: high-productivity/high-wage strategy in, 241; of 1958–59, 38, 118; of 1970–71, 40; of 1974–75, 40; of 1981–82, 48, 112, 113; union power weakened in, 38, 113; work rule bargaining and, 117–118
representation, alternative forms of: for nonunion workers, 222–223; for part-time and temporary workers, 221
representation elections, 76–78; anti-union tactics in, 94; appeals in, 233; coercive actions in, 232; decline in number of, 77; illegal employer activities in, 78, 232–234; labor law reform impulse stimulated by, 44; in new employment relationships, 78, 232; under NLRA, 25, 26; privileged electioneering in, 232; public policy on, 232–234; reforms needed in, 233–234; win rates in, 77–78; workers' views on unions in, 217
Republic Airlines, 123, 126
Republic Steel, 173
resident manager programs, 95
retail food industry, 183–187
Reuther, Walter, 33
right-to-work legislation, 70
Robertson, H. M., 26
robotics, 120
rubber industry, 31, 34

salary surveys, 248
Saturn project, General Motors, 199, 201, 202, 271n18
Schmenner, Roger, 67
Schneider National, 137, 139
Schneider Transport (subsidiary of Schneider National), 136–143; comparison pay provision at, 137–138; human resource management strategy at, 139–142; independent contractor operations established by, 138–139; Industrial Relations Group at, 141; management structure at, 139; NMFA at, 141, 142, 143; non-driving activities at, 141; ratification strategy at, 142–143; Schneider National, 136–143; supervisors at, 140–141; training programs at, 139–140
Schumpeter, Joseph A., 65
scientific management practices, 29, 89
seniority rules, 28–29, 36, 89
service sector, 54, 55
shop-floor militancy, 38–39
shop stewards, 135
skip-level interview program, 95
Slichter, Sumner, 9, 38, 88–89, 117–118, 255n21
socialist system of production, 22
social reformers, 23
social security, 28
sociotechnical theorists, 94
Southern states: employment growth in, 53,

Southern states: *(continued)*
54–55; general antiunion climate in, 70;
GM plants in, 59; management preference
for, 54–55
Spain, 169
speak-out and speak-up programs, 57, 83, 95
Spector, Bert, 42
steel industry, 115; contracts in, 34, 40; Experimental Negotiating Agreement in, 40;
LMPTs in, 172–174; pattern bargaining in,
128–129; strikes in, 32, 38; union organizing in, 30–31
Stern, Robert, 190
strategic business decisions, 15–18, 178–183;
banking interests in, 202–203; bargaining
agendas and, 178–179; business unionism
and, 178; corporate campaigns and, 195–
197; environmental pressures and, 201–
202; JLMC in, 186; labor-management
committees in, 182–183; worker attitudes
on, 211–213; worker participation in, 179
strategic-choice model of union participation,
179–205; in administrative teams, 198;
bargaining subjects and, 236; board representation in, 189–193; centralized bargaining and, 180; economic pressures and,
194–195; as experimental, 203–204; in
garment industry, 187–189; general patterns in, 201–203; at GM, 198–199; government policy on, 237–238; in highly
competitive industries, 182–183; at highly
unionized firms, 240–241; at industry level,
182–189; integrated effort required in, 204–
205; labor-management committees in,
182–183; management resistance to, 180,
237–238; membership evaluation of, 219–
220; in new technology, 187–189; obstacles
to, 237–238; at Packard Electric, 199–200;
in plant-level activities, 197–205; political
risks associated with, 179–180; at Rath
Meatpacking, 190–191; in retail food industry, 183–187; in Saturn project, 199,
201, 202; stock ownership plans in, 193–
195; success in, 202–203; Teamsters in,
193–195; trial-and-error period in, 180;
union debates over, 180; union leaders' attitudes towards, 179–182, 203; at Western
Airlines, 191–193; workers' attitudes on,
211–213
strikes: in auto industry, 32, 33, 40; decline
in, 134–135; in immediate postwar years,
32; at Phelps Dodge, 135–136; replacements hired in, 135–136; in steel industry,
32, 38; union representation eliminated in,
135; wildcat, 39
subcontracting, 66, 101, 119, 160, 164
suggestion systems, 89–90
supervisors, 101; in conflict management, 83;
individual bargaining power of, 249; job

security of, 236; perceived effects of
unionization on, 218; at Schneider Transport, 140–141; under Taft-Hartley definition, 235–236; in team work systems, 96–
97, 160; workers' attitudes towards, 87, 89
supplementary unemployment benefits, 38,
119

Taft-Hartley Act, 55; emergency dispute
resolution under, 38, 39–40; privileged
electioneering under, 232; union power
under, 32–33; worker/supervisor distinction under, 235–236
Tailored Clothing Technology Corporation
program (TC)², 187–189
team work systems, 96–99, 147; financial information received by, 160–162; at GM,
151, 158, 161–162, 199, 201; job classifications reduced in, 160, 162; local union
opposition to, 162; manager's role in, 96–
97; promotions in, 97–98; in Saturn project,
201; shop-floor relations in, 160; supervisors in, 96–97, 160; turnover in, 99; wages
in, 98–99
technician systems, 69
temporary workers, 221, 249
Texas International, 127
textile industry, 31, 187–189
Thompson Products, 34
3M, 49–50
training programs, 120; in clothing industry,
188; nonunion worker interest in, 223; for
professionals, 248; at Schneider Transport,
139–140
trucking industry: concession bargaining in,
193–195; decentralized bargaining in, 129–
130; deregulation of, 49, 129–130, 138–139;
employment guarantees in, 119; ESOPs in,
193–195; "full truckload" carriers in, 129,
130, 141–142; multiyear contracts in, 34;
Schneider Transport case study in, 137–
143; union decline in, 49; work-rule
changes in, 118
TRW, Inc., 34, 96–99
turnover rates, 104
TWA, 122, 123, 124, 125
two-tier pay systems, 132, 170

underconsumptionism, 26
unemployment insurance programs, 119
union-avoidance strategies, anti-union pressure groups and, 241; bargaining structure
constraints on, 59–62; decertification in,

76–78; different products pursued in, 69–70; disinvestment as, 72–76; employment concentration limits in, 68; of firms never organized, 56; at highly unionized firms, 239; labor law reform and, 233–234; line managers in, 64; matching union compensation in, 56; at new start-ups, 248; of partially organized firms, 59–62, 68–70; plant location decisions in, 54–55, 58, 67–68, 70; profiles of, 57, 59; public policy and, 232–233; QWL programs as, 150; reform strategy failure and, 241–242; wage differential incentives in, 70; for white-collar workers, 61; worker participation programs as, 57; workplace innovations in, 64, 150; work rules as incentive in, 72

Union Camp, 71

union leaders: corporate board representation and, 191, 192; on labor-management committees, 184–185; at local vs. national level, 240, 243; New Deal system and, 245; public policy and, 231, 232; public views on, 216; in strategic-choice participation, 179–182, 203

union members: expectations of, 220; in key industries, 30–31; maintenance policies for, 31; in new vs. old industries, 8; in 1954, 34–35; unions evaluated by, 218–220; during World War II, 30–31

union membership decline: alternative representation forms inspired by, 221–223; BLS statistics on, 48; business cycle and, 5; in coal industry, 49; at company level, 49–50; in construction industry, 49; decertification in, 76–78; economic growth sectors and, 8; employment cuts and, 115; on industry level, 49; labor-market changes and, 53–55; managerial strategies in, 8–9; new organizing strategies required by, 3–4; in 1960s, 5, 8, 39; in 1970s, 43–44; in petroleum refining industry, 49; prior history of organizing and, 52; regression estimate on, 53–54; representation election rejection rates and, 76–78; structural changes and, 51–52, 53–55, 262n11; theoretical framework for, 51–53; in trucking industry, 49

union organizing, 30–31, 76–78; human resource management practices and, 249–250; individual interest vs. majority support in, 217–218; job dissatisfaction and, 216–217; management adaptation and, 25–26, 254n11; modified strategies necessary for, 3–4, 250; negative image of unions and, 217; at new start-ups, 248; nonunion workers perceptions and, 217–218; workers' attitudes and, 205

unions: alternative forms of representation and, 221–223; basic questions faced by, 5–6; "Big Labor" stereotype of, 216; centralization of power in, 34; communists in, 33; company domination of, 234–235; dual images of, 216; environmental changes and, 12–13; independent, 34, 58, 69; individual membership options developed by, 250; internal political debates in, 33; legitimacy achieved by, 5; managerial ideology toward, 12, 14–15; market forces and, 13; median vs. marginal voters in, 114; membership evaluation of, 218–220; NLRA protections for, 25–26; nonunion workers' views on, 217–218; as part of democratic fabric, 15; personnel departments and, 35; prior to 1930s, 5; public opinion on, 216; public sector, 39; scenarios for future of, 251–253; specific views on, 216–218; in strategic business decisions, 178–179; strategic-choice ratings for, 218–220; wage targets of, 114; work-place level ratings for, 218–220; see also worker views on unions

union security clauses, 25, 36

Uniroyal, 71

United Airlines, 123, 124

United Auto Workers (UAW), 33; in administrative teams, 198; at Fiero plant, 161–162, 198–199; Ford and, 159–160; at GM's southern plants, 59, 61, 158–159; job bank negotiated by, 170; in job security agreements, 120, 121; 1948 GM contract with, 33; 1976 GM agreement with, 158–159; 1982 Ford and GM agreements with, 160; 1984 GM contract with, 170; operating teams opposed by, 158; QWL programs and, 151–152; in Saturn project, 201, 202; southern organizing campaigns by, 158–159; in strategic business decisions, 181, 182, 198–199; white-collar workers and, 61; under Woodcock, 40; worker participation and, 44

United Electrical Workers (UE), 58

United Mineworkers of America, 49

United Steelworkers (USW), 128–129; in LMPTs, 172–173; in Phelps Dodge strike, 136; on strategic-choice participation, 181

Urban Institute, 111

U.S. Air, 122, 123

U.S. Steel, 38, 172–173

value-added, 228

Veblen, Thorstein, 15

Verma, Anil, 101

Vietnam War, 38–39

Vroman, Wayne, 111

wage grades, 101, 102
wage norms, 111
wages: in airlines industry, 125–126; conces-
    sions in, 115–117; under contingent pay
    procedures, 134; employment cuts and,
    114; foreign competition and, 228; in gar-
    ment and textiles, 188; job classifications
    linked to, 28–29; in 1980s, 111–112, 116–
    117; nonunion firms influenced by union
    rates for, 30, 35; orbits of coercive com-
    parison for, 38; overprediction of, 111; at
    Packard Electric, 170; under pattern bar-
    gaining, 111; in pay-for-knowledge sys-
    tems, 96, 98–99; perceived effects of
    unionization on, 218; postwar formula for,
    26; profits and, 33; at Schneider Transport,
    141, 142; skilled/unskilled differentials in,
    41; standardization of, 26–27, 228; in team
    work systems, 98–99; two-tier systems for,
    132, 170; union/nonunion differentials in,
    41, 70, 103–104
Wagner Act, 33
Wall Street Journal, 76
Walsh, David, 24–25
War Labor Board, *see* National War Labor
    Board
Weintraub, Norman, 194
Weirton Steel, 190
Western Airlines, 123, 126, 134, 190, 191–
    193, 202–203
Westinghouse, 58
Weyerhauser, 71
Wheeling-Pittsburgh Steel Corporation, 173,
    190
white-collar workers: interest in worker par-
    ticipation among, 212; labor market for,
    53; management opposition to unioniza-
    tion of, 61; organizing efforts for, 30; union
    membership decline and, 53, 54; union ne-
    glect of, 55; work values of, 210–211
Wilson Meatpacking, 135
women workers: participation rates for, 53;
    perceived effects of unionization on, 218;
    unions as viewed by, 217
Woodcock, Leonard, 40
work assignments, 29
worker attitudes, 206–225; about accom-
    plishment, 210; on advancement, 210;
    about authority, 210; on bargaining issues,
    210–212; among clerical workers, 210; on
    corporate board representation, 191, 192;
    economic interests in, 207–208; empirical
    reflections of, 89–93; toward employers,
    213–215; on equality, 209; expressive
    theme in, 209; on grievance handling, 211;
    historical experience in, 207; of hourly
    workers, 210; human resource manage-
    ment theories on, 208; importance of, 207–
    208; on individual rights, 209; job-control

unionism and, 88–89; job satisfaction and,
    214–215; on job security, 210; management
    policies and, 208; New Deal system and,
    206–207, 208; about new skills, 210; on new
    technology, 212, 213; occupational group
    variations in, 210–211; ORC surveys on,
    214–215; on participation by areas of con-
    cern, 212; on pay and benefits, 210; per-
    formance and, 86–87, 93; on personnel de-
    cisions, 211, 212; political theme in, 209;
    pragmatic orientation of, 213; priorities
    assigned in, 207–208; production costs and,
    93; on product quality, 211; among profes-
    sionals, 210; on profit sharing, 192; psy-
    chological needs in, 207–208; QWL pro-
    grams and, 174, 211; representational
    structures and, 208; on respect, 209, 210;
    social context for, 207–208; on strategic
    management issues, 211–213; about su-
    pervision, 210; towards supervisors, 87, 89;
    on top management, 215; on work assign-
    ments, 211; on work methods and produc-
    tion procedures, 212; on work-organization
    designs, 211; on work rate, 212
worker participation: areas of concern in,
    212; in auto industry, 158–162; economic
    pressures and, 160; exclusive representa-
    tion and, 235; as experimental, 203–204;
    at Ford, 159–160; formal structures for,
    247; at GM Fiero plant, 199; government
    policy on, 17–18; industrial relations
    professionals and, 42; job security prob-
    lems in, 236; at new nonunion firms, 99–
    100; NLRA company domination prohi-
    bition and, 234–235; at Packard Electric
    200; at Saturn project, 199, 201, 202; in
    strategic business decisions, 179; strategic-
    choice participation as outgrowth of, 197;
    in three-tier framework, 17–18; in trans-
    formation of industrial relations, 160; in
    union-avoidance strategies, 57; union per-
    formance evaluated in, 220; union views
    on, 44, 240; worker attitudes on, 210–211;
    worker/supervisor legal distinctions and,
    235–236; *see also* labor-management par-
    ticipation teams (LMPTs); quality of
    working life programs (QWLs)
worker rights: classical view of, 22, 23; com-
    partmentalizing of, 229–230; contract
    codification of, 88–89; in developing na-
    tions, 228; institutional view of, 22–23;
    public policy and, 231
workers: legal definitions of, 235–236; low-
    wage, 217, 223; occupational identity of,
    248; older, 229; temporary, 221; *see also*
    blue-collar workers; nonunion workers;
    union members; white-collar workers;
    women workers
worker views on unions, 215–221; alternative

representation forms and, 221–223; bargaining vs. worker participation issues in, 211; dual image in, 216; expectations unfulfilled in, 220; general images vs. specific preferences in, 215–217; job dissatisfaction and, 216–217; among nonunion workers, 217–218; perceived effects of unionization on, 218–220; representational strategies and, 211; strategic performance in, 218–220; unionization effects as perceived in, 217–218; willingness to organize and, 216–217; worker participation and, 220; workplace performance in, 218–220
work-organization, 59; flexibility in, 101, 103–104, 239–240; under job-control unionism, 88; new models for, 94; after strikes, 135; union/nonunion comparisons in, 100–108; work rules and, 87
workplace innovations: at greenfield sites, 94; labor law reforms and, 234–236; local vs. national union leaders in, 240, 243; motivation theories in, 94; objectives of, 147; organizing incentive reduced by, 76–77; at partially organized firms, 99–100, 243; strategic level and, 153–154; top executive level commitment and, 247; types of, 149; in union-avoidance strategies, 64, 150
workplace level of industrial relations systems: business cycles and, 154; conflict management in, 82–85; decentralization in, 94; due process in, 82–85; evolution of, 88–93; generic functions of, 82–83; at highly unionized firms, 239; under job control unionism, 28–29; labor-management cooperation in, 18; lack of research on, 18; low-wage model for, 94; managerial flexibility in, 18; middle level and, 81–82; motivation in, 82–83, 86–88, 94; at nonunion firms, 81–82, 93–107; organizational change and, 87–88; perceptions of union performance at, 218–220; scope of, 81–82; shock-effect era in, 88–89; strategic level and, 81–82; in three-tier framework, 16, 17, 18, 19; at union firms, 88–93, 100–107; union/nonunion comparisons in, 100–108; union performance in, 218–220; union power in, 238; worker expectations and, 220; work rules at, 82, 85–86
work rules, 38, 65, 72; in airlines industry, 122–123, 125–126; bargaining structure and, 144–145; concessions in, 112, 113, 117–118; flexibility in, 86; in nonunion systems, 96; plant-level modifications in, 129; productivity and, 86, 104–107; during recessions, 117–118; scope of, 85–86; semi-autonomous work teams and, 174; as strike issue, 135; as union-avoidance incentive, 72; at union vs. nonunion plants, 104–107; at Western Airlines, 191, 192; at workplace level, 82, 85–86
work-sharing practices, 99, 100
work-system concepts, 94
World War II, 30–32, 35

Xerox Corporation, 120, 149, 163–168, 171–172, 176, 193

Zabala, Craig, 93